Total Internship Management

A Guide to Creating
the Ultimate Internship Program

By Richard Bottner &
Robert Shindell, Ph.D.

Intern Bridge

Total Internship Management
A Guide To Creating The Ultimate Internship Program

Authored by Richard Bottner & Robert Shindell, PH.D.

© Copyright 2016 by Intern Bridge, Inc.
All Rights Reserved

ISBN 978-0-692-61026-8
First Printing January 2016

This publication is designed to provide accurate and authoritative information in regard to the subject matter covered. It is sold with the understanding that neither the author nor the publisher is engaged in rendering legal, accounting, or other professional service. If legal advice or other expert assistance is required, the services of a competent professional should be sought.

Further, although every precaution has been taken in the preparation of this book, the author and publisher assume no responsibility for errors or omissions. Nor is any liability assumed for damages resulting from the use of the information contained herein.

Published by Intern Bridge, Inc.
2403 Steven Court
Cedar Park, TX 78613

For sales information, please email info@InternBridge.com or call 800-531-6091.

Cover design/layout/production: www.bookpackgraphics.com (Dan Berger)

Printed in The United States of America
2016

ABOUT THE AUTHORS

Richard Bottner is the Founder of Intern Bridge, a college relations consulting, research and outsourced staffing organization. In 2006, Richard founded the New England Internship Study, the largest survey ever to be conducted solely on the topic of internships. Backed by this research, Richard has consulted for several organizations, helping them build effective internship programs based on student expectations. He has spoken at numerous conferences including the Eastern Association of Colleges and Employers, the Mountain Pacific Association of Colleges and Employers and the New England Association for Cooperative Education and Field Experience.

Richard holds a Bachelor of Science in Business Administration from Babson College and a Master's Degree in Physician Assistant Studies from Quinniapac University.

Dr. Robert Shindell is the President & CEO for Intern Bridge, Inc. Dr. Shindell has successfully held a variety of professional leadership roles in higher education during his career and is a highly regarded expert in the area of the transition to the world-of-work for students. He developed three career centers and has consulted with more than 100 colleges and universities on the development of student and employer facing career initiatives. He has also worked with thousands of employers and higher education career centers in developing successful transition plans for students through both live and virtual presentations. Dr. Shindell's research and opinions are often quoted in the New York Times, The Chronicle of Higher Education, The Washington Post, Inside Higher Ed and many more.

Robert earned a Ph.D. in Higher Education Administration at Texas Tech University's College of Education, a master's degree in training and development from Midwestern State University, and a bachelor's degree in education from the University of Toledo.

TABLE OF CONTENTS

INTRODUCTION

A century ago, John Dewey made a compelling case for the integration of academic and experiential learning in the educational curriculum.[1] In Dewey's perspective, presenting students with experiential learning opportunities would mean that "the whole pupil is engaged, the artificial gap between life in school and out is reduced," and students draw motivation from exposure "to a large variety of materials and processes distinctly educative in effect,"[2] within the context of the larger society.

Scholars in the field of student learning outcomes or any discipline in which the academic knowledge provided in the classroom can be transferred to the world of work can acquire further understanding of the expectations of students seeking internships. Internships and other forms of experiential learning are key elements of the educational process in the United States today. The transfer of knowledge from classroom to worksite, regardless of the academic major, is a key component to student satisfaction. Experts in this field can eventually contribute to the effort of creating a meaningful link between the academic realm and the world of work.

Experiential learning experiences that combine academic learning with work experience have a long history in American education. A century ago, Dewey envisioned a fusion of classroom and community learning. Over the last 20 years, internships have become exceedingly popular and a growing number of colleges and universities are requiring that students take unpaid internships for credit. This trend has generated some controversy. There is evidence that students who take part in paid internships are more likely to be given challenging and relevant work and to have an advantage in gaining employment.[3] By design, an internship is meant to provide students with learning opportunities that allow them to develop the skills and competencies sought after by employers.

In the United States today, internships and other forms of experiential learning that integrate academic coursework with "real-world" work experience have become popular with currently enrolled students in higher education, employers, and students for a variety of reasons. For currently enrolled students participating in internships, the following benefits have been cited: higher starting salaries; higher job satisfaction; job offers sooner; more job offers; higher extrinsic success; development of communication skills; better career preparation; improved job-related skills; and improved creative thinking.

---

[1] Steffes, 2004; Swail & Kampits, 2004
[2] Dewey, 1916, cited in Swail & Kampits, 2004, p. 1
[3] Chatzsky & McGrath, 2011

A summary of employer benefits include the following: first choice of best students; best selection of future employees; better hiring decisions; exposure to new ideas; creating a college network; fulfilling social responsibilities; and receiving part-time help.

For higher education institutions, the benefits cited in the literature include the following: improved reputation; improved student recruiting; smarter students; new scholarships; other forms of funding; networking to the local community; external curriculum assessment and practitioner input.

To illustrate the rise in popularity of internships, consider that in 1980 only 1 in 36 students completed an internship, compared to 3 out of 4 students completing an internship just 20 years later.[4] Today, 94% of business colleges offer some form of internship opportunity to students, but only 6% require students to participate in an internship program.[5] The reasons why students participate in internships generally include, with some variation, the following: earn income to pay for tuition and other college expenses; gain a preview of the workplace; develop important skills and competencies to fulfill college graduation requirements; and complete community service obligations. For employers, internships and work-based learning opportunities are viewed as a cost-effective way to effectively support the business operations or mission of the organization.[6]

Methodology & Theoretical Framework

In today's business environment, for-profit, not-for-profit, and governmental organizations utilize internships as a means to access future talent through the recruitment of students from colleges and universities. Personnel management research is studied extensively by academics and industry experts in an attempt to identify employee characteristics desired most by corporate executives.[7] Although researchers might not agree on the rankings of the characteristics, the inclusion of employee attributes are similar among studies. Enthusiasm, motivation, interpersonal skills, work experience, initiative, oral communication skills, leadership, and maturity are important criteria in the decision to hire an employee.[8] This book and the Total Internship Management ideology is an in-depth look at best practices in developing, structuring, implementing and managing a successful internship program.

---

[4] Cook, Parker, & Pettijohn, 2004

[5] Weible, 2010

[6] Weible, 2010

[7] Boatwright & Stamps, 1988; Gaedeke & Tootelian, 1989; Kelley & Gaedeke, 1990; Raymond & McNabb, 1993

[8] Ibid.

Part of what makes this publication unique is that it is based on original, in-depth research into student expectations. The National Internship & Co-op Study has collected more than 450,000 responses from students representing more than 750 Colleges and Universities across the United States, creating one of the largest on-going internship research projects solely focused on experiential education. All of the statistics in this publication are from this on-going landmark research.

The research data was collected using two surveys: one for students and one for employers who host interns. The very first question on the survey for students was "Have you ever taken part in an internship experience?" Students who answered yes to this question were transferred to one set of questions, while students who answered no to this question were transferred to a different set of questions. Similarly, the very first question on the organizational survey was "Have you ever hosted an intern?" Individuals who answered yes to this question were transferred to one set of questions while others who answered no to this question were transferred to a different set of questions. Using this method, each survey was actually two surveys in one. In essence, a total of four surveys were conducted. (Both surveys contained a certain number of questions that were answered by both groups without branching. These questions were mostly demographic in nature.)

The survey design was accomplished by reviewing existing surveys on similar topics and has been revised each year since its creation in 2007 to capture new and trending data from the field. Initially, a group of human resources representatives from various industries and sized companies came together to review the questions and made recommendations that they thought would be useful to be included in the survey. The survey questions were then converted into an online format. All of the surveys were completed online using SurveyGizmo survey software. Questions were both quantitative and qualitative in nature. The survey for organizations contained over 100 questions, while the survey for students contained between 50 and 100 questions (certain responses allowed the skipping of particular questions).

Important Note:
There are over 100 student quotations in this publication, gathered directly from this research project. They are represented throughout this book by italicized quotations. (Due to our obligations to student survey takers and universities, we are unable to publish the student's name, or which university they attend.)

SHOULD MY ORGANIZATION HOST INTERNS?

The decision to host interns at your organization is not one to be taken lightly. The truth is, not every organization is a good fit to be an effective host for an internship program. The good news is that every organization can create a positive environment for an intern. However, there are several factors that you and your organization need to consider before making this important commitment.

As you start to assess whether your organization should host interns, the questions below may help you. Below you will find an organization audit that can be used to assess your organization's "internship readiness." As opposed to other business audits, this assessment focuses on an organization's ability to host an internship program, and will only take a few minutes. These questions need to be discussed with as many folks in your organization as possible, especially executive level leadership and the specific departments that may want to host an intern.

The following organizational audit can be a very useful tool in focusing your conversations with key leaders in your organization:

How serious is my organization about hosting an internship program?
- Is my organization committed to working with universities?
- Will my organizational culture be supportive of an internship program?

What can interns do for us? What are our goals?
- Does my organization have meaningful work for interns to complete?
- Are there special technical skills we need in interns?
- Do we want to use the internship program to identify, test, and recruit interns as potential new employees?
- Would an intern's naïveté and inexperience actually be an asset for our organization, providing a fresh perspective on our products or services? Or would a naïve intern actually be dangerous to self and to others in certain positions?

What human resources do we have to support an intern?
- Can my organization provide an individual with efficient supervisory skills to work with interns?
- Can my organization provide an individual with sufficient time to organize the program?
- In which departments might interns work?

Does my organization have the time to support an intern?
- What is the best time of year for my organization to host interns?
- What should the duration of individual internships be?

What physical resources do we have to support an intern? For example:
- A safe, adequate workspace
- Access to computers
- Internet access
- Telephone and fax
- Other communication resources
- Adequate reference resources
- Access to people who would be colleagues, resources, or internal clients
- Parking

What financial resources do we have?
- Will my organization be able to afford to pay a salary to interns? If so, how much?
- What remuneration, instead of salary, can we provide? (Parking, stipend, etc.)

As you read over the questions above and you start to formulate answers, you will begin to gain consensus with key stakeholders on the structure that your organization's internship will take. It is also important for you and your key stakeholders to understand why other organizations host interns and why millions of college students each year take part in these critical experiential education activities.

PURPOSE FOR ORGANIZATIONS

Each year hundreds of thousands of organizations make the decision to host interns. The significant majority of those organizations that host interns have indicated that it was a positive experience. Although each organization may have different reasons for hosting interns, the following reasons have been identified as the most important to their desired organizational outcomes. This list is not exhaustive, and through your organizational audit, you may identify other reasons why you should host interns. The following responses are the most generally agreed upon reasons to host interns.

Identify Future Hires

> *"I BELIEVE an internship is an unbelievable experience. It helps you get your foot in the door. I had completed an internship through my high school and I loved it so much, it turned into my job! And I've been working there for 3 years this month!"*

One of the most common reasons HR professionals say they host an internship program is for the opportunity to identify potential full-time employees. Depending on the structure and size of your organization, an internship may fit in perfectly with your entry-talent acquisition strategy or succession planning. As employees are promoted through the organization, interns (many of whom are soon-to-be seniors who will be seeking employment) could be perfect candidates to fill entry-level positions. Each year, about 65% of students who complete an internship report being offered a position with the organization that hosted their internship.

Conduct Recruiting Activities with Low Risk

There are few other scenarios where an individual participates in a twelve-week-long "interview" and where the organization can simply say "goodbye" at the end with no strings attached. Internships provide the opportunity for organizations to do just this. So long as you provide interns with the opportunity to learn, chances are that they will be satisfied with their overall experience. In that case, everyone goes home a winner: the student is able gain real-world experience in the workplace, and the organization is able to avoid hiring a candidate that may not be a good fit for the organization.

Provide Supervisory Experience

Internship programs can provide an organization with an internal training environment for current employees looking to ascend to higher-level positions and gain significant supervisory experience. This practice is popular with individuals who are moving from an individual contributor level to a management level. By having this individual manage an intern, it allows the employee to practice their management skills while allowing the organization to assess the employee prior to moving them into a full-time management role. As we will discuss later in the book, the practice of evaluating interns is critical and should be done consistently during their time within your organization. Using this method, it is easy to learn about potential problems with the supervisor and to coach that person through the learning process.

Pipeline for Additional Candidates

An effective internship program can build and sustain and effective pipeline for additional candidates. Even if an intern declines an offer for a repeat internship or full-time employment, that student can provide a pipeline for additional candidates. Students who pursue internships are often connected to their campus community in some manner: through a professor, the career office, an administrator, or maybe a student organization. By working to create long-lasting relationships with individual interns, an organization can almost guarantee to have a steady flow of applications.

Gain Short Term Talent

In today's dynamic business environment, your organization may have special projects or times during the year that have an increased workload. In each instance you may require a skilled individual with a special area of expertise. While some organizations may look to solve this issue by hiring a consultant or by engaging with a temporary staffing agency, doing so may be prohibitively expensive. Interns can often provide a great deal of valuable talent for these special projects.

Provide New Perspectives & Invigorate The Workforce

Every organization in every industry is looking for the "next big thing," be it a new technology application or a new service offering to customers. Today's college students have the ability to offer organizations with a unique insight, a new perspective, and fresh ideas that can spark innovation. Interns, based on their major and level in school, have been applying themselves in academic programs for several years. In many cases they possess an incredible amount of up-to-date knowledge from both inside and outside of the classroom. This knowledge and experience that interns bring to an organization often enable them to articulate new industry ideas and concepts in a manner that individuals who have been out of school for many years may struggle with. This is particularly true in the areas related to technology and social media, as today's students are comfortable with these areas and can be great assets in technology-related projects.

Increased Retention Rate

According to the data collected through the National Internship & Co-op Study, approximately 65% of students who have completed an internship with an organization were offered full-time positions at the conclusion of their experience. Although there is no direct research linking this to how long the individual might stay with their host organization as a full-time employee, anecdotal information gathered through conversations with former interns lead us to believe that they are more likely to stay with the organization for a longer period of time. As an intern transitions to full-time employment, they are more familiar with the culture, structure, and work of the organization. This comfort level tends to lead to a deeper connection to both the organization and co-workers. Interns who transition to full-time employment also require less training and orientation to reach full productivity.

Provide Students with Real Work Experience

Over two-thirds of students surveyed stated that the reason they were seeking an internship was to gain real-world work experience. As the host organization you have chosen to take the responsibility for providing this type of experience through an internship. How you provide this experience is solely dependent upon your business needs and the skill set that the intern brings to you. To assist you with creating tasks and activities that will help students gain the real-world work experience they are seeking, please refer to **Appendix E on page 233**. Remember, as an employer, the more you put into the internship program the more you will get out of it in terms of student satisfaction and productivity. One of the mistakes that many employers make is limiting the amount of "*real work*" that the interns actually do during their internship. Instead, they pack the internship experience with non-work related activities and "fluff" - as many students call it. So go ahead and pack as much "*real work*" into the internship as you can! This is what students crave most, but once this is achieved, the results are high-impact for the student's development, your organization's mission and goals, and the local economy and workforce development.

Low-Cost / High-Talent Labor

For many organizations, hosting interns is a low-cost solution to dynamic (and sometimes very expensive) human capital needs. Generally speaking, your organization can acquire interns at a much lower cost of labor than temporary, part-time, or full-time employees. From recruiting, to compensation, to benefits, hosting an intern simply costs less.

Problems occur for host organizations when they view the internships' sole purpose as a way to reduce labor costs. Hiring an intern just because it is a chance for your organization to cut or significantly reduce labor costs is a recipe for disaster. If your organization approaches internship programs with this mentality, it will damage relationships with universities and, ultimately, they will cease to send interns to your organization's program.

Completing "Back Burner" Projects

In every organization, regardless of size or industry, there are always instances of projects that get put on the back burner simply because there are not enough hours in the day for your existing staff to complete them. By hiring interns, your organization gains an "extra sets of hands and brains" to tackle these projects and get them accomplished. Some organizations choose to hire temporary employees to solve this problem; others have deep enough pockets to pay significant overtime or extra salaries. Hosting interns to assist in or even take the lead in getting these projects off the back burner is a great way to provide real-world work experience, while taking some workload off of your staff. However, be cautious that these "back-burner projects" are not just projects or work that other employees don't want to do. The real problem occurs when the purpose of hosting an internship program becomes an effort to complete work that full-time employees do not want to do. As with labor costs, this cannot become the primary goal of an internship program.

> *"SOMETIMES I FELT like I wasn't as respected as the rest of the employees and that people just threw projects at me that they had no interest in doing, instead of choosing ones that would be best for my learning experience."*

To Be a "Good Human Resources Organization"

Internships are gaining popularity by leaps and bounds. To illustrate the rise in popularity of internships, consider that in 1980 only 1 in 36 students completed an internship, compared to 3 out of 4 students completing an internship just 20 years later (Cook, Parker, & Pettijohn, 2004). Today, 94% of business colleges offer some form of internship opportunity to students (Weible, 2010). Regardless of the ebb and flow of our country's economy, your organization will always need talent. By providing opportunities for students to intern with your organization, you are helping transition students from college to the world of work. This is certainly a good thing for your community as the student that you bring on for an internship may one-day work there full-time, buy a home, and contribute to the overall tax base of the area.

Build Relationships with Local Higher Education

For many reasons, building relationships with local colleges and universities can be extremely important to your organization. Most importantly, it provides you with the chance to network directly with the individuals who can give you access to a wide range of talented young people. By building relationships with colleges, you are also opening the door for the institution to become involved with your organization, acting as consultants, guest speakers, and more. Hosting an internship program gives your organization the "in" and provides invaluable advertising.

Hosting an Internship Is Good For Public Relations

Providing internship opportunities for students in your community may lend itself to generating media for your organization. In the literature review portion of the research, hundreds of newspaper and magazine articles focusing on the structure of the program, spotlighting a particular intern, or announcing some sort of major organization-wide development accomplished by an intern were obtained. Internships, when hosted correctly, have the power to boost an organization's reputation through the power of the press.

Increase Diversity

For organizations that want to diversify their existing workforce, internship programs can be a valuable tool. Organizations such as InRoads are coupling experiential education with diversity. Students travel from all parts of the country and the world to take part in these highly selective and coveted programs. Tapping into local colleges and universities for interns is a tremendous opportunity to add diversity to the workforce. For more on this topic, please go to **page 151** for *"Internship Programs from a Diversity Recruiting Perspective"*

Work Opportunities for Employees' Children

While an internship program should not be implemented to serve as a "babysitting" service or to foster nepotism in the workplace, it is worthwhile to note that there can be additional sources of intern candidates other than just your local universities. The caveat to this is that children of employees rarely stay with the organization long-term, which is one of the main reported reasons to host an internship program. Depending on the culture of your organization, the internal politics relating to hiring employees' children can also become problematic.

SURVEY DISCUSSION

Table A on page 18 shows the ranked survey data for reasons why organizations choose to host internship programs. Column A represents organizations that have not yet hosted an internship program. Column B represents organizations that have hosted an internship program. This format allows for a comparison between the two groups.

Table A		
A		**B**
1	Identify future hires	2
2	Provides students with real work experience	1
3	To be a "good Human Resources organization"	10
4	Build relationships with local colleges	3
5	Conduct recruiting activities with low risk	9
6	Gain short-term talent	4
7	Hosting an internship program is good for public relations	7
8	Work needs to be completed that current employees do not have time to do	5
9	Provide the organization with fresh ideas	6
10	Increase diversity within my organization	8
11	Low-cost labor	12
12	No-cost labor	14
13	Reinvigorate the current work force	11
14	Completing work that employees don't have time or desire to do	13
15	Other organizations host interns, so my organization feels obligated to host interns too	15

Problematic Responses

Other organizations host interns, so the organization feels obligated to host interns too.

Several respondents to this survey answered "a great extent" or "a very great extent" to this topic. Organizations should not host interns solely on the basis of a perceived obligation. When an organization feels "obligated" to host an intern, it is doubtful that they will put the time and resources into it that will make it successful. The result will most likely be a very unpleasant experience for both the intern and the organization.

Low-cost labor and no-cost labor.

Looking closer at the data, 38 survey takers in total from both groups had agreed to a "great extent" or "a very great extent" that No Cost Labor was a purpose for hosting an intern. More than 60% of these responses came from organizations that have not hosted interns. While 38 individuals may not sound like a lot, it represents 38 different organizations that may host more than one intern, and may be setting themselves up for disappointment. Again, low-cost labor and no-cost labor can be purposes for hosting interns – but absolutely not on their own. This can create a very bad experience for the organization and the intern.

Completing work that employees don't have time or desire to do.
A total of 23 survey takers from both groups had agreed to a "great extent" or "a very great extent" that employees lacking desire to complete certain work was a motivating factor for hosting interns – a scary fact. The kinds of activities that employees do not want to participate in are usually the mundane ones such as stapling, collating, and filing; it would be a major disservice to the organization to farm these activities out as sole objectives in an internship program.

PURPOSE FOR STUDENTS

This section seeks to provide information for the many reasons that students pursue participation in an internship program. By gaining the perspective of a student, your organization can plan and implement an internship program capable of truly delivering experiences that exceed student expectations.

> *"IN ORDER for an internship to be meaningful I think the intern needs to walk away from it having enjoyed the time they spent, having gained knowledge and experience, maybe some contacts, and, in a perfect world, a job. That's what internships are for, right?"*

Gain Real Work Experience

In today's fast paced and dynamic work environment, students know that having earned a college degree is not the ticket it once was. Students know that to be successful in their transition to the world of work they need to have gained real world work experience before they graduate from college! While a college education does provide a valuable foundation in theory, it does not always help them to apply what they have learned in the classroom to what they may face in the working world. This skill, applying classroom knowledge in a real-world environment, can only be gained by having the opportunity to be immersed in a work setting through an internship or other experiential education experience. Students who take part in an internship program as part of their undergraduate curriculum have an amazing opportunity to build upon what they are learning in the classroom to make real decisions and solve relevant problems.

> *"THEY PROVIDED real work experience in an environment where learning was encouraged and contacts could be made."*
>
> *"I LEARNED a lot of things you cannot learn in a classroom. I am now steps ahead of my peers as I have a lot of contacts and real world experience."*
>
> *"I WAS ABLE to apply my college textbook learning to actual cases."*
>
> *"I REALLY ENJOYED the ability to get a sense for how theoretical knowledge I gain in school is applied to practical work in everyday situations."*
>
> *"AS LONG AS I'M LEARNING and gaining knowledge and experience, then I find the experience meaningful."*

Learn New Skills

As mentioned in the previous paragraph, gaining real-world experience is a key reason in which students choose to participate in internships. Students have indicated that one of the prominent reasons to engage in an internship is to learn new skills. Many students indicated that the skills they learned are specific to the industry that they have chosen to enter. For example, technical skills in an IT firm or utilizing a specific editing program in a graphic design company allow students to develop up-to-date abilities in those sectors. However, the significant majority of students across all majors indicate that it is the "soft-skills" they learn as the most important new skills obtained. These soft-skills include communication skills, teamwork and collaboration, adaptability, problem solving, critical observation and conflict resolution. While they may enter an internship with a particular skill set, there is the expectation that students will have the chance to either learn brand new skills or build upon an existing skill.

> *"I FEEL AS THOUGH internships are an excellent way for students to gain experience and knowledge in their specific area of study. I believe that hands-on training is the absolute best and most efficient way for a student to learn. There are a lot of careers in the real world. I would love to see what is out there, and I would especially like to examine which career I would excel at. I have a lot of great ideas, and would love to share them!"*

> *"WHAT I LIKED most about my internship was the freedom and chance to work with minimal supervision. Also the knowledge gained was incredible – more so than what I could have learned in any college classroom."*

Build the Résumé

Career advisors on college and university campuses across the country continually advise students that their résumé is the single most important document that they will ever write. However, without a significant balance in three specific areas (Academics, Leadership, and Experience) employers are sometimes hesitant to select the student for an interview. Students who take this advice seriously are also generally the students who choose to participate in internships. They know that by participating in this valuable experience they are able to build the experience and leadership sections of their résumé, thus making themselves more attractive to future employers. There is also an unquantifiable degree of expectation by family and future employers that a student should participate in at least one internship. Today, nearly 47% of colleges and universities also indicate that some form of experiential education is a requisite for graduation.

> *"THE PROFESSIONAL ENVIRONMENT of the organization was really great and the fact that I could use my experience and contacts as résumé builders afterwards was important."*
>
> *"I LIKED THE ITEMS that I was able to add to my résumé and talk about in interviews. I also liked that it gave me an idea of what people do in different job descriptions to help me decide what profession I want to go into."*

Make New Connections / Network

"It's not what you know, it's who you know." This is a statement that college students hear on a regular basis from their parents, faculty, and career advisors as they are making the transition to the world of work. Most jobs getting filled these days aren't even advertised. Instead, they're typically part of the hidden job market — those millions of openings that never get formally posted. To be considered for one of these jobs in the hidden market, a connection with someone within the hiring organization is critical. Students often hear about the power of networking throughout their university education, but do not get a chance to practice it as a skill on a regular basis. Without developing this skill they often miss opportunities simply because they do not know they are available. An internship can provide students with the opportunity to meet and connect with working professionals on a daily basis for an extended period of time. With this opportunity students have the chance to be exposed to jobs that go unposted and also provides them, with an opportunity to meet key decision makers within the organization. The bottom line is that participating in an internship can help students expand their network beyond family members and friends.

> *"I WAS ABLE to establish many contacts with prominent people in the finance industry."*
>
> *"WHAT I LIKED most about my internship was the countless opportunities to network, and [the] relationships with other interns."*

Experience Work With a Potential Full-Time Employer

As discussed in the previous section, one of the most common reasons HR professionals say they host an internship program is for the opportunity to identify potential full-time employees. Students are no different. Many students indicate that they take part in an internship at a specific organization where they may be interested in obtaining full-time employment after graduation. Just like organizations screen candidates to make sure they are a "good fit," students also want to make sure that the organization is a good choice for them as they transition out of college. They are essentially screening the organization for the kind of work and environment that they will be subject to if they were to accept a full-time position of employment.

> *"I THINK an internship would be great and I pray that I have a wonderful experience with mine when the time comes. I look forward to getting the inside scoop on the place I want/hope to work at before being committed. It will also help many people to get a foot in the door at their dream work place."*
>
> *"I GOT TO DO a variety of things, and they weren't menial jobs. I was actually a critical member of the team."*

Receive a Full-Time Job Offer from Employer

One of the key metrics of success for college students is whether or not they have a job offer (or multiple offers) at the time of graduation. According the National Internship & Co-op Study, from 2011 through 2014, 44% of students who participated in an internship self-reported that they were offered a full-time position from the organization that hosted them as an intern. Although the promise of a job at the completion of an internship is not a guarantee, most students know that if they perform well and exceed the expectations of their employer, they will most likely be offered a full-time position. For others, a full-time position from the host organization may not be an option. Thirty-two percent of these students have indicated that they feel "confident" or "extremely confident" that they will be offered a full-time position prior to graduation from another organization based on contacts and connections made during the internship.

Complete Interesting and Challenging Tasks

For some students, college based curriculum can be boring and tedious. These students are seeking to be challenged in ways that cannot be done in the classroom. For these students, experiential education provides that challenge! Give them an assignment and they will keep working on it until the job is done. An internship gives the self-motivated student a chance to be stimulated through interesting and challenging tasks.

> *"I LIKED LEARNING about different types of work and what is involved. Learning about what my co-workers/supervisors did on a daily basis really allowed me to think about whether I could do that job everyday."*

Earn Money

All students want it, and some students need to have it. The discussion of whether you provide interns with monetary compensation will come up later in this publication, but you should know that the demand certainly exists. Expectations have grown that internships are a chance to earn money.

Many students whole-heartedly believe that they deserve to be compensated monetarily for their work, and many of these students will not accept an internship unless it is paid. Other students simply need to earn money for life expenses such as rent, tuition, books, car payments, etc. Some students do receive scholarships, as well as federal grants and loan money. However, for many students this is simply not enough. These students seek paying internships because they need to be paid in order to complete their degree. It is always considered a best practice to offer interns monetary compensation.

Test Out a New Organization or Industry

Today's college student has spent a great deal of time learning about different organizations and industries through their curriculum. A significant number of courses in academia utilize case studies and current events to give examples of theoretical concepts in order to expose students to organizations and industries that may hire them after graduation. Although this is certainly good for students, it pales in comparison to having an opportunity to actually work within an industry or at a specific organization. Internships are often used to gain insight into a particular organization or industry. For example, being a business student is versatile: business students can take their degrees to a multitude of different industries, but picking which industry to work in is not easy.

By the time some students graduate, they will have experienced work in five, six, or as many as ten different industries. Some students have a more drastic shift as a result of participating in an internship. A story comes to mind from one student who was committed to the criminal justice program at a local university for over two years before an internship in the sales department of an electronics retailer changed his academic major and career path.

> *"THE LOCATION and type of work I was doing was different. I spent the summer in a different part of the country doing a completely new type of work."*
>
> *"I LEARNED a lot about the industry—but most of all I learned that it was not what I want to do for a career. I liked it and had a great time, but I wasn't passionate enough about it."*

Fulfill Degree Requirements / Receive College Credit

As illustrated earlier in this book, internships are growing in popularity for students and higher education institutions. A significant number of colleges and universities across the country have been adding some type of experiential education to their degree requirements. This used to be the case only with specific programs such as nursing, psychology, engineering, and education. More and more schools, however, are mandating that students complete internships for business, computer science, communication, and graphic design degrees – just to name a few. This has created an increase in the number of college students trying to secure internships in order to complete requirements for graduation. By implementing an internship program now, or by improving your existing program, your organization will be better prepared as colleges increase emphasis on experiential education.

Receiving college credit is different from an internship that is necessary to fulfill degree requirements. In the former case, the student is electing to pursue an internship in order to receive academic credit that they would not receive otherwise. Students typically do this for two reasons: first so that they can take a reduced course load during the school year. If they receive four credits for their internship experience, those are three less credits they need to achieve in the classroom.

The second reason is to broaden their transcript. If they are receiving academic credit for the internship, it will appear on their transcript as "experiential education," "internship seminar," or another variation. Universities that grant academic credit for internships tend to pay more attention to the actual content of the internship itself than schools that do not. When the student is not receiving credit, the university typically has less involvement.

Take Part in Community Service

For civic-minded students, there are few activities more worthwhile than giving back to the community. Many students specifically seek internships in the not-for-profit sector, hoping for a chance to make a difference either in their own community, somewhere else domestically, or even internationally. For example, one program at a business school in the Northeast offers the opportunity for business students to travel to disadvantaged countries around the world to teach business competencies for the summer. Many not-for-profit organizations, both small and large, offer some type of internship program.

> *"IT WAS REWARDING to help children with special needs."*
>
> *"THE PEOPLE I worked with were dedicated and sincere. I felt like I was making a positive, important impact on peoples' lives and I could see that positive change directly manifested in the work I performed."*
>
> *"AT THE END of the day I felt really good about what I had done, and how many kids I had helped. I liked watching my students' progress over the course of the sessions. I liked the interaction I had with the students and the other employees."*

Live in a Specific Area

While living in a specific area is not usually the main reason why a student seeks an internship, it is certainly a consideration – and one that more and more college students are seeking. In today's college curriculum, many degree programs and individual classes focus on issues like international affairs and globalization. Many students have never left their hometown region and are interested in what other parts of the country, or the world, have to offer. This may not compel you to market your internship to schools several hundred miles away (unless you have a large internship program, of course), but don't be surprised if you receive applications from students whose home addresses are several states away.

> *"MY INTERNSHIP was in Ireland!"*
>
> *"I GOT the chance to live in Boston."*
>
> *"MY INTERNSHIP was a wonderful experience because it was located in San Francisco."*
>
> *"I REALLY ENJOYED living in the Washington, D.C. area and learning a lot about the life that is lived down there by so many in our country. I enjoyed working side-by-side with so many people in the political arena."*

SURVEY DISCUSSION

Table B on page 27 shows the ranked survey data for reasons why students pursue internship programs. Column A represents students who have not yet taken part in an internship program. Column B represents students who have taken part in an internship program. This format allows for a comparison between the two groups.

Table B		
A		**B**
1	Gain real work experience	1
2	Learn new skills	3
3	Build résumé	2
4	Make new connections/network	5
5	Experience work at a potential full-time employer	6
6	Receive a full-time job offer from employer	10
7	Complete interesting and challenging tasks	4
8	Earn money	9
9	Test out a new organization or industry	7
10	Receive college credit	11
11	Have a fun and entertaining semester or summer	8
12	Required to fulfill degree requirements	13
13	Take part in community service	14
14	Live in a specific area	12

Money Does Not Come Out On Top

One of the most interesting pieces of data to come out of this portion of the research is where "earning money" fell in the ranking. Positions 8 and 9 shed a great deal of light on one of the largest apprehensions that organizations have about hosting interns. From this data we can learn that so long as many of the items ranked higher than earning money are fulfilled, students may be willing to accept less monetary compensation. The vast majority of reasons ranked higher than earning money are content- and structure-based, proving that you can have a successful and beneficial internship program without being tremendously concerned with monetary compensation, provided you work to ensure that your program is academically sound.

Please refer to **page 143** for more information on the importance (and benefits) of paying interns.

DEFINING YOUR INTERNSHIP PROGRAM

On the surface this probably appears to be a simple task. But if you ask different groups their opinion on how to define an internship program, you are guaranteed to receive highly conflicting responses. Students' perception of an internship will differ from organizations', and vice versa. The disparity increases when taking into consideration the different sizes of organizations and the industries they do business in, as well as the varying sizes of colleges and the degree programs they offer.

The idea of "brain drain" gains significant meaning when examined through the lens of workforce development and experiential education. Brain drain is the general concept of knowledgeable, well-educated individuals migrating from a specific geographic area and taking their talent elsewhere. Every year, hundreds of thousands of college students graduate and move back to their home states, or another region where they were offered employment. When this occurs, the region where the university is located loses out on the economic benefits that would have been realized had the student stayed. This is commonly referred to as *"brain drain."* Across the nation, more and more regions are recognizing that they have a serious problem retaining young, energetic talent. Not surprisingly, regionally-sponsored internship programs have consistently been one of the most broadly used, and most successful initiatives taken to combat the brain drain problem.

Intern Bridge has worked with hundreds of local and state government organizations as well as chambers of commerce to combat "brain drain" in communities. In each case, business leaders, university officials and government officials have gathered to discuss how to implement initiatives to generate and facilitate internships in the region. These individuals recognized that if more students took part in internship programs in their region, more of these students would network and seek employment in the area upon graduation.

What we learned was that one of the main barriers for internships to become a reality was that business leaders and university officials often find it difficult to come to an agreement on the definition for an internship.

Granted, there really is no true "one size fits all" definition for an internship. There are, however, some statements and generalizations that we can say about these experiences which at least allow us to have a shared understanding of their purpose and place in both business and career development.

Several National Organizations have sought to place a formal definition on internships. For example, The National Association of Colleges and Employers states that:

> *"An internship is a form of experiential learning that integrates knowledge and theory learned in the classroom with practical application and skills development in a professional setting. Internships give students the opportunity to gain valuable applied experience and make connections in professional fields they are considering for career paths; and give employers the opportunity to guide and evaluate talent."*

Another definition provided by The Council for the Advancement of Standards in Higher Education states:

> *"The primary mission of Internship Programs (IP) is to engage students in planned, educationally-related work and learning experiences that integrate knowledge and theory with practical application and skill development in a professional setting."*

In both of these definitions, we can summarize by stating that:

Internships Are...

Internships are structured, supervised, and short-term programs in which undergraduate or graduate students perform tasks and duties within an organization in order to gain knowledge and experience. The internship is usually performed over the course of one semester, or during a summer or winter break. The student may or may not earn monetary compensation from the company and/or academic credit from their university. Internship programs should benefit both the student and the organization.

Internships Are Not...

Internships are typically not repeated by the same student. They are also not an opportunity to hire part-time or full-time free labor to perform tasks that other employees do not have the time or desire to complete. Internships must have an educational component. In our survey, one HR representative wrote that an intern is a "sub-entry level temporary position," while another professional wrote that an internship is "when a student performs duties related to their studies for little or no compensation." Neither of these statements presents the right approach to an internship program.

Internships vs. Co-ops

Intern Bridge frequently receives requests for clarification on the distinction between internships and co-ops. Cooperative education, also known as a Co-op, is very similar to internships. However, co-ops usually link more closely to the academic institution. They are typically intensive full-time positions, and almost always part of a program that will allow the student to receive academic credit from their university.

The Cooperative Education & Internship Association defines cooperative education as follows:

"Cooperative education is a structured educational strategy integrating classroom studies with learning through productive work experiences in a field related to the student's academic or career goals. Co-op is a partnership among students, education institutions and employers with specific responsibilities for each party."

While an intern may work full-time during the summer months, most interns who work during the academic year do so on a part-time basis. Co-ops are often part of a five-year degree program and can last an entire year, instead of just one semester. While much of the research for this book is predominately focused on internships, much of the information can be applied to co-ops as well.

Is an Organized Internship Program Really That Important?
Absolutely! As one of the key determinants of the level of satisfaction with their internship experience, students indicate that the more structured the internship program is within their host organization, the higher their level of overall satisfaction. When an intern leaves your organization they will either become an ambassador or adversary. This outcome is largely dependent on how well your organization executes the processes and ideas outlined in this text. The job and internship search are the primary activities of college students, and therefore a chief topic of conversation among friends and families. Students will talk about their experiences; whether or not they have good things to say comes down to the dedication of your organization in creating a positive experience for the student. Giving interns a great experience in an organization has huge long-term benefits, such as great public relations on the intern's campus, as well as an edge when it comes time to recruit for full-time positions.

While well-organized and effective internship programs have the potential to greatly benefit a company, it is important to remember that unorganized programs have their consequences as well. Ninety-Two percent of surveyed professionals agreed that an internship could help the recruiting brand of an organization; yet only 29% thought that an internship program has the potential to hurt the recruiting brand. Of the students who reported having taken part in an internship, 96% agreed that they had shared their experiences with friends, and 99% of students who had not yet taken part in an internship agreed that they would share experiences with friends. This is one of the largest disconnects between organizations and students, which should caution organizations that a lack of knowledge and preparation could yield negative returns in recruiting talent.

Involvement from Others in Your Organization

I am sure that you have heard the old saying "It takes a village…," well nowhere is this statement more true than in developing an internship program in your organization. There are simply too many moving parts for one person to believe that they can tackle this alone. Through our extensive research into this area, we have identified three areas in which support is requisite to having a strong internship program: executives, supervisors and managers of the interns, and the general workforce of your organization.

First, the executives are the leadership and role models of an organization. It is extremely important to gain their support for an internship program. All successful internship programs in major organizations, as well as small to medium sized businesses, stem from executive buy-in and support; and executive buy-in with regard to an internship program must be more than just approving the funds to build the program's financial foundation.

Here are some ideas to show how executives can support an internship program:

- Have an organization-wide communication piece sent directly by an executive to all of the employees within the organization announcing the launch or improvement plan of the internship program. A simple email is highly effective. Don't miss out on this easy opportunity to provide executive support to a program.

- Have executives welcome interns on their first day.

- Provide an opportunity for interns to have lunch with an executive.

The second group of people within your organization that needs to demonstrate their support are the managers and supervisors of the departments or divisions of your organization that will host interns. Beginning on **page 47** of this text, we will spend a great deal of time focusing on the role of the internship supervisor. But they are not the only folks in your organization in leadership roles that need to show support for the internship program. Other departmental and divisional managers and supervisors need to have buy-in for the internship program as a whole for the organization, and the intern to have a positive experience.

Here are some ideas that supervisors and managers throughout the organization can support an internship program:

- Provide time off for folks in their department to serve on your internship steering committee.

- Provide input or information for the interns about what their department does and the role that their activities have on the overall organization.

- If the department is not hosting an intern, have them host other interns for a day so that they can get a feel for what that department does.

Finally, you will need to gain the support of other employees who will be working either directly or indirectly with the students that you bring into your organization to intern. This group of people can really make or break your internship program. Without their buy-in to the program and the intern there is very little chance that the student will have a positive experience.

Here are some ideas for non-managerial staff members throughout the organization who can support an internship program:

- Have them "host" the intern for job shadowing for a day.

- Ask for their input on the work plan for the interns in their department.

- Ask them to be mentors.

- Solicit their feedback on the success of the internship program.

Remember, it is highly unlikely that your program can be a success without the support and collaboration from these three groups. Once you gain the support and commitment from these groups, make sure to keep them in the loop about developments within your program, especially with examples of how interns are providing value to the organization.

"THE PLACE where I interned was not a good place for interns to work. It was a small company and they didn't take the time to show me around. They just pushed the interns aside."

"THE CULTURE WAS positive for interns – respect, professional behavior, and meaningful work were all a part of my experience."

"THE CULTURE of the firm was unbelievable."

"I LOVED the environment and the amount of responsibility put on me. I felt as though I played a role in the company and wasn't just an intern."

"I LIKED the overall environment of the office the best. All of my co-workers were supportive, hard-working, and became great friends of mine."

STRUCTURING AN INTERNSHIP PROGRAM

Just as there is no single definition of an internship, there is also not one single way to structure an internship program, either. However, creating a structure that works with your organization and that coincides with a structure put forth by the college or university, this certainly sets the tone for a successful experience for all involved. The bottom line: *Structure is, by far, one of the key ingredients to a successful internship program.*

Choosing A Semester

To begin developing a structure for your internship program, it is a good idea to start with when you will actually have the intern in your organization. There are four general time frames when students attempt to obtain an internship. These times are typically in line with the academic calendar and are broken down into two categories: when classes are in session, and when classes are not in session.

Summer and Winter Semesters

Historically the most popular semester for internships for both students and organizations is the summer semester. Generally, this time frame runs between May and August, depending on the school's academic calendar and starts when students complete their final exams. The summer concludes when classes begin again in the fall, usually meaning the last week in August or first week of September. Students typically request at least one week on each end of the internship to take a vacation or prepare for upcoming activities. Therefore, most students have between twelve and fourteen weeks in the summer to work at an internship site. With the summer being the most popular time students seek internships, the candidate pool will also be the largest for this period. Summer internships have the potential to allow the student to work with the organization for the longest length of time, allowing the organization to accomplish larger, more long-term projects.

The winter semester is the time between the completion of final exams from the fall semester and the start of classes in the spring semester. Hosting an internship program during the winter semester tends to be tricky. The time period is extremely brief (three to six weeks), depending on the university. You will be competing with family vacations and the holiday season. Some students just want a break during the winter session. The pool of potential candidates for winter semester internships will be at its lowest. However, winter semester internships do lend themselves nicely to short-term special projects. It may be best to reserve winter session internships for students who have already been interns within your organization, since they have already become acclimated to the environment. In addition, many schools will not recognize such a brief internship for academic credit.

Based on data from the National Internship and Co-op Study, students ranked a summer internship as the most desired. Organizations, based on work available for interns, also ranked summer as the best time to host interns.

Fall and Spring Semesters

From a student's perspective, there is not a large difference between taking part in an internship program in the fall or spring semesters. Students will be enrolled in classes and also participating in collegiate activities at their academic institutions during these time periods. Interns will be attending classes where instructors will assign them homework and often obligate them to take part in group work. Furthermore, students may be working another job to financially support themselves. As a result of these other commitments, it can be slightly more difficult to host interns during the fall and spring semesters.

On the other hand, some students will take part in an internship in lieu of a class during the school months. While this type of activity is traditionally more of a co-op (not directly covered in this publication), some students will connect a part-time internship experience to an independent study project or a university-administered internship seminar course to earn academic credits.

How Much Time Can I Expect Interns to Commit to My Organization?

The amount of time that an intern has to work for your organization is largely dependent upon which semester you choose to host the program. As previously stated, students will have less time to work when classes are in session. As shown by the data collected as part of the National Internship and Co-op Study, the majority of past interns would prefer to work between 5 and 20 hours per week during the fall and spring semesters. Students who are taking classes will not have time to perform high quality work for your organization much more than 20 hours per week.

Based on the data for summer and winter, it can be observed that when classes are not in session, students are willing to work more hours. A closer look at winter session shows that unlike summer, most students are willing to work fewer hours. This can be attributed to a higher number of distractions during this time period.

"NEITHER OF [my internships] were paid; at times, both organizations expected me to put the internship as a priority over my class work and familial responsibilities (as a student in an unpaid internship position!), especially the most recent one, which is why I gave it bad reviews. The most recent one tried to fail me when I wouldn't commit to more time than originally agreed upon, even when I explained to them that I could not due to schoolwork responsibilities."

"MAKE THE INTERN happy to walk in every day that they have to work. The work that should be required of an intern should be work that is enjoyable to complete and will teach valuable skills. Interns typically have a lot to do, especially during the school year, and it should not be a chore for the intern to complete unmanageable and inappropriate tasks."

Here is a summation of the points outlined above:

	Starts	Ends
Fall	Beginning of September	Mid-December
Winter	Mid-December	Mid-January
Spring	Mid-January	Beginning of May
Summer	Beginning of May	End of August

	Winter	Spring	Fall	Summer
PROS	Great opportunity for short-term special projects.	Second most common time students seek internships; tends to be a busier time in many organizations when projects need to be completed.	Tends to be a slower period in many industries, allowing staff to be more attentive.	Largest candidate pool; best opportunity for completing larger projects; Easier to provide a consistent program.
CONS	Extremely brief period of time; competition with vacations and holiday season; much smaller candidate pool.	Competing with class time, homework, school activities, and possibly other jobs.	Same as spring. In addition, students are just returning from summer.	Requires the most structure and planning.

The Key Players

Two key players from within your organization must commit fully to the internship program in order for its launching to succeed: the internship coordinator and supervisors. The internship coordinator does the legwork related to the internship program. He or she decides which departments receive interns, assigns supervisors, reviews intern work plans, writes job descriptions, conducts recruiting activities, and maintains the contact with universities that require organization follow-up.

Interns directly report to supervisors who establish their day-to-day activities and conduct evaluations of the interns' work when necessary. Depending on the size of your organization, you may find that you are playing the role of the coordinator and the supervisor. In larger organizations, however, supervisors (typically line managers) and the individual who coordinates the entire process (typically someone in Human Resources) are usually separate.

The Work Itself

Students expect a reasonable amount of work. In fact, they want it. In the student survey, 99% of students agreed that by the time they complete an internship program, they should be better prepared to work in that particular field. The level of preparation that a student ultimately gains from an internship is attributed mainly to the work that they fulfill.

Employers also report higher levels of satisfaction with internship programs where more work - *not less* - is required of the intern.

> "*I FEEL THAT INTERNSHIPS expect too little from a participant and they get dragged down with menial tasks that provide little, if any, valuable work experience. On the other hand, I also feel like they can be on the exact opposite end- that certain programs expect too much from a participant; that they assign too much work or assign projects that are way over one's head. It is important to find a place or come to an understanding about a middle ground. A balance should be made between putting forth an effort and being involved in projects and tasks so that one feels useful and helpful; however, it should also be recognized that most internships are occurring while a student has an entire other life to worry about at the same time.*"

> "*INTERNSHIPS NEED TO ENSURE that students will receive the learning experience that they are looking for. There is nothing worse than saying that you interned somewhere and then have to explain that you just filed documents all summer. The intern needs to have something to take away from the experience, not just sore fingers or paper cuts.*"

"THEY SHOULD MAKE SURE that the intern feels as though they're an employee and not just some college kid that they can dump their dirty, boring paperwork on. A real part of the experience of an internship is to see what it would be like doing that job – not doing administrative work."

Creating a Work Plan

Deciding specific assignments interns will complete during their tenure is one of the most important and delicate processes an organization will accomplish in regards to internship programming. Keep in mind that the top three reasons students pursue internships are educationally based – in other words, ***they want to learn***. The Intern Work Plan details the projects that the interns will be completing and it helps to ensure that all activities contain some degree of learning. While clerical work in an internship is to be expected, this type of work should be kept to a minimum. However, even clerical work should be entered into the work plan. All proposed work for the intern should be in the work plan. The job description used for marketing the internship should be ultimately based on the Intern Work Plan.

In many cases, especially if the student is earning academic credit as part of their internship experience, the school may require you, as the employer, to submit your Intern Work Plan to the faculty member who is supervising the intern for approval. **Please refer to a Sample Intern Work Plan on page 246.**

Short-Term vs. Long-Term Projects

From our research, it can be seen that there is a general disconnect between the amount of time that supervisors anticipate an assignment will take an intern to complete, and the actual time necessary for the intern to finish. Generally, *interns finish work much quicker than supervisors predict.* It is recommended that students be given mostly short-term projects (one hour to a few days turnaround time) along with one or two long-term projects (due towards the end of the term).

With this format, students always have something to work on, even if the supervisor is unavailable to answer questions regarding a short-term project. This is considered a best practice. Students want to be useful, with 97% agreeing that they should be given enough work to be kept busy.

> *"MY SUPERVISOR had very good insights but was often busy with work. I had to wait before finishing something because I had a lot of little questions to ask but he was often on the phone."*
>
> *"I WOULD OFTEN do work faster than it would be assigned to me, so there was a good chunk of time I didn't have much to do."*
>
> *"SOME OF THE PROJECTS were long and boring and sometimes my supervisor was too busy to give me something else to do when I was done with a project."*

Learning Objectives

The Association of Talent Development defines learning objectives as:

> *"A statement establishing a measurable behavioral outcome, used as an advanced organizer to indicate how the learner's acquisition of skills and knowledge is being measured."*

Well-written learning objectives form the foundation of any learning experience and set the stage for both the organization and the intern to have a successful experience. However, crafting effective objectives is easier said than done, and even the most seasoned practitioners may find the process challenging. The learning objective needs to describe what you expect the intern to learn upon the successful completion of the activity. For example, suppose you host an intern in your organization's training department. A long-term project that the intern might complete is the creation of a training manual for a new e-learning software package. The learning objective might be to "develop e-learning skills." A short-term project an intern might complete in the finance department is creating graphs based on daily sales levels. The learning objective here might be to "gain an understanding of sales reporting." Maybe the intern will have contact with industry professionals outside of your organization. The objective for this might be "enhance overall knowledge of the restaurant industry." As you can see, objectives can be either narrow or broad in focus, but nonetheless they should be clear to both the organization and the intern.

By developing solid learning objectives for your internship program you provide direction, focus, and guidance. By spelling out expectations, creating commitment, and positioning your initiatives for success, you'll help your organization align the internship program with its results and leap forward into the state-of-the-art world of measurable performance.

> *"I FELT AS THOUGH there was not enough for me to do when my supervisor was away all day at meetings or conferences. Those days were relaxing but I wasn't there to relax, I was there to learn."*

Learning Tasks

Learning tasks describe the *"how"* of an internship activity. They provide for a specific description of what the intern will do in order to accomplish the learning objective. A single learning objective may be accompanied by more than one learning task. Let's look back at the long-term project example mentioned above. A learning task associated with developing e-learning skills might be to "write a learning guide for employees." The learning task for achieving a greater depth in sales reporting might be to "produce daily sales reports with graphs." Lastly, a learning task for an intern working, meeting, or speaking with external industry professionals might be to "correspond with personnel within the restaurant industry."

Evaluation Methods

Evaluation methods describe how the supervisor will measure the output from the learning tasks; to explore if the learning objective has been reached. While there is a whole section in this publication providing suggestions on the topic of evaluating interns, it is important to note here that it is a critical, and often overlooked, responsibility of the organization. Evaluation methods may include a review by the supervisor (in person, on the phone, or through email), intern self-assessment, and/or gauging overall acceptance of the work by other employees in the organization. It is considered a best practice to provide evaluations in writing whenever possible so the student has something of record that they can show to their university and future employers.

Importance of Developing Objectives & Tasks

Learning objectives and tasks are the most important pieces of developing and facilitating a successful internship program. It is also the most overlooked. They represent the actual work that the interns will perform while they are with your organization. As mentioned earlier, many employers overlook this critical factor because of the time it takes to develop them. However, you may already have these learning objectives and tasks developed and might not realize it!

In many cases, you have already determined tasks for part-time employees, full-time employees, and temporary employees, even if your organization doesn't refer to them as "learning tasks." One of the keys to a successful internship program is relating each and every proposed task into a learning objective that can be related to the intern and evaluated. This is often a prerequisite for the intern to earn academic credit from their college or university. It may be helpful to actually start in the middle (learning tasks) to determine objectives and evaluation methods.

Meaning of Menial Tasks

We have all heard of *"menial tasks"* and their impact on internship programs. When students and seasoned internship coordinators refer to menial tasks, they are referring to administrative work that does not provide the student with any educational benefit. Most of the time, the term directly refers to filing, stapling, collating, hanging flyers, etc. An important distinction is that interns expect menial tasks.

As indicated by both students and supervisors, a key metric of success for an internship program is balancing the amount of menial tasks with the amount of genuine work, which leads to learning opportunities. Menial tasks can provide significant learning for students, but host sites tend to rush students through menial tasks, which eliminate any possible learning outcomes. By allowing students some extra time to absorb the information, menial tasks may become beneficial. Provide students with the big picture aspect and explain to them the importance of what they are doing. For example, if one the tasks that you are having your intern do is entering data into a spreadsheet, explain where that data goes after they enter it, who uses it and its importance to an overall project or how this fits into decision making by the department or organization.

> *"MY INTERNSHIP was an odd mix of both extremely interesting work about 5-10% of the time, and INCREDIBLY boring, menial work for the other 90-95%."*
>
> *"I LIKED THE FACT that I got experience within the field. I wasn't stuck making copies and getting coffee all the time (although I did have to do those things sometimes, as was expected.) I was improving my writing skills and getting a feel for what a public relations job would be like."*

Increased Experience Should Be Met with Increased Responsibility

As the internship experience progresses, students should have the opportunity to demonstrate an increased level of responsibility. This is a sign of good faith from the organization, in that they have confidence in the abilities of the student. Of the students who had participated in internships, 72% agreed or strongly agreed that they were able to assume additional responsibility as their level of experience increased.

> *"I WAS GIVEN the opportunity to prove myself. Initially they did not plan on me completing work similar to an Account Coordinator, seeing as I was hired as an intern; but they were impressed with my work and I was given the chance to complete more complicated projects once I proved myself."*

Don't Leave Things Out

It is an overall best practice in the Human Resources field to provide job candidates with a realistic preview of their potential job duties. It was once routine for recruiters to make jobs sound highly alluring and exciting. The candidate would accept a job offer only to be disappointed with their employment and leave the company prematurely, leading to a high turnover rate and high acquisition costs. In an internship program, a realistic job preview is just as, if not more, important. Students are present to learn more about a specific job in a particular industry, with the hopes of possibly being offered a full-time position. By hiding certain tasks of a particular job function, an organization can only harm their relationships with these potential full-time employees. Virtually all (98%) of students agreed that they must be given a realistic preview of the field during an internship program. Approximately 1 in every 5 interns reported that they only slightly agreed, or did not agree at all, that they were actually given this realistic preview.

> *"WHAT I LIKED THE MOST was that it was very hands on. I had goals and objectives to accomplish, my supervisor helped me to design the right kind of experiment, but I got to carry it out, and even learn the technique, on my own. In a way, that was very empowering."*

Provide for Group Work

Interns place a great deal of value on feeling like they are a part of the organization, as opposed to just feeling like outsider who are not really "part" of the organization. One opportunity to provide them with a more "at home" feeling is to assign them group work. Group work can be completed with other interns from within your organization or with employees that are working on similar projects. About 90% of students agreed that they should be given the opportunity to work in groups during an internship, while over half (54%) of interns surveyed disagreed or only slightly agreed that they were actually provided with group work.

Don't Be Afraid to Challenge Interns

Many organizations choose not to provide interns with challenging projects or work assignments, for two main reasons: the work that needs to be completed is by nature not challenging; or staff members lack faith in the ability of interns to effectively complete the work. However, the fact remains that 98% of students agree that the work completed should be challenging and stimulating, and 14% of interns felt that it was not.

There are two key components to ensure that work is challenging. First is the development of learning objectives and tasks as discussed earlier in this chapter. The other is allowing interns the opportunity to work on a project from creation to completion.

Assist Interns with Setting Priorities

The vast majority of students (92%) agreed that they must be given the opportunity to set priorities. Of the interns surveyed, 86% agreed that they were actually given the opportunity to set priorities. The data suggests that while setting priorities is important to students, they may need some help. This can simply be done by supervisors suggesting to interns the projects that need to be completed first.

"I REALLY LIKED the openness of the internship project. I was able to design my own program and carry it out with my own timeline/objectives, while still working closely with my supervisors."

Providing for "Core Competencies"

The idea of core competencies as it relates to interns is that students wish to build upon their existing skill sets during the internship experience. While much of what they will learn is work-related and industry/job-specific, there is something to be said about assisting interns in improving upon "core competency" skills such as writing, presenting, etc. When structuring an internship program, it is best to keep the core competency list below in mind, and try to match as many competencies as possible with the activities and tasks that are planned. From the survey data, it is apparent that students who took part in an internship recognized that the experience helped them improve on all of the listed competencies and skills to some degree, with the only exception being reading and writing.

SURVEY DISCUSSION

Table C shows the mean ranking of core competencies, based on students who had completed an internship, in order of most to least improved. Column A displays the rank and Column B presents the mean response (based on a 5 scale rating) from the survey takers.

Table C		B
A		
1	Communicating	4.03
2	Listening	3.85
3	Taking Direction	3.85
4	Problem Solving	3.75
5	Decision Making	3.70
6	Critical Thinking	3.67
7	Teamwork	3.65
8	Networking	3.55
9	Leadership	3.44
10	Ethics	3.35
11	Presenting	3.14
12	Reading	2.99
13	Writing	2.98

A Long-Term Goal: Rotational Internships

One of the largest and most recent trends in internship programming is the idea of rotational internships. A rotational internship is one where the intern has the opportunity to experience work in either different areas of a specific discipline or, in very broad rotational programs–different areas of an entire company. The recent growth in rotational internships is directly related to their unique ability to provide students with the most workplace experience.

A departmental rotational program would allow the intern to experience different areas of a department for a specific period of time. For example, a rotational internship program in an HR department may have the intern working three weeks in compensation, three weeks in recruiting, three weeks in benefits, and three weeks in training.

An agency-wide rotational program would have the intern working for a specific period of time in different function areas. For example, the intern might work three weeks in HR, three weeks in marketing, three weeks in accounting, and three weeks in legal.

45

Total Internship Management

The major advantage of a rotational program is that it guarantees that the intern will be exposed to as many people as possible within a department or an organization. If the main goal of your internship program is to potentially hire interns as full-time employees after they graduate, few models could be better than a rotational program.

However, rotational programs are not right for every organization. If you are just starting to implement an overall internship program or college relations plan, working with a rotational model is probably not the best choice for your organization at the present time. Gaining proficiency in a one-job internship model first will aid greatly in the proper implementation of a rotational program. The question of an organization's culture also comes into focus when dealing with a rotational program. Since the intern will be handed off several times between departments and supervisors, the chance for problems in continuity of the student's learning experience increases. There is also a greater time commitment on the part of the internship coordinator to recruit four or five total supervisors per intern, as opposed to just one supervisor for the non-rotational program.

> *"I WAS ABLE to experience the company's atmosphere as a whole, because I was brought out into the field to work with other areas of the business. I enjoy working with people and my supervisor made sure I met almost everyone."*
>
> *"IT WAS GREAT to gain different views of the jobs within the organization (client relations, receptionist, inventory/ordering, maintenance, etc.)"*

SUPERVISORS

As discussed in the earlier section regarding program structure, there are separate key individuals in the management process of an internship program: the internship coordinator and the internship supervisor. The internship supervisor is the individual from whom the intern receives job assignments, work-related feedback, and evaluations. The supervisor is the individual who will have the most contact with the intern on a daily basis throughout the internship.

> *"I WANT AN INTERNSHIP that will have a good supervisor willing to teach their interns everything they need to know and be willing to answer any questions they may have. I also want an internship that I learn something in and where I am able to use my skills that I have learned from my courses."*

If you were to perform an Internet search for "best practices in internships" you would find a list of varying best practices from universities, associations, and some employers. However, the selection of a supervisor will most likely not be mentioned even once on the list. In almost all cases, the supervisor is the direct manager of the intern. The relationship is identical to the relationship between a manager and line employee; and the latest research shows that the way employees are treated by their manager is often the sole determinant in whether an organization retains that employee. The same applies in an internship.

Remember, interns are going to represent your organization. The supervisor has a great deal to do with whether the student will have a positive or negative influence on your campus recruiting strategies. Therefore, choosing and properly training a supervisor is an extremely important, yet currently under-appreciated, component to an internship program. So under-appreciated, in fact, that *less than five percent* of organizations reported that the supervisor for interns is evaluated for their ability to act in a supervisory role for students. The vast majority (81%) of organizational survey respondents strongly disagreed, disagreed, or were neutral when asked if they evaluated potential internship supervisors. Choosing a supervisor, and evaluating that person for the ability to perform as an internship supervisor is an important step in the process that must not be overlooked - and a key determinant of a positive experience for both the student and the organization.

Just over two-thirds of interns reported that their supervisor was involved in their internship. Almost 10% reported that their supervisor's involvement in the internship was minimal, if any. Just under 70% of students agreed or strongly agreed that they would want their supervisor to be involved in the internship. Interestingly, 27% of students were stuck in the middle and unsure if they would want their supervisor to be involved in the internship at all. This disconnect speaks loudly to students' expectations of supervisor involvement in internships. It is likely that these students have the expectation, based on the experiences of their peers and friends, that supervisors do not, and should not, have a strong involvement in the internship. Many students fail to realize the importance of the supervisor's role, as do many organizations.

A Cautionary Note

Because the process of choosing an intern's supervisor is delicate, this publication would be incomplete without making an important distinction. An individual who is an excellent supervisor of full-time, experienced individuals may not necessarily be the most effective internship supervisor. Providing supervision of a college student with little or no work experience is considerably different than managing full-time employees. Through our workshops, presentations and work with employers and higher education institutions from across the country, we have had the chance to present best practices to audiences from both entities. In each interaction, the universities generally recognize the difference, while the employer organizations almost always miss it. Thus, this is one of the largest gaps that require special attention. Organizations need to evaluate their expectations and adjust them as appropriate.

Supervisor Skill Sets

As discussed above, the role of an intern supervisor is one that requires a very special and unique skill set for the relationship with the student – and the eventual successful outcome of the internship experience for both the student and the host organization. The following are some skills that intern supervisors should possess to be as effective as possible.

Allow Time for Questions and Making Sure They Get Answered

Interns, being brand new to an organization, will have several questions relating to work assignments, industry standards, and the organization itself. Keep in mind that one of the key reasons the student is working for the organization in the first place is to gain a deeper understanding of the industry and organization. If they do not ask questions, they will not have that chance, which will ultimately lead to an unsatisfied experience for the intern. Equally as important is providing the intern with answers to their questions. This will ensure that they can properly do their job and that they are being provided an educationally sound and meaningful experience.

According to the aggregate results of the National Internship and Co-op Study from 2007-2014, 81% of the students that participated in an internship either agreed or strongly agreed that they were given the opportunity to ask questions of their supervisor. However, nearly 40% of these same students did not agree that they were given the chance to have their questions answered. This is a strong indication that one of the strongest skills that intern supervisors need to exhibit is allowing time for their intern to ask questions and for the supervisor to provide answers to those questions.

> *"MY SUPERVISOR WAS EXCELLENT! He always made sure I knew what I was doing, never thought any question was stupid, and always treated me with respect."*
>
> *"WHAT I LIKED BEST about my internship was that once I had been given proper instructions on what to do, I was set free to do work on my own with little supervision. I felt as though I had gained the trust and respect of my supervisor, and he always seemed pleased."*
>
> *"WHAT I LIKED BEST about my internship was how my supervisor made it her priority to find time to help me with any questions or problems that may have been an obstacle for me to overcome."*
>
> *"IT WAS A LAID BACK environment. My supervisor was very accessible to me and eager to answer any questions I had about the organization or my tasks."*

Be Available for Consultation

Being available for consultation is similar to being available for questions, the only difference being that a consultation tends to take a bit more time than simply answering a question or two during the day. A consultation is an involved conversation that provides the intern with greater insight to the operation of the department or in-depth discussion about the organization. There is a great opportunity to provide the intern with valuable knowledge when consulting with them. An effective consultation will allow the intern to be better at their jobs and fulfill the requirements of their internship experience. It will allow them to continue their assigned work in a more efficient manner.

Nearly three quarters of interns surveyed agreed or strongly agreed that their supervisor was available for consultation, while 7% of interns strongly disagreed or disagreed with the same statement. Not surprisingly, 98% of students strongly agreed or agreed that they would want their supervisors to be available for a consultation, should they take part in an internship program.

This does not mean that the supervisor needs to be available for the intern whenever the intern requests attention. It does, however, stress the importance of the communication and relationship between the supervisor and their intern. To be an effective supervisor, one needs to respond to the intern in a timely manner if a consultation is either requested or deemed necessary. If the supervisor cannot consult with the intern, he or she should remind the student of other available projects to work on in the meantime.

> *"MY ADVISOR WAS DISORGANIZED and, after assigning me over 2,500 contracts to go through, disappeared for the duration of the internship."*
>
> *"MY SUPERVISOR WAS HORRIBLE. She was not present physically 70% of the time, so I would have no direction."*
>
> *"MY SUPERVISOR WAS based out of Paris, so we only got to see him for four days over the course of five weeks."*

Supervisors Must also Be Instructors

As with any other managerial role, the supervisor must not only provide the intern with work, but also explain in detail what they are expecting the intern to actually accomplish. If the supervisor simply hands the intern an assignment, or emails it with little description, the intern may be able to complete the assigned task but may not fully learn why this assignment was important! By providing the intern with *outcome expectations*, the supervisor can be assured that the intern will be on the right track when completing the assignment. It is in this role that the supervisor is also acting as an instructor.

The data suggests that supervisors may need assistance being effective instructors. In response to the question "is being given adequate explanation concerning assigned tasks is of importance?" the mean response (on a 5 scale) from students was 4.16, as opposed to interns whose mean response was a 3.86. Students expect far more explanation to be given than what is currently being provided by supervisors. This is a gap that must be addressed and accounted for if the internship experience is to be successful in the long run.

To further illustrate this point, as we look closer at the aggregate data for 2007-2014, just under 70% of interns report that they agree or strongly agree that they were given adequate explanation of work tasks and assignments at the time that they were received. A striking 83% of students agree or strongly agree that they should be given adequate explanation.

> *"I WASN'T GIVEN enough guidance. I was thrown into the sales world with no experience and asked to sell a product I understood very little about."*
>
> *"I THINK THE KEY is to have a well-structured program with an enthusiastic supervisor that possesses strong communication skills."*

Treat the Intern Professionally and Respectfully

Although interns may not be full-time employees of the organizations for which they work, it is critically important to understand that the way interns are treated reflects on the overall organization. Interns who are treated poorly by their supervisor will believe that the organization is an undesirable place to work.

Approximately 13% of interns strongly disagree or disagree that their supervisor treated them respectfully during the internship program. About 16% of interns felt the same way when asked if their supervisor treated them professionally. While the percentages are low, they represent a significant population who feel were not treated with a reasonable degree of respect. Being that this is easily correctable by the organization, it is highly recommended that a supervisor is chosen who will treat interns with the professionalism and respect any employee or contractor of the organization deserves.

> *"IT'S NOT NECESSARY to hold the intern's hand, but that doesn't mean they don't require some supervision. Many employers don't understand the difference, and that's important."*
>
> *"MY DIRECT SUPERVISOR was not respectful and offered no opportunities for personal growth during the internship."*
>
> *"I UNFORTUNATELY did not get the respect I believed I deserved from my supervisor. He did not treat me like an employee and made inappropriate comments. Other than that, I was treated great by the other employees and felt welcomed by them."*
>
> *"I REALLY ENJOYED working with the amazing people that I did. They treated me very professionally and allowed me to take on genuine responsibilities."*

Supervisors Should Be Approachable Individuals

Aside from a possible mentor that is assigned to the intern, the supervisor is typically their only contact within the organization that they will have a significant relationship. If the intern is having a problem, whether it is related to a work assignment or another employee, it is likely that the intern will want to approach their supervisor regarding the situation. If the supervisor is an unapproachable individual, the intern will hold back, which would be detrimental to their internship experience. More than three quarters of intern respondents (77%) agreed or strongly agreed that they did feel comfortable talking to their supervisor regarding problems they had encountered.

"MY BOSS ... would tell us to do something, we'd do it, then she'd change her mind and do everything over the way she wanted it, usually throwing out everything we did. It made us feel terrible. We put so much effort into all the projects and she'd throw them away in seconds without even consulting us. She was also very disrespectful when someone's personal opinion differed from her own. At one point she singled me out about a certain issue and sent me more than 10 emails a day trying to 'educate' me."

"I REALLY ENJOYED the professional relationship I had with my supervisor. She was reliable, open, and understanding. It made working at the internship easier to adjust."

"MY SUPERVISOR WAS a very good mentor and friend towards me. I did not feel out of place or unable to talk about a problem."

MENTORING INTERNS

An essential component of designing a comprehensive internship program at your organization, it is important to include a deliberate and detailed mentoring component. As discussed earlier, the primary reasons why a student chooses to participate in an internship all focus on the development of new skills, gaining experience in their field of study and to gain a realistic preview of the workplace. All areas in which a relationship with a mentor can make an incredible difference in the experience an intern has with your organization.

Much like the development of the internship program itself, the mentoring component requires a significant commitment of time, energy, and effort. The overall positive outcomes of effectively mentoring interns far outweigh any costs associated with its development. It is likewise helpful to remember that organizations with reputations for being good training grounds will get more-talented interns who can do better work! The added benefit to the company is to have a pipeline for home-grown talent that can be socialized to the ways of the organization and familiarized with its methodologies, which can be great for your organization.

Mentoring is Focused on Career Development

Many of the premier scholars in the field of mentoring note that what distinguishes mentoring is its primary focus on development and growth in the context of the career of the individual being mentored, and the fact that the relationship comprises an experienced practitioner and a novice. Mentoring can also include sponsorship, which is more focused on entry into the field and career advancement, and apprenticeship, which is experiential learning that exposes apprentices to the processes and characteristics of the profession. "Mentoring" tends to be a catch-all phrase for all three types of relationships, but it is important to note that it is the career development and growth that is part of the overall experience interns desire.

The Basic Functions of a Mentor:
Career, Psychosocial, and Role-Modeling

Researchers in the field of mentoring have described three primary functions of a mentor: namely career, psychosocial, and role-modeling. Many of the career functions are similar to sponsorship, and usually include promoting the intern's advancement by making the intern more visible to key people throughout the organization during the internship experience. This often involves making introductions and highlighting the work of the intern, the latter of which coincides with challenging tasks that showcase their strengths and help develop new knowledge, skills, and/or attitudes – commonly referred to as KSA's. Additionally, mentors generally protect their interns from harmful forces and politics within the organization. The psychosocial functions refer to the ways in which the relationship promotes personal and professional growth, especially in terms of identity and self-efficacy. This often involves an emotional relationship with the mentor that is predicated upon trust and respect. Role-modeling is about being the kind of professional that the intern would want to become; it is walking the talk and leading by example. In doing so, the mentor makes the world in which (s)he works a lesson in and of itself.

The Mechanics of a Good Mentoring Relationship

The role of the intern's mentor is one that requires a very special and unique skill set for the relationship with the student – and the eventual successful outcome of the internship experience for both the student and the host organization.

The following are the basic mechanics of an effective mentoring program.

Matching Mentors and Protégés:
Let Mentors and Interns Choose for Themselves

One of the most common errors that organizations make is assigning mentor-intern pairs. While it is expedient in the short term, it is often ineffective, if not disastrous, in the long term. Because of the emotional bonds and trust that are necessary for effective mentoring, this is not the kind of relationship that can be dictated, and the selection needs to be up to the two individuals who will build the relationship. One helpful way to initiate this process is to introduce the Intern to potential mentors within the organization based on their goals, attitudes, interests, and personality, and let the intern have the opportunity to chat with several possible choices. Pragmatically, there may be only one person available, but then it becomes important to respect the fact that this may need to be more of an apprenticeship than a mentoring relationship. Under such circumstances, the organization is advised to frame the experience as such, and focus on building specific skills rather than on general career development. When there are large intern pools, as in the case of summer internship programs, it is often fun and informative to have a mentor showcase in which all of the possible mentors describe themselves and their work, after which everyone mingles for a while so that interns and potential mentors can informally assess the style/cultural fit.

Two other pitfalls are worth noting. The first is that companies sometimes set relationships in stone after they are chosen, and do not allow interns to change mentors. Sometimes, the initial fit appears strong, but turns out to be superficial, and keeping an intern with a bad mentor is going to have a negative impact on the intern, the employee mentor and the overall internship experience for all involved. The second major pitfall is putting the onus on the intern to make the mentoring relationship work – while it takes two to make any relationship function, the senior member of the partnership must take the lead in mentoring.

Keep the Mentoring Relationship Informal

Just as it is impossible to dictate whom a person will trust, it is unrealistic to try to force mentoring to happen on a schedule. The most effective mentoring occurs spontaneously, and sometimes happens outside of the formal office environment and traditional supervisor-intern context. To promote such interactions, the organization can sponsor off-site events or create a framework for interactions to occur. For example, look at the intern's work plan and the dedicated times that the mentor and intern can meet. Much like supervisor availability, mentors should also be available, keep an open-door policy, and encourage the intern to take the initiative on when to have a meeting.

Tailor Teaching and Advising to the Needs of the Intern

A one-size-fits-all mentoring program is rarely effective; each mentor needs to tailor the instruction and advising to their intern. The mentoring relationship is a great opportunity to work with the intern to craft the job in accordance with the needs of the company and the capacities/interests of the intern as well as the requirements from their college or university. The mentor should work with the intern to establish a set of developmental goals that they co-create – these may be based on established goals within the organization, but should not be exact copies thereof. It may be helpful to arrange the goals under the rubric of KSAs: knowledge, skills, and attitudes (perspectives), and likewise to remember that the goals should be flexible enough to change with the interests of the intern yet meet the requirements of the academic constructs put forth by the school and the interns work plan.

Provide Detailed and Effective Feedback

One of the key responsibilities of a mentor is to provide the intern with clear and honest feedback. This means giving feedback that is detailed, explicit, and non-personal (i.e., focus on the action/results instead of the individual), and presenting it as close to the relevant activities as possible. Mentors should make sure to comment on what the intern does well with the same clarity and specificity with which (s)he provides criticism. Too often, organizations pay lip service to what people do well and focus on what needs to be developed.

If anything, the balance should be toward praising the positive. Help interns to do even better, and enhance their strengths and capabilities. Again, this promotes loyalty to the company and enjoyment of the job tasks. It is also important for the mentor to coordinate this feedback with job related performance measures from the interns supervisor (in the case where the intern has a separate supervisor and mentor).

A Good Mentor is Both Respected and Respectful

It goes without saying that one's superior should be respected, but it is likewise incumbent upon the superior to be respectable and respectful. In addition to being someone whom the intern can admire and emulate (which is a function of behavior and ethics, not rank!), a mentor should treat interns fairly and appropriately. Specifically, this means showing respect for the intern's uniqueness, ideas, work, and contributions, and likewise for his or her goals and circumstances. It is important to remember that the aim is to develop the intern into future colleagues, and a key step in doing so is respecting them as key players in the organization's future.

Be Supportive by Providing and Building Positive Psychological Resources

Keeping up with the fast pace of the current business environment takes a lot of psychological and emotional resources. Mistakes can be very costly, pressure is high, and this can be a lot for an intern to handle. Mentors can soften the impact of these realities by providing encouragement, conveying empathy, and protecting the intern from some of the dangers and politics of the working world. Another important means of support is providing trust; the company has already put the intern through an interview process and determined that (s)he is capable of doing the job and fits with the company. As such, the mentor should show confidence in the intern's ability to do what (s)he needs to do, and help them develop his/her own confidence and self-efficacy. It is also very important to understand the intern's motivation, to nurture it, and to encourage the intern to feel genuinely positive about the meaning and importance of the work (s)he does. The result will be an employee who is ready, willing, and able to expand his/her capacities, job tasks, and responsibilities.

Emotional Safety

One of the hardest, and yet most important, duties of a mentor is to foster an emotionally safe environment. With the high pressure that is common in most organizational environments, there is a tendency for mistakes to receive very harsh reprisals and for people to be bullied and humiliated in the office. When people are afraid of making mistakes, they are not going to be innovative, creative, productive, or willing to take initiative. The mentor can best prevent these effects by avoiding overly harsh or curt criticism, and protecting the intern from others who might be forceful in their admonishment or be overly/unnecessarily judgmental. There is plenty of room for constructive criticism, and there are even gentle and effective ways for indicating that someone has made some serious errors. It is also critical to remember that mistakes are occasions for learning, and that they are part of any learning process. As such, they should be handled with tact and grace.

Another key form of support is giving the intern time to think, act, and learn. There are very few work environments in which it would be earth-shattering to give the intern more time to answer a question, or to let them think for a moment (in fact, it might be a good idea to encourage the intern to take more time to think!). Overall, an emotionally safe environment reduces the amount of pressure and harshness that interns face, and enables them to bring their fullest capabilities to bear.

The Developmental Behaviors Enabled by a Good Mentor

The work environment for an intern is a learning environment, and it should foster positive developments in knowledge, skills, and attitudes.

There are four key developmental behaviors that a mentor enables: exercising independence, reflection, synthesis, and extrapolation.

Increase Interns' Opportunities for Independence

Interns often need a significant amount of training, and can need a lot of hand-holding at the outset. Yet, even from the beginning, the mentor should look for opportunities for the intern to do tasks independently, and to increase gradually the complexity of the tasks and level of responsibility as their comfort and skill level improves. One of the best models for this is having the intern perform job tasks with increasing amounts of responsibility each time, and maintaining an open-door policy that leaves the intern feeling free to come with questions. A great framework for this can be developed within the intern work plan.

Facilitate Opportunities for Reflection

The optimal mentoring environment encourages interns to reflect upon past actions, experiences, and behaviors, and then consider how they may apply in future contexts and use them as a springboard for improving performance.

Reflection is also one of the best ways to learn from mistakes, and requires trust and constructive feedback to work most effectively. Mentors should create opportunities for reflecting on knowledge, skills, and attitudes (KSAs) both in terms of the tasks that need to be done and in the contexts of both the company's mission and the individual's personal and career goals.

Facilitate Opportunities for Reflection

The optimal mentoring environment encourages interns to reflect upon past actions, experiences, and behaviors, and then consider how they may apply in future contexts and use them as a springboard for improving performance. Reflection is also one of the best ways to learn from mistakes, and requires trust and constructive feedback to work most effectively. Mentors should create opportunities for reflecting on knowledge, skills, and attitudes (KSAs) both in terms of the tasks that need to be done and in the contexts of both the company's mission and the individual's personal and career goals.

Synthesis and Extrapolation Tie KSAs Together

Synthesizing and extrapolating are both key developmental behaviors that promote the intern's evolution into a full-fledged professional. Synthesizing integrates established KSAs with each other or with new KSAs, thereby increasing the depth/strength of both. Most job tasks that come with a promotion will require combinations of KSAs, and a mentor should help the intern to unite his/her KSAs into a coherent picture of the task, and job, as a whole. This is a great opportunity to tie in the mission of the organization and the professional/personal goals of the intern.

Extrapolating involves applying KSAs to novel contexts, which results in the intern developing new KSAs or improving established KSAs, and expands his/her skill set so that (s)he can do new tasks and take on more responsibilities. A great way to do this is to ask questions that require the intern to think beyond the task at hand and into the meaning of the task relative to the activities of the unit/department/company, and also consider how the products of the intern work will be the input for other important tasks or aims.

Promote Positive Professional Development

When a mentoring relationship is built on the six mechanisms that underlie good mentorship, it enables the intern to engage in key developmental behaviors that will promote positive professional development. For example, synthesizing and extrapolating can occur through tasks that are tailored to the intern. When these exercises are presented in an emotionally safe and supportive environment, the intern may have the self-confidence to try extending his/her knowledge despite the many opportunities for error inherent in novel contexts. If the mentoring relationship is informal, collegiality can foster open dialogue between the mentor and intern, and the mentor's provision of timely and constructive feedback can emphasize both the points that the intern needs to grasp and the areas that need additional work and development.

Similarly, a supportive and emotionally safe environment, in which the mentor conveys empathy, listens, and offers opportunities to reframe ideas, can enable the intern to feel more comfortable engaging in reflection. Removing conditions that cause self-consciousness, fear of failure, and the like allows the intern to feel free to ask questions and receive criticism. Moreover, informality can augment emotional safety by moving the reflection process to a non-work setting, which facilitates reflecting from an "outside-looking-in" perspective. When the intern is confident of the mentor's respect and support, they can feel comfortable being open and honest in the reflection process, secure in the knowledge that the mentor wants them to succeed and that the mentor is trying to effect improvement for a future colleague rather than belittle a subordinate.

The National Internship and Co-op Study consistently finds support for all factors of this model and adds two key mentoring functions: Challenge and Connecting. As interns are consistently looking for growth, one of the best ways to foster this is through challenging assignments that are aligned with their career interests and growth trajectory. In meeting these challenges, they learn new behaviors and skills, which add to the competencies and services they can provide, and they are also more likely to have high job engagement. The other important developmental opportunity is connecting – while an intern needs to be protected from harmful forces, (s)he also needs to be directed toward positive relationships within the organization. A mentor can help the intern build a network of important people who can help promote their career and introduce him/her to additional opportunities, challenges, and experiences.

Mentoring is a Feasible and Worthwhile Investment

While it may seem that many of these suggestions require a significant investment, mostly it involves the mentor paying attention to their own actions and being a role model. Especially when time is tight, being a person that the intern can emulate accomplishes most of these suggestions. Having an open door actually saves time when it is combined with promoting the interns independence, because (s)he will feel encouraged to try things alone before coming to the mentor with questions, and will be able to learn from mistakes instead of having the mentor clean up an assignment afterward. Most importantly, good mentoring will promote strong job engagement and company loyalty, which in turn fosters high productivity, innovation, creativity, and high initiative, which makes a very positive impact on the bottom line!

MARKETING YOUR INTERNSHIP PROGRAM

Before you can begin marketing the internship program to universities (and their students), a decision must be made as to which universities will be targeted. One of the things to keep in mind is that every university is different in their approach to how they handle internships and communication with their student population. The best method for targeting universities is to get to know the ones in immediate geographical area.

On the most basic level, at least investigating what majors are offered by a college is the beginning of an important part of college recruiting - targeting the correct college. Just as a career counselor advises students to not take a scattershot approach to applying for jobs or internships, and to avoid blasting a generic cover letter and résumé to every company on earth, we also know that there are benefits to building a stronger relationship with specific colleges that offers students with the majors, demographics, geographic preferences, and other qualities you seek in candidates.

Targeting Universities

Targeting the right colleges can reduce the expenses of your recruiting efforts by focusing time, travel budgets, job fair registration fees, and so on, to those schools where you are most likely to succeed in finding talent that fits your needs. Also, other employers meticulously target; if you don't target you may be on the losing side in the impending "war for talent," as the Baby Boomer generation continues to exit the workforce through retirement. (This is not to say an employer should ignore applications from students from schools that aren't on their target school list; but to create a logical list of target schools can still be a good investment of time and energy.)

Of course, in the age of mass job postings and online application processes, it doesn't cost that much more to post a job at hundreds of schools, but beyond a quick broadcasting of an internship listing, where do you really want to expend your effort? Today, when almost all recruiting efforts can take place online which makes the job application process more impersonal, how can you win the war for talent by building a more personal relationship with a specific college or even specific students?

Some questions that you should consider are:

- What makes each university unique?

- What degree programs does the university offer?

- What makes each university unique?

- What resources are available within the institution to support the students taking part in the degree programs that you will be recruiting from?

- Does the university have any sort of research center dedicated to any of its degree programs?

- Is it easy to find information about how the university interacts with employers?

Granted, learning details about all of the universities in a region can be difficult, if not nearly impossible. In the United States today, there are nearly 4,300 institutions of higher learning. It would be an impossible task to learn all of the pertinent information about every university! Your best bet is to target those that are close to you geographically and grow from there.

How to Target

A first step in the process of choosing target schools is to determine your organization's hiring needs, and to project where they will be in the next few years. It's important to remember, for example, that students usually make a decision about a choice of their college major in their sophomore year. Employers might be able to influence a student's choice of major by providing presentations on campus about careers in that field. However, an employer will not reap the benefits of this type of "seeding" for at least two more years, when the student finally graduates and enters the workforce.

So, thinking ahead at least a few years, look around your organization. Are certain parts of your workforce nearing retirement in the next several years? Where are your greatest needs for entry-level and management track hires? What skills or qualities are important to you in new hires? Are there particular majors that are most essential? Do you foresee changes in your organization's business model, product line, or structure, which will influence your college recruiting? Does your company have a commitment to hiring and retaining a diverse workforce?

A good way to determine hiring needs is to survey hiring managers throughout your organization. In this survey you should be asking about specific skills, degrees, and demographics they seek in their hires. Of course, integrating this information into your organization's long-term or strategic plan, with input from the highest levels of leadership in the organization, will help you make an informed decision about what kinds of candidates you seek.

Where to Look

Now that you have a sense of how many candidates, and from what backgrounds, are needed in your organization, you can begin the search for schools that offer a population you're seeking. It is very tempting, and sometimes logical, to look to the past for where you have had previous success. Surveying your current staff to see where they went to college it is one place to start. It may also be helpful to look at the success of prior college hires from certain schools – do graduates of certain schools get promoted more quickly than others?

However, there can be pitfalls with relying entirely on this data. For example, demographics and majors, and even the curriculum, can change dramatically within a college or university over time. Additionally, there may be excellent opportunities at colleges where your staff did not go to college, and in some cases these colleges may not be receiving attention from competitor firms and therefore can provide an excellent opportunity to gather the "cream of the crop" of the graduating class.

In addition to looking for which colleges have many alumni among your current staff, it is important to look at not only which majors are offered at the college, but how many students actually choose those specific majors, and what actual courses are required for those majors. Most college career centers will be able to help you if you call to ask them this kind of question, and can at least provide some anecdotal information about what the most popular majors are at the college. Or, they may be able to refer you to an office of institutional research at the college that can provide you with detailed demographic information. This type of information can also be quite helpful when assessing a college for the diversity of the students.

College rankings can sometimes be helpful, though it is also important to remember that the top candidates from a lower-ranked, possibly regional college, may be just as competitive as many of the students from a high ranked college (and again, students from the high ranked college may be courted by numerous other competitor companies, whereas a regional college might get overlooked). Also, not all college rankings are based on criteria that are helpful when it comes to hiring. It might be worth looking at things besides the U.S. News & World Report rankings, such as whether a school is AACSB-accredited if you are seeking business majors.

Geographic information is also important. There are some colleges that naturally have a population of students who are willing to relocate. A good question to ask the college career center representative is "where do students come from to attend your college?" If students from all over the nation, or perhaps all over the world, attend that college or university, there is a chance that those students may be flexible about relocating to your organization's location. Or, it is helpful to know whether most students who graduate from that university tend to stay in the surrounding area or whether they prefer to relocate elsewhere. It is important to remain open-minded, though; if a college has all of the other qualities you seek, it is quite possible to maintain an excellent "long-distance" relationship with that college if you put the effort in, and to still show excellent hiring results.

Other criteria might include the potential to build other types of partnerships with a college or university, such as being able to support their research programs, or ability to provide corporate contributions that will have a larger impact both on the university and your company.

Once you've determined which criteria are most important to you, it is helpful to rank these criteria in order of importance. Perhaps it is helpful to give each criterion a numerical weight, which you can use later to make ranking decisions. The next step is to produce some research and analysis to determine how the various schools on your list have ranked according to your various criteria. Balancing your list with the number of schools you can feasibly recruit at within your recruiting budget, and remembering the non-quantifiable factors (like where your CEO went to school!) is also important.

Building a Relationship Once You've Chosen

Once you've determined the schools that you want to recruit from, it is important to consistently continue relationship-building activities with them. Sometimes it can take a couple of years of effort to institutionalize a relationship with a college or university, due to the complexity of their organizations, turnover of staff within the career centers and other offices on campus. It is important to remember that students are constantly cycling through the university, and the ones you may have tried very hard to impress will soon be graduating. To truly build a presence on a college campus and ultimately a relationship with students, staff and faculty you will need to be diligent in your efforts.

It is a good idea to start your relationship with a phone call or an introductory email to the college career center director or head of employer relations. The goal of this initial dialogue is to schedule an in-person meeting with them to discuss the goals that you have for recruiting their students and also to learn as much as you can from them if possible. It is also a good idea to bring the college career center staff to your organization to give them a sense of what you do. Since many college career center staff members may not have worked in the corporate world, they may not understand the lingo of your industry. Yet these individuals are responsible for explaining to numerous college students what it is that you do. With this in mind, try to provide information in a way that a layperson can understand.

Remember that the career center staff may have tremendous influence over whether a student chooses to work for you, so making a good impression with them can only help your organization. Also, try to be realistic in what the career center can do for you. The significant majority of career centers are underfunded and understaffed compared to others, and most of them are not in the "placement" business. One of the misnomers that many HR people have is that career centers function as headhunters. This represents one of the largest expectation gaps in these relationships. Career center staff members don't make a commission, and they cannot just send you résumés in an instant, nor can they typically provide recommendations for specific candidates. Most career center staff members aren't doing this work for the money, they're doing it because it's a rewarding job. At the minimum, at least tell the career center who you hired. At the end of the day, that is how career centers are assessed — by where the students got internships and jobs — and they might depend on you to report this information to them.

It is also important to understand that every college and university is completely different from each other in how their career services office is structured and how it operates. Many have specific policies and procedures, especially related to internships, and it is important to learn as much as you can about what they expect from your organization. Colleges may also have a specific internship recruiting time-frame, often corresponding with the academic calendar. Additionally, different colleges have different relationships with student organizations on campus, or with college professors, and may use different procedures for posting internship positions, organizing on campus presentations, or setting up on campus interviews. It is a good idea to simply ask what the school's calendar year and school policies are as they relate to internship and job recruiting.

After an initial meeting, the simplest way to begin the relationship is to post an internship with the school. Follow up and communicate with the career center staff to ensure that the position will get enough publicity with the student population that meets the criteria of your posting. This could be accomplished through targeted emails or other social media that the career center utilizes. If you are sure that you want to build a long-term relationship, consider signing up for a job fair, corporate presentation, or campus interview schedule.

As the recruiting season winds up, it is important to assess how your internship hiring is going, how many interns convert to full-time hires, and whether your full-time recruiting initiatives have been successful. If the recruiting wasn't successful, try to survey the career center staff and even the students to see if you might be able to improve the efforts on your side, before giving up on the school. If the relationship with the school is going well, consider what it involves to become an "employer of choice" on campus; possibilities for going above and beyond the typical employer might include sponsoring scholarships, speaking on campus, volunteering for interview preparation events, volunteering for advisory boards, getting a student who was previously an intern to be your on campus recruiting ambassador, and so on. If all goes well, you will have made an excellent choice of targets schools, and will begin to see excellent returns on your investment of time, energy, and research — and you will be achieving all your target goals.

Identify Universities by Specific Degree Programs

Another approach is to visit the website for The College Board. You may recognize the name if you know of high school students that have recently taken the PSAT/NMSQT and the SAT. The College Board, based in New York City, is the educational testing organization in charge of the college admissions test. Over the past several years, the College Board has also begun offering a resource to its website visitors. The "college search" portion of the website allows individuals to perform a college search based on specific search criteria including geographic area, student clubs offered, financial information, and average test scores. While the website is geared specifically to help high school students target universities where they wish to apply, it is also a tremendous resource for you to target universities for your internship program.

To use this method, first see Appendix A in this publication. This is a list of the degree programs that the College Board has available on their website. You will notice that the list is extremely specific. This should help weed out the universities that might not be best for your internship program. Make a list of the degree programs that you would like to target. (You may perform several searches if your internship program involves positions that are vastly different from each other – for example a position in marketing and a position in engineering.)

Visit www.CollegeBoard.com and find the link for the "College Match-Maker". Once you click the link, you will be in the College MatchMaker interface. You don't want your search to be too specific, because you want to receive a good number of candidate schools.

At the top of the interface, click "location." Select the states where you would like the university to be located. Then click "Majors and Academics." Using the list in **Appendix A**, you can search for specific degree programs. By clicking on "show results" a list will be generated with all of the colleges that fit your criteria.

You can get as specific as you would like with the search criteria to generate different results. Once you are satisfied with the search results, you now have your list of colleges to target for the program.

Do Not Choose Only "Feeder Schools"

Intern Bridge recently worked with an organization that had just been acquired, and the new CEO was determined to implement an internship program – something that had never been done before in this large organization. In speaking with the HR staff about the best way to implement their program, a comment was made that when he first started working for the organization several years before, the culture was to do their very best to obtain MBA applicants from the top business schools for all of their positions. He jokingly remarked that even the mailroom worker had an MBA.

This represents one of the largest gaps in employing graduates of our higher education system. Employers typically reach out to the "big name" schools that achieve high rankings, and the schools without the brand name tend to lose out. When you seriously think about this, it doesn't make sense. Once an entry-level employee enters an organization, they become just that – an entry level employee. At the entry level, someone from a well-known school and someone from a school that might not be as recognizable will most likely end up working next to each other, performing the same tasks.

Are all colleges and universities created equal? Of course not. But to only recruit interns from the popular schools would be making a serious mistake. Your organization will ultimately lose out on highly qualified candidates and the chance to increase diversity within your internship program and organization. Further, the brand name schools do not usually have a problem with attracting organizations to recruit their students – the employers are always knocking at these colleges' doors. Their students are saturated with options. Smaller, and often less known schools often have to go out and recruit organizations to come to their campus. If you recruit at these schools, you will have less competition for students that can do fantastic work.

WORKING WITH COLLEGES & UNIVERSITIES

Time-Consuming, Yet Critical!

Marketing your available internship program to students at specific universities will require the most time on your part. As we illustrated in the previous section, every school will have different policies and procedures, but generally the process works something like this:

Step 1:
Contact the college career office and determine who is in charge of internships.

Step 2:
Contact the internship coordinator to open a dialogue about your internship program.

Step 3:
Submit your pre-formatted job description OR complete the college's detailed internship form.

Step 4:
Select a date and time to conduct interviews (possibly on-campus).

Step 5:
Review cover letters and résumés from applicants.

Step 6:
Conduct interviews (possibly on-campus).

Although this process seems simple, this process will be repeated, with some level of difference, for every college that you choose to recruit! For the most part, you will have to post the position with the college even if you plan on recruiting interns through methods other than the campus career development office. If you plan on having multiple rounds of interviews, it is common for the first round to take place on-campus or over the phone, and for the second round to take place at the host site.

How Closely Does My Organization Have to Work with Colleges?

The answer to this question depends on the college you are contacting. Different colleges have different standards for their internship programs. Almost every college you contact will require that some legwork is completed before the internship is posted to their students; it's just a matter of how detailed and time-consuming the process is.

Some colleges will just have you send a copy of the internal job description, and then they will do the rest of the marketing and scheduling work. Other colleges will require that you not only complete one of their internal forms, but also that you arrange a meeting with someone from their career office who will come on-site and inspect the space where the intern will be working.

The college has a particular interest in ensuring that the intern will remain safe at all times while taking part in an internship experience. Therefore, you must be flexible when working with the college. Depending on the institution that you target and the brand of your organization, the college may not find it worth their time to negotiate their process with you. As harsh as this might sound, it is a reality. For the most part, the colleges hold the key to potential intern candidates and you must adhere to their guidelines for your program to be a complete success.

It is also important to remember that the college or university may not do the legwork for you when it comes to posting, advertising or recruiting candidates. Organizations often have the misconception that universities will offer a "matching service," and that it will be done on a moment's notice. This is not the job of the career center or the university; there are very few, if any, that actually offer this type of service. Universities will help you develop job descriptions and discuss your program with you, but do not expect them to recommend specific students. The role of match-making is up to you, and it will allow you to make informed decisions leading to a mutually beneficial experience.

Interesting Note Relating to Paying Interns

You may be able to get around some of the red tape with the universities if you choose to pay interns and not offer them academic credit through the institution. Sometimes, when the college is offering credit to the student, there are more stringent guidelines put in place by faculty members and other members of the college community. However, you must also keep in mind that there is a very large candidate pool of college students in the nation who are required to complete an internship as part of an academic program, and these are almost always unpaid and for academic credit, as mandated by the school.

Collaboration Plague

The following scenario, albeit purely hypothetical, is a fairly common occurrence:

An organization decides to host interns. They contact a local university for advice on how to reach out to their student population. The organization is greeted excitedly by the college. However, the college has several guidelines that they wish the organization to follow before they are able to market the position to students. The organization, unable or unwilling to abide by the guidelines, decides not to target the university for their internship program.

This has been affectionately named "collaboration plague" by Intern Bridge. Across the country, universities and organizations are trying to collaborate on the "ideal" internship program. Organizations want more flexibility, whereas the universities generally prefer a rigid program with a high degree of supervision. The interests of the two groups are common, but not necessarily equally weighted. Unfortunately, it is the students who suffer, because internship programs in some cases simply don't happen, or operate at a level of unrealized potential.

The truth is that total 100% agreement is often difficult (while not entirely impossible). This is, of course, not meant to discourage you, but rather to reiterate that you should expect the universities you contact to have procedures and requirements that your organization will need to fulfill before they will allow the position to be posted to students.

SURVEY DISCUSSION

Table D on page 72 represents how intern respondents learned about their opportunities.

Column A reflects the ranked responses of how interns learned about the opportunity. Column B represents the matching response from students who have not taken part in an internship experience.

Table D		
A		**B**
1	Friend or family contact	1
2	Personal contact	2
3	Campus Career Development Office or Field Placement Office	6
4	Faculty contact	3
5	Organization website	10
6	Online career directory (Monster.com, etc.)	14
7	Campus internship information session	5
8	Fellow student who was a past or current intern with the organization	4
9	Fellow student	9
10	Career fair	8
11	Student organization	12
12	Internship fair	7
13	Advertisement in print	13
14	Organization open house	11

Table E shows which resources organizations who host interns find most useful.

Column A represents the ranked responses of methods organizations use to market their opportunity.

Table E	
A	
1	Working with the career development office at local colleges
2	Word of mouth from past or current interns
3	Faculty contacts at local colleges
4	Organization website
5	College campus internship information sessions
6	Career fairs
7	Outreaching to student clubs on local college campuses
8	Internship fairs
9	Commercial career websites (such as Monster.com)
10	Hosting an open house
11	Direct email marketing
12	Advertisement in print

Utilizing the Campus Career Center

As previously discussed, the campus career center is a great resource, and in most cases, a mandatory one. Employers ranked using the career office most effective when trying to recruit interns for the program. A glimpse at student responses shows that both students who have had an internship, and those that have not, did not use the campus career office as their primary point of contact. In fact 86.4% of students that participated in an internship indicated that they secured their internship through their campuses' career center.

A bit of caution as we move forward...

The ranked data is based on the feedback from students at all of the colleges and universities where the National Internship and Co-op study has been implemented. It is important to note that while the overall ranks are important, each college's career office operates differently. In some universities, the career office is an integral part of the student experience. Students may be required to meet with a representative from the career office before they can even post their résumé for employers to review. At other institutions, however, the career office may have a less prominent place in the community and have less contact with students.

In many colleges across the country, the career office is staffed by only one person. This person is in charge of full-time recruiting, internships, career advising, student workshops, and often many other activities that may not be directly related to students transitioning from college to the world-of-work. At colleges such as these, where the career office is a less centralized unit of the college community, students may seek one of the alternate sources listed above. It is always a good practice to work with the university career office, in addition to other methods you decide to pursue.

Power of Networking

Interestingly, both former interns and students desiring to participate in an internship found great value in tapping into their network to pursue an internship. Whether it was a friend, family member, or a personal or faculty contact, students found that networking with these individuals was more beneficial than seeking an internship through a source such as a campus career center.

On the other hand, organizations resorted to the traditional method of contacting the career office as their main point of entry into the college. *The internship program should be marketed internally so employees are empowered to share information with potential intern candidates.*

While organizations should certainly continue to work closely with the college career office, you should also have an understanding that, depending on the size of your organization, effectively marketing an internship may be as simple as broadcasting an internal email.

Faculty Contacts

Faculty members of a university are an incredible resource. Not only do they typically teach in a specific discipline, but they also have been exposed to a large part of the student body and are familiar with students' strengths and weaknesses. These individuals can help identify great candidates for your internship program. Students often turn to faculty members when they are seeking an internship. Students assume that faculty are a part of large industry-related networks and have several contacts that can lead to an internship offer (which is usually a reality).

The challenge can be connecting with faculty in a meaningful way. Some colleges make it easier than others. If you visit the university website, you may find a "faculty search" option that will let you search for faculty members based on the disciplines they teach. You can contact the person via email or telephone (some websites will only provide you with the extension number and no email address). You may need to be aggressive with follow-ups as faculty members are usually very busy individuals with multiple research projects and classes on their plates. Faculty want what is best for their students, so if you have a quality opportunity to offer they will contact you and at least point you in the right direction.

For colleges that do not provide an online directory, call the main college number and ask who the Department Chair is for the specific discipline you are looking for (for example, the Accounting Department Chair or the Engineering Department Chair). The position of Department Chair is typically only given to faculty members who have been members of the college community for a considerable amount of time. The Chair should be able to recommend a faculty contact (if not themselves) and possibly students as well. Don't be afraid to ask if the Chair or faculty member would forward an email message from you to the students in their classes or in other classes studying the same discipline.

Empowering Full-Time Employees to Help

Again, empower your employees to recommend family members and college students they may know. Allowing employees to help with the process may open the doors to connections at local universities. To help lighten the load, you may wish to ask full-time employees if they would be in charge of researching candidates from their *alma mater*. An employee who graduated from a specific college or university would know how the system works at that particular school. They may also know, and have strong relationships with, specific faculty members and administrators who can help single out students.

Get on Campus

One of the best things you can do to promote your internship program to students is to increase the awareness of your brand on the campuses you target. The single best way to accomplish this is to work with the career center and ask them about opportunities to be on campus. Let's face it, it is nearly impossible to build your organization's brand and develop relationships with students if you are not physically on campus! There are many ways for you to be on campus, but remember that individual schools may have specific limitations and rules that need to be followed - this is another good reason to meet with the career center! They can generally help you to navigate the approach that is best for your organization and fits into their existing structure.

The following are several ways that employers have indicated are successful ways to be on campus:

Sponsor an Information Session

When you decide to recruit interns at a specific college or university, you have the option of contacting the career center to post the internship and then sitting back and hoping that the résumés, cover letters, and applications come to you. This passive approach will most likely not produce the results that you desire. One of the best ways to get on campus is to sponsor an information session, which many college campuses will help you to plan. The sessions, which usually take place in the evening, will be marketed to the student body through the career office. Even if a student is unable to attend the program due to prior obligations, seeing your organization's name in campus-wide email or on flyers will increase brand awareness. Furthermore, students who do attend the program will receive a great deal of information about your organization and internship opportunities, thus increasing the number of qualified applicants.

Be sure to ask colleges whether or not they require students to attend your information session prior to interviewing with you. This will allow you to cater your presentation in regards to how detailed you want to be about the specific job, or if you want to give a wider company overview. Of course, if candidates will be interviewing the next day, you want to focus more on the job that interests them, while a more general presentation can be given for non-applicants who just want to learn more about the company.

Career Fairs

Most colleges host at least one job or internship fair for either their specific school, or for a group of schools through a consortium effort on an annual (if not semesterly) basis. For many years, these fairs have been focused on the full-time recruiting of graduating seniors. A recent trend is a completely separate fair geared specifically for internships. These "internship fairs" follow the same model as the full-time fairs. Employers set up booths, hand out promotional items and business cards, and try to portray a positive image to students. In most cases, there are fees associated with exhibiting at internship fairs, but the fees are nominal. There may be a substantial time commitment, however, depending on how many universities you choose to target for internship fairs.

Sponsor Student Organization Events

Sponsoring an event that is organized by a student club or organization can bolster brand awareness as well. Students tend to form clubs around the same disciplines that you are recruiting. Contact the college's Campus Life or Student Activities office for a complete list of clubs. You may wish to contact a student officer, as opposed to the advisor, who is typically a faculty member. Faculty advisors are usually also professors with a multitude of other responsibilities. While any type of sponsorship is subject to the advisor's approval, you should try to make a student officer a primary contact.

If you do not wish to increase expenses by monetarily sponsoring an event, you can also volunteer some time to the organization as a guest speaker. Many student clubs offer career exploration seminars in the evening where they invite guest speakers from a specific industry. Becoming a guest speaker will give students the opportunity to learn more about your industry, organization, and available intern positions.

For a sample list of student organizations, refer to Appendix B on page 219.

RÉSUMÉS, INTERVIEWING, SELECTION & HIRING

Evaluating Student Résumés

Students look toward internships to provide them with their first professional experience. Résumés submitted for internship opportunities may not contain prior experience working in a career field; rather, they may comprise part-time employment, academic achievements or campus involvement. For this reason, employers must search for evidence of skills using other strategies.

Campus Involvement

Students who have taken the time to get involved in campus organizations and activities have usually developed strong time management and organization skills, as well as the ability to work within teams and groups.

A résumé that highlights a great deal of campus involvement is also a great indicator of a student's pride and loyalty to their institution. Students who take the time to get involved on campus are invested in their institution in the same way an employee is invested in a company.

Leadership Roles

For many students, taking on a leadership role is practice for leadership in the workplace. Students who have served as orientation leaders, campus tour guides, student government representatives or mentors have developed the skills necessary to lead others and communicate ideas effectively. Look for positions within organizations as well, such as chair of a committee or vice-president of a group or organization. These positions show responsibility and require a certain level of professionalism.

Academic Performance and Coursework

A high grade point average (GPA) does not always indicate a good internship candidate, but it does show that the student finds value in knowledge and education. GPA is also a good indicator of a student's work ethic and organization.

When searching for an intern, make sure that the potential candidate has completed any coursework that may be necessary to successfully work within the professional setting. If your industry requires background knowledge in a particular subject area, make sure the student has achieved that level before hiring them to fill an intern position.

Always keep in mind that although GPA is an important factor in screening candidates, it is only one piece of the puzzle. Make sure a student also possesses the other qualities you are looking for in an intern.

A word about GPA...

GPAs vary between institutions. A student in a more difficult academic program may have a GPA that is lower than his or her peers.

Many of today's students are juggling external responsibilities along with going to college. A student who does not have a high GPA may be working during the semester to pay for school.

GPAs take time to improve. A student who struggled early on may have had difficulty bringing up his or her GPA, even when performing well.

High GPAs are more difficult to achieve in college than in high school. Average GPAs vary by institution, but generally only a small fraction of students carry a 3.5 GPA or higher.

Prior Work Experience

Obviously, most students applying for internships do not have résumés full of professional work experience. However, the jobs a student has worked can tell you a little something about his or her work ethic, dedication, and skill set. In addition, working any type of job requires punctuality and responsibility—two qualities any employer would want in an intern.

Fast food, retail, summer camps—these are just some of the jobs seen most frequently on college student résumés. Look beyond the job title and think about what skills and knowledge the student had to possess to succeed in a particular environment. The student probably developed communication skills while working with the public, trustworthiness while handling money transactions, patience while working with children, etc.

Athletic Involvement

Students who have participated in college athletic programs typically possess a great deal of personal discipline because they have had to balance demanding practice schedules with coursework and classes. Athletes are also accustomed to working as members of a team, and those skills can transfer easily into the workplace.

Application Process

Depending on the number of schools you decide to target and the popularity of the internship's discipline, you could receive hundreds of applications for each position. Be sure to acknowledge the receipt of each application, with a specific contact person. Students are persistent. They will follow-up with you repeatedly until you answer. For those candidates who do not receive an interview, be sure to email them explaining that at this time you don't believe they would be a fit for your organization but that you will keep their résumé on file.

Interviewing & Selection

Interviewing candidates for the internship program with your organization is an important step that, surprisingly, some organizations choose to skip. If you choose not to interview candidates, you will not truly know if they are a good fit for the culture of your organization, or if they have the right combination of skills and abilities to be successful in their role as an intern. Having an effective interview process is critical, and it needs to be treated professionally.

Through subsequent interviews of students who participated in the National Internship and Co-op, one student told the story regarding when she applied to work for a nationwide restaurant organization. She initially met the company representatives when they attended the job fair on her campus. The job fair booth was tended to by the manager of the local establishment, but if students were interested in applying, they had to contact someone else, whose business card was available. The company offered an in-depth management-training program, part of which included time spent in the Wine Country of California. She eagerly applied.

She never received acknowledgement that her résumé and cover letter had been received. Two weeks later, the recruitment manager emailed her to setup an interview time. When she called him at their scheduled time, the call went to voicemail. He returned the call the next day at a random time and somehow expected her to be ready for the interview without notice. Luckily, she was. He was traveling and conducting the interview over his cell phone. The reception was lousy. About ten minutes into the interview he had to disconnect to go through airport security. He promised he would call back in a couple of minutes, but he did not call back for half an hour. The interview continued, on his cell phone, with the noise of airport announcements and travelers talking in the background. She also stated that the interviewer didn't take a genuine interest in anything about her – her educational experiences, leadership experiences, etc. All he asked was "what do you know about us" and "what would make you a good fit to work for us?"

To make a long story short, she wasn't offered a position. But she also stated that even if she had been offered a position, she was so dissatisfied with the lack of professionalism from the interviewer that she wouldn't have accepted anyway. And, to further speak to our point that students are representatives no matter what (even at an early stage, such as an interview), she did tell all of her friends about her experience.

Although the previous story is not a common occurrence, it does illustrate how at least one organization treated the potential intern less than professionally. The point we are making with the previous story is not that students will be offended by phone interviews (in many cases, students prefer them, as it is less of a time commitment), but that you must treat the interview process as you would treat it for a full-time candidate – professionally and respectfully.

BEHAVIORAL INTERVIEWING

Important for Interviewing Intern Candidates

Behavioral interviewing as part of the selection process leads to a successful internship experience for both the student and the employer. Although the benefits of behavioral interviewing are many, they are determinant upon your individual organization and to the degree in which you utilize it. Behavioral interviewing has become a customary and well-respected best practice for interviewing and the advantages are numerous - for both the candidate and the hiring organization. Behavioral interviewing provides the means for employers to gain a very clear and honest glimpse into the potential of a job candidate.

In college and university career centers across the country, students are being educated and coached regarding the prevalence of behavioral interviews. Many students take part in mandatory education programs geared toward teaching them how to analyze a behavioral interview question and apply techniques to best answer the questions presented by hiring managers. They participate in student-to-student mock interviews, and many universities tap into their alumni pool for special student-to-employer practice scenarios.

The bottom line is that students are going to enter an interview with the high expectation of being asked behavioral questions. Their judgment of the internship opportunity may become skewed if their expectation of the interview is not met. In the research, the vast majority of organizations responded that they ask behavioral questions of intern candidates during the interview process.

The Basics

The basic idea behind behavioral interviewing is that past performance is the best predictor of future behavior. For years, HR professionals asked candidates questions such as "what are your strengths?" or "what is your weakness?" And, for years, they received the same generic answers: "I'm a team player" or "I can't say no." Behavioral interviewing demands that the candidate provide examples of past behaviors to substantiate their claims. Using the examples above, a behavioral interviewer may ask the candidate to describe a time when they used their skills as a team player to achieve a goal, or to describe a time when the candidate didn't say no, and the outcome of a project that suffered as a result. Students are often taught the STAR method of how to respond to a behavioral interview question. STAR stands for Situation, Task, Action, Result.

The STAR method lays the groundwork for students to discuss the *Situation* they were in, the *Task* that needed to be completed, the *Action* they took to complete the task, and the *Result* they attained.

Please refer to **Appendix C on page 228** for a detailed guide of behavioral based questions and what you, as the interviewer should be looking for in the candidates answers.

Interviewing a Student

The steps taken to interview college students seeking an internship are similar to that of a full-time, experienced potential employee that you are seeking to hire. One important difference to keep in mind is that when you are interviewing a college student, it could be *their first job interview ever!* That might change the dynamic of the interview a bit, and it may require that your questions be more probing in nature.

The following six-step process has been specifically designed to assist you with interviewing students for internship opportunities.

Step 1: Build Rapport

Building rapport with the candidate is important in any interview, but especially when working with college students. This is your chance to give the student a feeling of calm so that they will open up to you. Remember, the purpose of the interview is to determine if the student is a good fit for the organization. Presumably, you have already decided based on their cover letter and résumé that they have the necessary skill set. Making small talk will give you the opportunity to learn more about the candidates past behaviors, and it may provide you with a basis to ask questions you may not have considered prior to the interview.

Step 2: Explain Note-Taking

If it is the student's first interview, you may create an increased level of anxiety as you frequently pause to take notes. The student may become confused, and think that they are performing poorly. It is important to briefly explain that taking notes is a necessary part of how you remember the qualifications of a candidate.

Step 3: Ask About Past Experiences

In a standard interview, this step would most likely read, "ask about past employment." However, depending on where the student is in his or her education, they may not have an extensive job history, or one that connects with the internship. On the flip side, they will most likely have taken part in unique experiences as part of their college experience. If it appears on their résumé, it is what the student is most proud of in terms of non-classroom experience. Be sure to ask questions about it.

Step 4: Ask if the Student Has Any Questions
Students are coached by career departments to make sure they investigate an organization (via their website, news articles, etc.) before they go for an interview. They are also coached to have at least one question ready for the interviewer. Chances are that if the student has a genuine interest in the opportunity, they will have at least one question based solely on information learned in the interview process.

Step 5: Close the Interview
Thank the student for their interest in the position. It is in your best interest to give the student a timeline of when they will hear from you regarding a decision. Today's students are very persistent. Without a timeline, you will probably hear from the student several times per week until they are given a definitive answer.

Step 6: Send a Thank You
This is one trick that could set your opportunity apart from the rest. You may expect to receive a thank you note from the applicant; but what is rare, however, is the employer sending a thank you note. This is a great opportunity for you to reiterate the details of the position, thank the student for their interest, and remind them of when they are likely to hear a decision.

Selecting Your Intern
Now that the interviews are complete, it is time to select which candidates will become part of your internship program. Just like selecting a candidate to fill a full-time position, selecting the intern you would like to hire requires an objective, as well as subjective approach. The following section provides best practices to formulate a comprehensive selection strategy.

Create a Selection Strategy
The first step in selecting the interns for your program is to create a strategy. The main goal of creating a selection strategy is to ensure that you are being consistent with the applicants that are extended offers of employment. Before proceeding, create a list of specific criteria that you are looking for each candi-

date to possess. Then grade each remaining candidate on a rubric with a clear delineation of criteria. This will help you after the interview when you may not remember everything about a particular candidate. This will also help the process to be objective.

Background Checks
Depending on your organization, it may be a prerequisite for employment that every employee submit to a background check. If that is the case, the policy most likely will lead to background checks having to be conducted for interns.

Type of Check	Number of Organizations
Reference Check	107
College Enrollment Confirmation	79
Criminal / CORI	70
Job History Confirmation	62
College Transcript	36
Drug Screening	29
Credit Check	16

College Enrollment and Transcript Confirmations
Verifications that are completed through the college take time. It would work better with the recruiting timeline if you have all applicants request enrollment and transcription verifications when they apply to your organization. Most colleges require that the request come from the student, especially transcripts, and under the Department of Education's Family Educational Rights and Privacy Act, commonly referred to as FERPA. Universities are not permitted to release transcripts without the consent of the student. The school, however, is permitted to release enrollment verification without permission. It will take a significant amount of time on your part to call each Registrar's office for every candidate to confirm enrollment or transcripts. It is best to notify students that this will be required as a part of the application process.

Note: *College transcripts will come in an envelope with some sort of official seal. You should not accept transcripts that students print from their computers.*

Selection Criteria
Your organization probably already has well-established selection criteria for full-time positions. These criteria were probably derived over time and have

been proven to address the key competencies, both skills and attitudinal, that your organization wants to see in employees. The process of selecting interns is really no different than selecting full-time employees. Remember, one of the things that interns are looking for as they engage in an internship is an "accurate preview of the organization and the industry." Part of providing that "real-world" experience should extend to the hiring process as well.

By now you should have some idea of how you will be picking interns before the selection process begins. By having this idea in mind before the selection process starts, you will minimize the likelihood of going with a "gut feeling" and maximize the opportunity to select fantastic interns.

Table F shows how employers rank each criterion according to most used in the selection of interns.

Table F	
1	Interview
2	People skills
3	Availability
4	Technical skills
5	Student's major
6	Level of education
7	Job experience
8	Recommendation(s) from professors
9	Recommendation(s) from previous employers
10	Grades
11	Volunteer experience
12	Student's expectations of monetary compensation

Student Availability

During the interview process it is important to make clear what your expectations are in terms of the level of commitment from the student. If your internship will be during the fall or spring semesters, then the internship will not be the top priority of the student as they will be attending classes, engaged in clubs and organizations as well as other college related activities. However, you need to make it clear that even though classes are in session, there is still an expectation that the student will create a schedule and stick to it, with the exception of emergencies. Be sure to explain that an emergency is not a mid-term exam or an assignment that is due since, in almost all cases, they are given ample notice from their professors.

Since the student's availability is one of the topics you should be covering in an interview, you will have a good basis to see if the student is too overextended with other responsibilities (class, student clubs, etc.) to dedicate the amount of time that you feel is necessary. The student's availability should be a key factor in the selection process, as issues that arise during the internship pertaining to the student's schedule can become messy. It is best to figure out availability before the start of the program. If you are unsure that the student will have satisfactory availability, it is best to hire a different candidate.

COMPENSATION AND BENEFITS

The topic that causes the most consternation with employers regarding an internship program is that of compensation. Many organizations continually ask questions like: *"Should we pay interns? If we do, how much should we pay them? Maybe they can just get college credit?"* And if you are like the majority of your peers, just when you think you have the answer someone says something that challenges your decision and makes you uncertain that you made the right one. If you are anxious about compensation when you are planning your internship program, you should be. Compensating interns, as with considering compensation for full-time employees, is a very sensitive and real issue.

> *"TOO MANY INTERNSHIPS are unrealistic. They are positions that are not well-defined, and often students are not paid for them. It is unrealistic to think that a student can manage classes and an internship, and still try to work a job to get by. I think many programs forget that students need to make money, too. It's very important to think about."*
>
> *"I THINK THAT getting paid is important. It is difficult for poor students to gain access to opportunities such as an internship when they also have to work a paying job."*
>
> *"IT WAS DIFFICULT to complete an internship that consumed so much of my time and not being paid for it. It's hard to work 50 hours a week and at the end of the week not have a pay check to take home. Having to commute to the internship each day cost me money in gas and it's difficult when the money to pay for that gas is not returned. The internship put me at a financial loss."*
>
> *"I DIDN'T LIKE how little I was paid for the amount of work I did. I knew that people who did less work than me were making more money because they were hired through a temp agency."*

All Internship Compensation Should Be Created Equal

If your organization is intent on hiring more than one intern in a given discipline, be sure to pay the interns the same and offer them the same benefits. If interns are being hired in different areas of the organization, it is not necessary to pay the same wages. Some internship positions traditionally earn considerably more (sometimes double) other positions.

College Credit Is Not Compensation

As an employer, you cannot compensate an intern by providing them college credit. This is an easy way to create significant problems with university partners. Remember, the college or university can grant college credit, you, as the employer of the intern, cannot. Different universities have different requirements regarding what the student needs to do in order to earn academic credit. The student may be required to take a class or write essays. Furthermore, many universities require that students pay in order to receive credit as the result of an internship experience.

Are Organizations Creating a Disparate Impact?

Disparate impact is a legal theory used for proving unlawful employment discrimination. Time and time again, we hear stories of students working several jobs just to be able to stay in college. Some students are in such a financial bind that they simply cannot afford to take part in an unpaid internship program. Even if the internship program is the absolute best program on earth, the bottom line here is that by making that program unpaid, an organization is excluding a large group of highly qualified candidates.

In 2008, an editorial in the Chronicle of Higher Education brought forth the idea that unpaid internships resulted in a disparate impact on individuals who can't afford them and thus do not have access to the value they provide. The editorial boldly suggested that, in the long term, unpaid internships contribute to making wealthy students wealthier and poor students poorer. This claim was based on the fact that employers are more likely to hire a graduate with internship experience for a full-time job; and wealthier students are more likely to take part in unpaid internships. There is a real skills gap between someone with internship experience who has practiced before entering the workplace and the student whose first job is also their first practical work experience.

The article stirred up a great deal of discussion from the university community. Universities expressed frustration that they had been trying for years to encourage students from lower socioeconomic backgrounds to increase their marketability in the job market, while employers were not doing their part to ensure jobs were available to the same group. The chart below illustrates an interesting connection between socio-economic status and internship salaries.

In further exploration of this topic, we found that students from high-income families were more likely to be found in paid internships with for-profit companies, compared to lower income students who received paid internships at a significantly lower rate and were more likely to have paid internships with non-profits than high-income students. It was also noted that high income students were less likely to be in paid internships with government agencies, and among students in unpaid internships, no significant difference was found in the distribution among their host organization by income.

It is important to note that 74% of students whose family's household income is less than $80,000 per year believe earning money is an important consideration when choosing an internship. The numbers suggest organizations that choose to provide monetary compensation often favor their wages towards students of higher socioeconomic status. This practice needs to be further evaluated and will be a topic of future Intern Bridge studies.

To ensure that your internship program is non-discriminatory, that the candidate pool is as large as possible, and to show universities and students that you value the contributions of interns and that your organization takes the program seriously, paying your interns should be a very important consideration.

Compensation Data
The average intern compensation is $11.96 across all academic majors, industries, and positions. **Please refer to Appendix D on page 231 for a breakdown and specific details.**

Legal Implications
There is a discussion of the legal impact of unpaid internships in the chapter "Employment Law Issues Regarding Internship Programs" on **page 171**. This topic is one that is changing regularly with new court decisions. Intern Bridge remains at the forefront of this discussion and regularly hosts programs to keep both employers and higher education up to date.

Benefits
Having a great benefits package is what could separate your internship program from the rest. Benefits, in the case of internships, are slightly different than the type of benefits that an employer might consider for full-time or part-time employees. While there are several "standard" benefits that should be offered to interns (for example, vacation days), there are also benefits that could most likely be ignored when dealing with an internship program (for example, health insurance).

When dealing with benefits in an internship program, we are referring to any compensation or benefit for the intern, not including any compensation arising from their regular wage (if any). This includes typical benefits as well as intern-only "perks."

Benefits are one of the main material ways in which an organization can show appreciation for work done. Interns, sometimes the most overworked employees in an organization, should certainly be considered.

SURVEY DISCUSSION

Table G shows the benefits available to interns,
as reported by organizations.

Table G - Benefits Available to Interns - Reported by Organizations		
Rank	Benefits to Interns: Reported by Organizations	% of Organizations
1	Free/subsidized parking	41%
2	Social events for interns to meet one another	21%
3	Discounted organization merchandise or services	12%
4	Internship work counts towards time worked if job offer is extended	12%
5	Transportation stipend	9%
6	Free organization merchandise or services	8%
7	Fitness center membership	8%
8	Meal allowance	7%
9	Vacation pay	7%
10	Sporting event tickets	6%
11	Partial housing assistance	4%
12	Theater tickets	3%
13	Partial relocation assistance	2%
14	Complete housing assistance	2%
15	Health insurance	2%
16	Commission on sales (if applicable)	2%
17	Uniform stipend	1%
18	Full benefits (same as full time employees)	1%
19	Tuition reimbursement	1%

Table H shows the benefits available to interns,
as reported by interns.

Rank	Benefits to Interns: Reported by Interns	% of Interns
1	Free/subsidized parking	37%
2	Social events for interns to meet one another	23%
3	Free organization merchandise or services	15%
4	Transportation stipend	13%
5	Discounted organization merchandise or services	12%
6	Meal allowance	12%
7	Fitness center membership	9%
8	Sporting event tickets	9%
9	Internship work counts towards time worked if job offer is extended	6%
10	Theater tickets	5%
11	Complete housing assistance	5%
12	Vacation pay	5%
13	Uniform stipend	4%
14	Full benefits (same as full time employees)	3%
15	Health insurance	3%
16	Partial housing assistance	2%
17	Commission on sales (if applicable)	2%
18	Complete relocation assistance	2%
19	Tuition reimbursement	1%
20	Partial relocation assistance	1%

The table title, spanning the header, reads: **Table H - Benefits Available to Interns - Reported by Interns**

*As the data from the survey is self-explanatory, we will not be going into detail here about each of the items listed on **pages 90-91** (with a few exceptions).*

Internship Work Counts Towards Time Worked if Job Offer Is Extended

This is a fantastic way to reward interns for their work with your organization. It is also a great way to entice an intern to accept an offer of full-time employment after graduation. Depending upon how your organization operates, you may have rigid policies regarding promotions based on the length of time an employee works. The work an intern completes could be quite substantial when applied to this time. For example, if a summer intern working full-time were allowed to have "intern time" counted, it could account for almost 4,000 hours of completed employment.

Brown Bag Lunches

The idea of "brown bag lunches" have been a part of internship programs of all sizes, industries, and job functions for many years. The main purpose of the brown bag lunch is to give interns the opportunity to meet different director-level and higher-up professionals within the organization. In many organizations, the brown bag lunches are led by "chief" level personnel. From information gathered from the National Internship and Co-op Study, 98% of students believed that the organization should provide a chance for them to explore other career opportunities outside of the department where they are assigned during the internship. Seventy-Seven percent of interns reported that they were actually given this chance, a 21% gap.

Brown bag lunches are an inexpensive way to give interns a glimpse into other job functions within your organization. Depending on cost constraints, students can be asked to bring their own lunch, or the organization can provide lunch. Brown bag lunches usually last for one hour. The presenter will typically speak about how they became involved in that particular field of work, how they rose to the top, and offer advice for the interns. Be sure to provide ample time for interns to ask questions. Brown bag lunches are almost always semi-informal events.

> *"THE COMPANY I WORKED FOR was both small and on the cutting edge of their industry. It was great to have direct access to the people who were making important decisions and leading the pack in the field."*
>
> *"MY FAVORITE PART of the internship was the weekly meetings with all of the interns to learn about the different aspects of the business."*

Organizational Gifts

Almost every single intern who was employed by an organization that provides a service or sold a product reported receiving some sort of gift of that organization's service or product. For example, interns reported receiving free shoes from a shoe manufacturer, tickets to a concert from a radio station, branded hats and jackets from a television station, and food from a restaurant business. This is yet another inexpensive way to show interns appreciation.

Off-site Organization Functions

When an organization conducts an off-site function, the interns should be included. Whether it is the summer barbecue or the annual meeting, interns appreciate being invited to these events. It provides them with a sense of belonging, and it gives them a great feeling of community. It will also give them the chance to network with additional personnel and to learn more about the organization.

Tour of Organization or Industry-Related Sites and Buildings

Some interns reported being given access to special "behind the scenes" tours of organizations or industry-related sites. Interns working in theater were given tours of the backstage area; interns working in event management were given the chance to go backstage at concerts; and interns working in the finance area report being given tours of high-security areas in the New York Stock Exchange. These types of tours provide an intern with an even more in-depth preview of what it might be like to work in that particular industry.

Opportunity to Attend Company Trainings

An easy and inexpensive way for an organization to show that they care is to provide lunches and birthday cake for interns. As simple as this may sound, it was one of the most noted benefits when interns were asked open-ended questions relating to benefits they received. In particular, there appeared to be a high level of intern satisfaction when their supervisor took them out to (and paid for) lunch, or brought them coffee in the morning. When the intern applies to work for the organization, they will provide their birth date. A special note should be made in the supervisor's calendar if the birthday falls during the internship time frame. Several interns reported that they were given birthday cake, birthday cards, balloons, a surprise party within their department, and small gifts such as a gift basket or movie tickets.

Idea Presentations

As discussed earlier, one of the main reasons for hosting an internship program is to allow students with a fresh prospective and the most up-to-date education to have an impact within an organization. One method to ensure that interns are contributing their innovative ideas is to provide them with a forum to present those ideas. This presentation technique can take on many forms. It can be in a report form that is submitted to the director of the department, or the vice president. Several interns reported that their host organizations held an "internship idea fair." In this setting, similar to a grade school science fair, interns would create poster boards of their ideas for employees of the organization to view and inquire about.

The idea can also be large scale. One intern noted that his host organization provided for a competition. Interns presented various ideas to top-level officials. If even a small part of the idea was ultimately implemented, the intern received special recognition and some sort of prize. The opportunity to envision an idea for an organization, and then have that idea exhibited to employees of the organization is very exciting for interns.

Preferential Interview

Offering interns the chance for preferential interview times is perceived to be a great benefit. If an organization either has high turnover, or is growing quickly, allowing current (or past) interns to have a preference in the interview process is an easy benefit to implement with a relatively large impact to interns. From an organization's perspective, this benefit should make sense. After all, the intern would have been "interviewing" over the course of many weeks. Most organizations give internal employees the opportunity to fill positions before the organization looks externally. Interns should be treated the same in this practice.

Skill Development Sessions

Skills workshops can be of great value to an intern. In particular, students are almost always interested in learning ways to better apply their leadership, presentation, and communication skills. Providing a workshop for interns geared toward the improvement of these skills (or several others) can help an intern become more confident, and more effective in the work they complete for their host organization.

These programs should be conducted towards the beginning of the internship experience so that the organization can maximize their benefit. It is not necessary to bring in a special consultant or trainer to carry out the programming. Remember that interns are impressionable students, eager to learn more about the world of work. Having someone within your organization manage the workshops would certainly be sufficient.

Résumé Workshops

While most colleges and universities have career development departments that will critique a student's résumé, the opportunity to have their résumé critiqued by a professional in the industry is a huge benefit. A résumé workshop could be conducted by someone in the HR department or by several different individuals on a rotating basis. If individuals are hired in an organization by department managers, having a rotation where the résumé is critiqued by managers from different departments will provide the intern with constructive criticism from several different angles.

Industry Exams and Credentials

Several interns reported that their organizations assisted them in obtaining certain industry certifications and licensure. For example, if the intern works in the Human Resources department, the department may wish to assist the intern obtaining their PHR credentials by reimbursing the student for a prep class or for the exam fee. Several students working in the financial sector reported that their employers helped them to pay for their Series 7 examination.

ON-BOARDING

Only 56% of interns agreed or strongly agreed that they were satisfied with the quality of the orientation that they received, and only 43% of organizations agreed that the quality of the orientation they received was high.

On-boarding, or orientation, is your chance to show off your organization and prepare students for their internship experience. It serves a multitude of purposes. First, it provides the student with a chance to relieve some anxiety: few things can be more stressful for a college aged student than being placed in an environment with individuals older than they are who have been working with the organization or within the industry for several years. Without the on-boarding process, supervisors would be responsible for all of the topics covered within the program. Therefore, the process can save time for the intern's supervisors.

The on-boarding program also helps to set realistic expectations for the intern. Remember that some students have had part-time jobs in the past to finance their education or social lives, but this doesn't mean that they are familiar with other aspects such as organizational culture and politics, the need for confidentiality, or other items specific to your organization. Organizations must be committed to the on-boarding process, including supervisors, who need to provide students with concentrated time at the beginning of the program. This level of direct supervision will decrease as interns become more independent and productive colleagues.

> **"SUPERVISORS CAN MAKE one feel welcome from the start. I think a great start would lead to a great finish."**
>
> **"THE MOST IMPORTANT THING an organization can do to make the internship experience meaningful is to train the person well and allow them to explore the field they are interested in."**

What to Include

Most organizations already have some sort of orientation in place for their new hires, and with a few tweaks, these are usually sufficient for an internship. Some important items to include especially, for an internship orientation, are industry language that the student may not know on their own, acceptable dress for your organization's workplace, confidentiality issues, who the intern can go to with problems, if overtime is acceptable, and how to fill out timesheets.

One of the most beneficial pieces of information you can provide an intern is an organizational chart. Often an intern will be meeting with their supervisor when a colleague interrupts the meeting. The supervisor introduces the intern to Joe Smith. By providing the intern with an organizational chart, the student can then go back to his or her desk and use the chart to see where that person works and what his or her position is. Having access to the chart is a great way to acclimate your interns to the people within your organization.

Do Not Just Orient Students

If you are moving ahead with the internship program, then hopefully you have the support of the executive level personnel within your organization. However, most organizations do not currently provide any sort of employee orientation as it relates to the internship program. In fact, less than one-third of surveyed employers agreed or strongly agreed that the quality of how employees are oriented about the internship program was high.

> *"IN ORDER TO MAKE an internship experience meaningful an organization must be happy to have the intern there. It is obvious when someone is not wanted, and that causes uncomfortable feelings. Employees of the organization must be willing to tell the student all that they know and have learned from working in the environment and the student must also have some responsibility so that in the end he or she can feel as if something was accomplished."*

Introduce Students to Employees

It is incredibly important to make the intern feel welcome. There is no better way to do this than to provide the intern with a chance to meet employees, especially employees who work within the same department as the intern. Sixty-three percent of interns reported that they agreed or strongly agreed that they were given a good introduction to the other employees when they first started the internship. One way to encourage introductions is to post interns' names, pictures, and bios on your organization's intranet. An employee with similar interests, or one who graduated from the same university, might reach out to the intern and make them feel welcome.

> *"AN ORGANIZATION can put more stress on internship programs and educate employees that such a program is an important part of the interns' experience and the company's image. They should also have well-planned tasks to help the intern gain experience as they work for the firm and promote a comfortable environment for the intern."*
>
> *"I TRIED TO GET an array of opportunities so that I was not only getting experience in one area. The best internships were ones that took me seriously, as a valuable asset to the organization with a distinct perspective."*
>
> *"IT WAS UPSETTING that sometimes I wasn't taken seriously by other employees. I was looked at as just an intern."*

Opportunity to Set Expectations

The on-boarding process is the perfect time to set forth expectations. These expectations include everything from the intern's availability, to expectations for dress code and professional conduct. Sixty-three percent of interns reported that the organization's expectations of them were clear when they began their internship.

If your organization has an internship coordinator in addition to separate supervisors, you most likely need to have two orientation programs. The first program would be for all of the interns. At this program, you would gather all of the interns together and provide them with information about your organization. The second orientation is intern-specific, and is individualized time that the intern will spend with the supervisors. This is the time when the supervisors need to lay out what activities and projects the intern will be involved in. Only 54% of interns reported that the activities or projects of their internship were made clear to them from the start. It should also be noted that a significant majority of students surveyed (74%) stated that having written goals for their daily, weekly, and overall for the period of the internship would be helpful.

> *"HAVE THE PURPOSE and goals of the internship noted and reviewed to ensure each student completes those goals."*
>
> *"I WAS GIVEN a work load larger then I originally was lead to believe at the beginning of the internship."*

> *"I DIDN'T LIKE the pacing of my internship; at first, we got off to a slow start, barely getting anything accomplished. Then, toward the end of the second week, my boss turned up the tempo and decided that we had to get X, Y, and Z done. Almost unrealistic in its nature, the timeline he had laid out in his head was undisclosed to me, so I had a difficult time imagining a) what his final goals were, b) how he wanted me to complete those goals, and c) how long he expected it to take me. I didn't like the complete lack of structure/training."*

> *"EACH INTERN WORKED for a specific researcher and I felt that mine was not specific enough when she explained my tasks. She expected me to learn how to use a complicated computer program in a few weeks which she herself didn't even understand. When I wasn't successful she was very disappointed and I was left feeling very frustrated. Also, we were to complete our own personal projects during that time as well, but it was difficult to balance the time."*

> *"I THINK the orientation describing my exact job description could have been better."*

Beyond the Ordinary Presentation

Here is a list of some things you can do for interns to make them feel welcome beyond the informational presentation:

- Ask the Vice President of the division where the intern is working, or even the CEO, to stop by the interns' work-space and personally welcome them. The brief greeting should only take a couple of minutes.

- Create a "Welcome Fall/Spring/Summer Interns" banner and display it somewhere the interns and full-time employees will see it.

> *"MY ORIENTATION was horrible, especially because the first week was really confusing and discouraging."*

Think Twice About Icebreakers

A keystone of many orientation programs is to have employees take part in icebreaking activities. These activities, while they are effective at building morale and friendships, tend to be childish. The problem with having interns take part in such programs is that their goal is to enter an organization and be taken seriously as a professional. These icebreaking activities may make them feel that they are being patronized. This is not to say that icebreakers should not be conducted, but the ones that are chosen should be as professional as possible.

> *"MAKE AN INTERN feel welcome, but not uncomfortable by treating them like a child. Give them appropriate work and allow for feedback in both directions."*

Alcohol & Interns

> *"MY INTERNSHIP ROCKED because I loved my boss and colleagues. I got to attend meetings and represent [the company], I got to do research and create websites, write reports, go out to bars with the entire team, and make presentations."*

The quote above represents a recurring theme found in the research data. Many interns reported that they were provided alcohol by their host sites. Sometimes the beverages were provided during meals, and other times at organization-wide events. Generally speaking, interns appreciate the gesture and will take an employer up on their offer. The main reason for this stems from the obvious social context of acceptance into a group. In many cases, interns feel that sharing a drink with the boss means they have earned their keep.

But there is more than just providing the alcohol that needs to be considered. The National Association of Colleges and Employers, the largest nationwide association for bringing together the two entities, issued a "principle document" in 1998 regarding this very issue. The bottom line is this: employers are discouraged from furnishing alcohol to interns, and for good reason.

First there is the obvious legal implication – how closely will your organization monitor the age of your interns? You can't ask it during an interview, so how likely is it that you will go back and review internal documents to figure out their age based on their birthday? Providing alcohol to minors is a serious crime, and it will open your organization up to an incredible amount of criminal and civil liability.

Then there are the ethical arguments. Take into consideration the student who chooses not to drink alcohol in general, but, when offered by their employer, feels obligated to do so to fit in. What if that individual is unfamiliar with their "alcohol tolerance?" They could embarrass themselves, or worse.

There also needs to be consideration of the university where the student attends. Many colleges have strictly "alcohol free" campuses. By offering alcohol to interns in violation of these policies, you could seriously jeopardize the relationships that your organization has with the college moving forward.

The principle document was adopted by the ethics committee of NACE. As an employer who is either a member of NACE, or is thinking of joining (**more information in Appendix J**), you may end up adopting a position that you comply with the NACE "Principles of Professional Conduct." (You should – it means a lot to universities.) If your organization does take that position, you should strongly consider not serving alcohol to interns.

OFF-BOARDING

Unlike full-time, part-time, or temporary employees, the off-boarding process in an internship program is something to be celebrated. With an internship program, there is a definitive end to the time the student will be spending with your organization (at least as an intern). Just over 60% of interns reported that the organization provided them with an appropriate farewell at the conclusion of the program.

Showing Appreciation

Off-boarding correctly is very important. It is an organization's last opportunity to show appreciation to the students for the work that they have done. While off-boarding won't make or break the ambassadorship of a student, it could certainly bolster the organization in the student's mind as a great place to work. The process is simple, and does not have to be expensive. Several students reported that the organization took them out to lunch, or gave them company products with a thank you note. Whatever you choose to do, be sure to show appreciation!

Gain Valuable Feedback

The other critical component to the off-boarding process is your opportunity to gain valuable feedback from the student as to what they thought the strengths and weaknesses of your program were. This "exit information" will allow you to identify which pieces of your program are successful and which parts need improvement. You will be able to use quantitative and qualitative information from these exit interviews and surveys when marketing the internship program to prospective candidates.

Extending Job Offers

If your internship program is geared towards students that will be graduating soon, you may want to consider offering a full-time position as the program wraps up. Depending on the major of the student, there are traditional times of the year when official offers are made. For example, financial positions tend to be offered during the fall semester, while marketing and HR offers are traditionally made in the spring. It is best to speak with a professional association within your industry to determine what time of year is best to extend the official offer. However, there is nothing precluding you from informing an intern at the conclusion of the program that you will be extending them an offer at some point. Students place great value in receiving this opportunity, and you should provide it before another organization has the chance to.

What if my organization extends a full-time offer and it is rejected? Is our program a failure?

Absolutely not! This is an expectation that your organization must have from the outset of your program. Not every student who participates in your program will accept a full-time job offer. This should not discourage you from continuing your program. There are many benefits to hosting an internship program, even when students do not accept full-time positions.

Keep these important points in mind:

- Your organization is creating an extensive network of colleagues and students. Assuming that your interns have a positive experience and become ambassadors to your organization, they will share these experiences on-campus and your organization will achieve tremendous positive public relations and improve your campus recruiting brand.

- Would you rather have a well-informed candidate decline an offer because they know your organization is not a good fit for them, or an ill-informed candidate who accepts a job offer only to quit six months down the road?

- The program has provided an excellent opportunity for young managers and executives to gain a deep understanding of how to manage people, millennials in particular.

- Your organization has been able to complete work at a fraction of the cost of a full-time employee.

- The intern provided a fresh perspective and brought the most cutting-edge education and technology to the table.

- The intern could very well return to work for your organization at some point.

PROGRAM EVALUATION

What Is Assessment?

Simply stated, assessment is the process of measuring individual or program outcomes. Assessment can be conducted using a systematic approach in which both quantitative and qualitative data is collected, or by using a less formal method. While the former is more likely to yield valid results, data collected from the latter method also has merit. In fact, depending upon the culture of an organization, the philosophical views of a particular manager/supervisor (referred to as manager throughout the remainder of this chapter), or the reason(s) for conducting assessment, one of the aforementioned processes for collecting the data may be perceived as having more value.

The bottom line is that most organizations and colleges/universities, as well as managers and career service professionals (and faculty, when appropriate), use assessment data to guide decision-making in partnerships, strategic business initiatives, and staffing.

Why Is Assessment Important?

In recent years, there has been an increased focus on assessment. In addition to evaluating the performance of team members, managers have been instructed to provide evidence of program success that goes beyond anecdotal stories and to demonstrate the value-add of programs in order to secure additional financial resources. This directive to measure outcomes on individual and programmatic levels is not limited to Fortune 500 companies, but is also strongly encouraged and even required at small, mid-size, and large organizations that recruit and hire interns and maintain internship programs.

Managers assess interns and internship programs for a wide variety of reasons:

- To provide evidence regarding whether or not a student benefited from an internship.
- To demonstrate the degree to which a student learned or gained new skills.
- To guide the student in identifying areas for improvement.
- To provide data regarding the overall program.
- To demonstrate value-add.
- To offer suggestions for program improvement.

There is great variability regarding the degree to which managers conduct and ultimately utilize data collected from the various assessment tools. Managers who seek to recruit the best talent for their organizations or strive to strengthen the quality of their internship programs will likely leverage assessment data to inform hiring decisions, guide recruiting strategies, and make modifications to their program, be it the position description, orientation program, or strategic integration within the organizational culture.

Data from the Intern Bridge research reinforces the notion that managers not only conduct but also value assessment. More than fifty percent (54%) of managers surveyed in the study reported that their organization actively solicits feedback from interns about their experiences. Student feedback reinforced this finding. Nearly fifty percent (50%) of interns reported that their organization actively solicited feedback regarding the internship experience. Noteworthy is that nearly fifty percent (45%) of managers who responded to the survey reported that their organizations strive to make changes to the program based on feedback received from interns.

Individual Assessment (a.k.a. Performance Appraisals)

Perhaps the type of assessment that we are most familiar with is performance appraisals. Depending on the organization, the performance appraisal process, including the frequency and timeline, as well as the degree to which the process is formalized, will vary.

In general, consistently evaluating staff performance using organizational guidelines is essential for monitoring progress, supporting staff to improve performance, and meeting departmental/organizational goals. In a similar manner, providing consistent and timely feedback to interns ensures that they have an opportunity to demonstrate success or improve performance during the short duration of their internship experience.

It is interesting to note that less than thirty percent (26%) of managers who participated in the research reported that interns are evaluated often. Conversely, seventy percent (70%) of interns reported that they were provided with constructive feedback. This discrepancy may be explained, in part, by a manager's style –interns may have interpreted constructive feedback, whether formal or informal, as a type of evaluation and therefore responded with favorable comments regarding assessment.

Managers assess interns' performance and contributions to an organization in numerous ways:

Observation: Managers observe how interns carry out responsibilities and the ways in which they collaborate with members of the organization. These observations provide valuable feedback about a wide variety of skills valued by the organization, including teamwork and project management.

Consultation: Because managers cannot be in all places at all times, they solicit feedback from their colleagues in all levels of the organization to provide input regarding interns' performance on tasks and accomplishments. Depending upon the intern's specific role, the manager may also consult with external constituents to gain a deeper understanding of the intern's impact.

Skills Training: In addition to a general orientation to an organization, most likely an intern will participate in a training program at the outset of an internship. Typically, training programs provide an opportunity to learn new skills (e.g. analysis using particular statistical software, web site development). Interns' ability to demonstrate skills following the training is another measure of assessment that a manager may document.

While collecting this data is valuable, more important is sharing the feedback with the intern(s). The particulars of the performance appraisal process will vary depending upon the organization, and perhaps even the manager's style. Nevertheless, it is critical for a manager to provide timely feedback regardless of whether the process is a formal mid-internship performance review or in the context of an informal discussion. Best practices for assessing interns' performance include the following:

- Setting clear expectations at the outset of the internship regarding desired outcomes.
- Establishing the parameters for providing formal feedback.
- Articulating the specific timeline for delivering feedback.
- Providing informal feedback throughout the duration of the internship experience.
- Delivering the feedback according to the pre-determined parameters.

In addition to the performance appraisal process mandated by organizations, colleges often conduct individual assessments. More specifically, colleges administer surveys to interns and to employers to solicit interns' observations of skills improvement and to gather employers' input regarding interns' performance. When colleges administer similarly structured surveys to interns and employers – often referred to as "companion surveys" – the data collected provides comparative quantitative assessment. At some colleges/universities, this information is utilized to determine letter grades or to award credit for an internship course. Depending upon the particular questions posed, the survey tool may also provide insights into program assessment.

Program Assessment

While data regarding the performance of interns and their individual contributions is important, particularly for informing hiring decisions, collecting data regarding the internship program overall is equally important. Program assessment is essential for several reasons. More specifically, program assessment:

- Assists managers to identify best practices in internship programs.

- Guides managers to identify areas for program improvement.

- Aides career services professionals to identify employers that offer quality internship programs.

A variety of tools, including surveys and focus groups, are utilized to measure program satisfaction and effectiveness. Surveys, frequently conducted online (e.g. Survey Monkey, Perseus), are a cost-effective method for collecting large quantities of data from multiple constituents – interns and employers – in a timely manner. The following are guidelines for developing the survey instrument:

- Create a short survey.

- Use a rating scale for most questions (it is easier to tally and score the data).

- Incorporate open-ended questions to collect qualitative data.

Focus groups are another method for collecting data. Focus groups may be structured, in which the facilitator asks participants to respond to pre-determined questions, or informal, in which the facilitator sets the stage and thereafter poses targeted questions in response to comments shared by participants.

Needs assessment is another type of evaluation. This form of assessment may be of particular use to managers and/or career service professionals when developing new internship programs. More specifically, the questions posed in a needs assessment survey focus on interns' desires or desired program outcomes.

Similar to individual assessment in which feedback is solicited from interns as well as managers, program assessment should solicit feedback from both. While assessment tools may need to be tailored for interns versus managers, it is important to provide comparative assessment. The aggregate data may inform decisions pertaining to recruiting strategies, hiring practices, intern assignments, and continued partnerships between a particular organization and a specific college/university.

Best Practices in Individual and Program Assessments

While a manager can solicit feedback from multiple sources in numerous ways, to be most effective, the assessment should incorporate several best practices:

Best Practice #1: Create a systematic process for conducting assessment. It is not sufficient to administer satisfaction surveys, host focus groups, or conduct needs assessment; assessment needs to be an on-going and planned process. This ensures that individual contributions and program satisfaction and outcomes are documented in a timely and consistent manner in order to reward performance, as well as to facilitate resource allocation or demonstrate value-add to the bottom line.

Best Practice #2: Establish guidelines regarding frequency and timeline for collecting data. There are several reasons why this is good practice. First, creating a data collection schedule ensures that assessment-related projects are high priority on the task list, rather than completed as an afterthought. Second, compiling information collected over a period of time provides managers and organizations with historical data which may serve as a vehicle to support the hiring or promotion of an individual, or an effective planning tool pertaining to program delivery and improvement.

On a related note, compiling information over a period of time provides colleges/universities with insights regarding organizations that offer quality internship programs versus those that do not. Finally, the design and implementation of an assessment plan ensures the data is valid and reliable.

Best Practice #3: Establish specific, measurable goals/objectives at the outset. By defining intended outcomes, interns have a clear understanding of management's expectations and their responsibilities. At the conclusion of the internship experience, using various assessment tools, they can articulate their progress on various projects and skills developed. Furthermore, establishing goals/objectives not only provides managers with a clear vision of the internship program but also a means to effectively evaluate all components of the internship program, including structure and intern responsibilities. It is important to note that during the course of an internship, managers and interns may agree to modify goals and objectives for a wide variety of reasons.

Components of Good Internship Programs

Many organizations offer internship programs, but some programs are better than others. For an internship program to be great, it requires that you:

- Solicit support from all levels of management within your organization. Interns value the opportunity to meet and interact with key decision makers in the organization. These forums not only provide insights about operations and strategy, but also showcase the types of leadership roles that they may aspire to. Effectively engaging all levels of management in the various facets of the internship program is a primary way to demonstrate to interns that their presence and contributions are valued by the organization.

- Call on your best people to orient interns to your organization, to supervise them, and to mentor them. This will ensure that your interns have the best training and are connected to the individuals who give your organization the reputation that it has. Pairing interns with poor managers can reflect negatively on the organization and may be a contributing factor to an intern's decision to decline a job offer if one is made.

- Assign meaningful work to your intern(s). If you are using interns as a pipeline strategy for recruiting full-time hires, you will want to assign work that gives the intern an accurate picture of the work he/she would perform in their first year of employment.

And most importantly, a good internship program will provide timely feedback to an intern regarding his/her performance, as well as solicit impressions regarding the overall internship experience from both interns and the managers and others involved in the internship program.

Final Thoughts . . .

While the purpose and scope of assessment will vary depending upon the organization or college/university, there will continue to be a demand for managers and career service professionals (and/or faculty) to assess interns and internship programs. Conducting assessment can be time-consuming and even intimidating, but the more assessment you do, the more comfortable you will become with it, and perhaps most importantly, the more likely you are to see its value.

Acceptable ◆ *Accomplished* ◆ Adaptable ◆ *Adequate* ◆ Advancing ◆ *Adve*

Authentic ◆ *Average* ◆ Awesome ◆ *Bad* ◆ Beautiful ◆ *Beneficial* ◆ Borde

Chaotic ◆ Chill ◆ *Confusing* ◆ Connective ◆ *Constructive* ◆ Consultar

Determination ◆ *Developmental* ◆ Different ◆ *Difficult* ◆ Disappointing ◆

Dynamite ◆ *Easy* ◆ Eclectic ◆ *Educational* ◆ Edutainment ◆ *Effect*

Enlightening ◆ Entertaining ◆ *Equipping* ◆ Essential ◆ *Eventful* ◆ Exce

Exposure ◆ *Eye Opening* ◆ Fabulous ◆ *Fair* ◆ Fantastic ◆ *Fascinating* ◆

Fruitful ◆ Frustrating ◆ *Fulfilling* ◆ Fun ◆ *Good* ◆ Gratifying ◆ *Great* ◆

Horrible ◆ *Humorous* ◆ Important ◆ *Impressive* ◆ Incredible ◆ *Indescr*

Insincere ◆ Inspirational ◆ *Inspiring* ◆ Intellectual ◆ *Intense* ◆ Interacti

Invigorating ◆ *Involved* ◆ Knowledge ◆ *Learning* ◆ Learning-Experie

Mandatory ◆ Meaningful ◆ *Meaningless* ◆ Mediocre ◆ *Memorable* ◆ Meni

Motivating ◆ Motivational ◆ *Multidimensional* ◆ Multi-Faceted ◆ *Neg*

Opportunistic ◆ *Opportunity* ◆ Outstanding ◆ *Overview* ◆ Overwhelming

Powerful ◆ *Practical* ◆ Priceless ◆ *Productive* ◆ Professional ◆ *Realistic* ◆

Required ◆ *Research* ◆ Resourceful ◆ *Response* ◆ Resume-Builder ◆ *

Satisfying ◆ Scam ◆ *Scientific* ◆ Semi-Rewarding ◆ *Sensational* ◆ Simp

Stimulating ◆ *Stressful* ◆ Structured ◆ *Sub-Par* ◆ Successful ◆ *Sufficien*

Terrifying ◆ Thrilling ◆ *Time-Consuming* ◆ Tiring ◆ *Tolerable* ◆ Transfor

Unforgettable ◆ *Unfulfilling* ◆ Uninteresting ◆ *Unique* ◆ Unpaid ◆ *Unparal*

Useful ◆ Useless ◆ *Valuable* ◆ Varied ◆ *Versatile* ◆ Wake-Up-Call ◆ *Warn*

e ◆ Aesthetic ◆ *Affirming* ◆ Amazing ◆ *Ambitious* ◆ Amusing ◆ *Arousing*

e ◆ *Boring* ◆ Breathtaking ◆ *Busy* ◆ Careerism ◆ *Challenging* ◆ Changing

Cool ◆ *Creative* ◆ Crucial ◆ *Decent* ◆ Decision-Changing ◆ *Delightful*

mal ◆ Disorganized ◆ *Dissatisfied* ◆ Diverse ◆ *Draining* ◆ Dull ◆ *Dynamic*

◆ Empowering ◆ *Encouraging* ◆ Energizing ◆ *Engaging* ◆ Enjoyable

t ◆ *Exceptional* ◆ Exhausting ◆ *Exhilarating* ◆ Experience ◆ *Exploratory*

st-Paced ◆ *Fine* ◆ Flattering ◆ *Flexible* ◆ Focusing ◆ *Fresh* ◆ Friendly

wth ◆ *Grueling* ◆ Happy ◆ *Hard* ◆ Hectic ◆ *Hell* ◆ Helpful ◆ *Horrendous*

ble ◆ Influential ◆ *Informal* ◆ Informational ◆ *Innovative* ◆ Insightful

◆ *Interdisciplinary* ◆ Interested ◆ *International* ◆ Intriguing ◆ *Invaluable*

e ◆ *Lesson* ◆ Life Changing ◆ *Life-Altering* ◆ Long ◆ *Lousy* ◆ Magical

◆ *Mentorship* ◆ Misleading ◆ *Mixed* ◆ Mixture ◆ *Moderate* ◆ Monotonous

ve ◆ Networking ◆ *New* ◆ Nice ◆ *Nightmare* ◆ Observational ◆ *Okay*

Paid ◆ Paperwork ◆ *Perfect* ◆ Phenomenal ◆ *Pointless* ◆ Poor ◆ *Positive*

eality ◆ *Reality Check* ◆ Relationships ◆ *Relaxed* ◆ Relevant ◆ *Remarkable*

ealing ◆ Rewarding ◆ *Rollercoaster* ◆ Routine ◆ *Sales* ◆ Satisfactory

◆ *Slow* ◆ Spectacular ◆ *Spine-Tingling* ◆ Spontaneous ◆ *Stepping Stone*

Suitable ◆ *Superb* ◆ Surprising ◆ *Sweet* ◆ Tedious ◆ *Terrible* ◆ Terrific

tive ◆ *Tremendous* ◆ Trying ◆ *Tumultuous* ◆ Unbelievable ◆ *Unexpected*

ed ◆ Unproductive ◆ *Unrelated* ◆ Unsatisfactory ◆ *Unstructured* ◆ Uplifting

◆ Waste ◆ *Well- Rounded* ◆ Wonderful ◆ *Work* ◆ Worthless ◆ *Worthwhile*

MY NOTES

MY NOTES

MY NOTES

READINGS TO ENHANCE YOUR INTERNSHIP PROGRAM

STAPLE THAT. HANG THIS. COLLATE THESE.

By Richard Bottner

Unfortunately, these are my fondest memories of an internship I had while attending Babson College, a business school located in Wellesley, Massachusetts, about 14 miles west of Boston. I had somewhat fallen on the field of human resources after almost two years of trying to figure out what I ultimately wanted to do upon graduation. It was the Fall Semester of 2005 when I completed the college's Human Resources Management class, and realized it was something for which I had a growing passion.

At the time, I was enthusiastic and eager to learn more about the field. I approached my professor, a practicing leadership consultant with a great deal of experience and an enormous number of HR contacts. I explained that I was excited to have finally found a field that interested me, and I was looking for some "what now" guidance.

He quickly made two suggestions. The first was to join the regional HR association. He had done some presentations to their membership a few years prior, and felt that there was potential for me to assist with some of their professional development programs. His second suggestion was to obtain an HR internship for the Spring semester. It sounded like great advice to me.

In the Career Development office, I explained to the director my newfound mission. Interestingly enough, she had spoken earlier that day with the people who managed the internship program in one of Boston's largest corporations, Byron Industries.[1] They mentioned that the internships for their popular business functions always had a high application rate, but they were trying to increase the applicant pool for their HR internship program. She handed me the flashy application which provided a detailed description of the company and the various HR internships that were being offered. I was impressed with the marketing materials and convinced that HR was my career goal; I feverishly completed the entire application later that night and sent it in the following morning. The semester was just concluding, and I was preparing to return to my home state of New Jersey for winter break.

As this was occurring, I was also making contact with the regional HR organization that my professor had discussed with me. They were intrigued by my interest and invited me for a meeting to discuss potential opportunities. I was to meet with the Executive Director and the Director of Conferences. As a junior in college, the chance to meet with executive level personnel from the

---

[1] Byron Industries and Delightful Desserts are fictitious names, (mentioned later in this section) representing the companies where I was an intern.

organization that represented my desired profession was, to say the least, very exciting.

I learned from the meeting that the organization hosted professional development seminars several times per month at various locations throughout the Metro Boston area. At least once a month, these programs were held at Babson. The headquarters for the HR association also happened to be located in the same town as the college. Normally, the Director of Conferences would have to travel back and forth from the office several times per day to manage the event. Realizing the inconvenience, the Executive Director and Conference Director were delighted for me to help. The deal was that I would spend the entire day at the conference, including setup and breakdown, and in return I would have the chance to network with attendees, have lunch, and observe the actual programming. It was definitely a great deal. I was to begin my duties at the start of the Spring semester, in 2006.

I entered the winter recess with a great deal of hope that I had answered the college student's most feared question of "what will I do after the four years is up?" About a week into Winter break I received a call from Byron. They left a friendly voicemail informing me that the organization was interested in interviewing me for a position in their Spring 2006 internship program. The phone interview took place a few days later, and, not to my surprise, I was asked the sort of questions that my college's career department had prepared me for.

With the expectation that I would work 12 to 15 hours per week at the downtown Boston office, I was offered an internship position in the Human Resources department. I would not earn a salary or wage, and it was required that I receive academic credit from Babson. I was notified which sub-department of human resources I would be interning for, but not the specific work I would be doing. I was told to come in for an orientation session, which was to take place the week before the official start of the Spring internship program.

My experience at Byron left a lot to be desired; and to say the least, my expectations were not met. At the start of the program, I was given a list of exciting tasks that I was to accomplish as part of my internship. However, I ended up spending most of my time hanging up flyers, collating, stapling, and filing. The amount of time that I actually spent performing non-menial tasks was at an extreme minimum. The internship was unpaid and I had to drive to and park in Boston. By the end of the internship, I had lost several hundred dollars taking into account parking, gas, and tolls. Byron didn't even provide a parking stipend.

To make matters worse, Byron's overall culture was not supportive of an internship program. Interns were assigned to their respective departments, but every morning, department leaders would send the internship coordinator an email if they needed an extra set of hands for the day. If an intern's supervisor gave permission, the intern would essentially be transferred for the day to an unfamiliar department, with no introduction, to complete - you guessed it - more menial tasks. I was transferred one day through this "intern marketplace" and my supervisor-for-a-day didn't even bother to ask my name. Instead, she referred to me as "intern."

It was not until March of 2006, when I was two months into the Byron Industries internship that I realized that there was an overall disconnect between employers and interns. On March 16th, 2006, I attended my third professional development seminar on behalf of the regional HR organization. The topic of the program was "Strategic Staffing." There were about fifty human resources personnel present, all of whom were at least at the manager level. The first half of the program focused on overall staffing strategies, and the second half of the program provided specific tools that organizations could use to implement the strategies. One of the main tools that the presenter suggested was an organization-wide internship program.

Currently being in an internship that I found less than satisfying, I was intrigued by his proposal and hoped that the HR professionals in the room could shed some light on my situation. To my surprise, the exact opposite occurred. The HR managers in the room looked dumbfounded. They proceeded to ask questions such as "where do we find interns?" and "what kind of work should they do?"

Meanwhile, Byron Industries was investing a large amount of time and money, into what they presumably thought was a successful program, through hiring, training, and utilizing interns, with the hopes that they would be ambassadors for their organization. But that was not going to happen with me. When friends asked how my internship was, I told them how I truly felt. Friends that were thinking of applying to Byron Industries for an internship or full-time employment were told to reconsider. I was not trying to hurt the company; I was simply trying to be candid with my friends by informing what I thought of the organization, which was solely based on my internship experience. I began to think that perhaps there was a large underlying problem when it came to organizations putting together internship programs for students.

I went home and immediately fired off an email to some of the Special Interest Groups of the HR association. That email is what started it all. I explained my situation and my observation during the professional development program. I threw out the idea of conducting research into internship management, hoping to receive just a few responses. The response was overwhelming. I received emails from several HR managers supporting the idea. As one HR manager wrote, "I would LOVE to see a survey like this done and its results.

I've been trying to figure out the 'formula' for college recruiting!"

Returning to my professor, I asked him if he would sponsor an independent research project for the following semester. He was excited about the idea and signed off on my research plan. Interestingly, the original plan was to research a small number of schools and organizations. I realized soon after starting the project that the plan was actually quite scalable. I thought "why not add more schools, if I can?" What was supposed to be a small survey ended up being one of the largest surveys to ever be conducted that focused solely on internships.

And then there was Delightful Desserts, my internship in summer of 2006. Delightful Desserts is in the food-service business, operating hundreds of café-style establishments throughout the world. I worked in the training department, and it was a truly excellent experience; mainly because I was given meaningful work assignments and had a terrific supervisor and great co-workers.

At the time I came on board, Delightful Desserts was rolling out a series of new products, and it was my job to update the training materials. "Updating" in most internships would probably mean taking the old page out of the training manual and replacing it with the one that someone else made. At Delightful Desserts, it was my responsibility to create brand-new training materials. To complete the task, I worked directly with high-level personnel from almost every department in the organization. By the end of the internship, I had overhauled almost all of the training materials and job aids that Delightful Desserts used in all of their stores. About six month later, I took a trip with friends to Florida. Delightful Desserts had just opened a new location in the airport. Missing their delicious food, I went over to place an order. As I watched the employees fill orders for the customers in front of me, I noticed that they were using the job aids and materials that I had created in Boston during the previous summer. It was extremely satisfying.

My supervisor was great, as he took the time to understand what my abilities were. Ultimately, this saved him a great deal of time and made me as productive as I could be. From day one I was brought into the organization as an equal employee. My name was added to the "culture committee" list so when it came time in July to celebrate employee birthdays, my name was included on the giant card that sat next to the ice cream cake, and I received two movie tickets. My department also bought me a cake for a smaller party inside my supervisor's office. I was also given access to the employee discount on the food I purchased. At the conclusion of the program, I even had lunch with the CEO. I left the organization with the utmost respect for how they view internships, student employment, and overall employee relations.

Here is the truly shocking part. Byron Industries hosted a highly-structured, substantial internship program that provided experiences to at least 40 students in each of the Fall, Spring, and Summer semesters. The organization also employed two full-time individuals; a large part of their responsibility being dedicated to managing the program. On the other hand, Delight Desserts did not have a formal program. They had hired interns from time-to-time but it was not a steady flow or a highly structured program – yet, they did it better and more effectively than the organization that was spending tens of thousands of dollars in salaries and opportunity costs.

The bottom line is that almost every organization can benefit from an internship program, and as complicated as it might sound, once you've done it, it will become a seamless part of your organization's culture.

The information contained in this publication is largely based on the available data from the landmark Intern Bridge research. I hope that you will find the information in this publication interesting and useful. Furthermore, I hope you will leverage it within your organization. An internship program can be an incredible tool for creating a pipeline of fresh talent for an organization. Together, we can create new programs and improve existing programs that are win-win situations, for both the organization and the student.

Let's close the gap.

THE MILLENNIAL GENERATION, V 2.0

Rachel I. Reiser
Founder and Principal, Generationally Speaking

We've heard of them as Generation Y, Generation NeXt, Echo Boomers, Boomlets, and Millennials, among other nomenclature, but I can never forget the first time I heard about them as a group. It was November of 2001, and I was in Chicago at a professional conference about undergraduate business curriculum. One of the available breakout sessions, entitled "Understanding & Responding to the New Millennials," was offered by colleagues from Virginia Tech. In this session, they discussed the work of Neil Howe and William Strauss, well known experts on the field of generational studies. My passion was born that day!

This session introduced me, in a salient and cohesive way, to research that explained this generation of students' unique and influential psychographic dynamics. My professional life has been spent in many facets of higher education administration, educating students, and supervising employees of all ages. During this time I have worked directly with college students and really experienced firsthand the changing characteristics of today's late adolescent. But never, until this session in Chicago, had I been presented with information that so immediately resonated with what I was experiencing with my students. I now had concrete language that described the growing trends towards ultra-achievement, hyper-scheduling, excessive parental involvement and attachment, high expectations for themselves and others, team-approach, optimism, and a disproportionate orientation toward technology. I immediately began reading whatever I could find that helped to explain this particular brand of student.

And wow, has there been a lot to read! In these intervening years, I have found no shortage of research, articles, and publications that have helped me to further my understanding of the Millennial Generation; the attention on the Millennials has been intense and unwavering. (In fact, I find it interesting that no prior generation had been identified from their very beginning, nor has any generation since – we are about ten years into the birth span of the generation that follows Millennials and we see little, if any, literature about whoever they are.) As the first of the Millennial Generation began graduating and entering the work force, my research turned to this issue, resulting in my 2010 book, **Millennials on Board: The Impact of the Rising Generation on the Workplace**. This book, and much of my work since then, centers around the ways in which societal influences and systems have contributed to the generational characteristics and the resulting implications for the workplace.

And the implications are far-reaching. Not only do we need to consider how, as managers of this new generation, it is incumbent upon us to understand Millennials in order to most effectively supervise them, but we also need to consider the ways in which our organizations can – *and should* – evolve in response to the needs of today's employees…of all generations. In the last ten years, we have seen tremendous changes in business culture, not exclusively driven by the arrival of Millennials as interns and full-time employees, but certainly informed by it. Their outlooks and experiences are a part of what makes them who they are, along with the basic demographics, and those characteristics have already had a major impact. But there is of course so much more to discuss regarding what gives them a generational culture, and what that means for today's businesses and organizations. As Lynne C. Lancaster and David Stillman write, "What most people overlook is that each generation brings its own set of values, beliefs, life experiences, and attitudes to the workplace, and that can be the problem. … Different generations won't become more alike with age. They will carry their 'generational personalities' with them throughout their lives. In fact, when hard times hit, the generations are more likely to entrench themselves even more deeply into the attitudes and behaviors that have been ingrained in them."[1]

So, some of the basics: their birth years are generally defined as 1982 to 2002; they are a large population and, with immigration, are about one-third larger than the Baby Boomer Generation; also as a result of immigration, along with other factors, they are racially and ethnically more diverse than any previous generation; the initial Millennials were raised by Boomer parents, while the latter Millennials will be raised by Generation X-ers. According to "Millennials: A Portrait of Generation Next" from the Pew Research Center (2010), when describing what makes them unique as a generation, Millennials cite their use of technology, their music and popular culture, their liberal and tolerant attitudes, being "smarter," and their clothes as the top five identifiers. When I talk with various groups and organizations, adjectives such as these resound most deeply as characteristic of Millennials: optimistic; multitaskers; overachievers; protected; politically active; nurtured; fearful of boredom; accustomed to structure and order; socially conscious; in need of instant gratification. A real mixed bag of qualities.

But there is much more to this picture, with just a bit more digging. Howe and Strauss detailed seven core characteristics of Millennials: special, sheltered,

---

[1] Lynne C. Lancaster and David Stillman, <u>When Generations Collide: Who They Are. Why They Clash. How to Solve the Generational Puzzle at Work</u> (New York: HarperCollins Publishers, 2002).

confident, team-oriented, conventional, pressured, and achieving.[2] In my own research I have found it useful to frame Millennial attributes somewhat differently, explaining their psychography and drives based on the societal influences that have informed their development, and considering ways in which businesses and organizations can respond to these features.

The Hovered Generation

Wake Forest College Dean Mary Gerardy originated the term "helicopter parents," referring to those parents with whom we college administrators have unfortunately become all too familiar: the intrusive, hovering parent. In fact, in more recent years, I have found the more appropriate moniker to be "snowplow parent," those who clear the path for the child of all hurdles and obstacles, and of course it goes without saying the unintended consequences of such an approach. I could go on and on with hundreds of stories from my experiences and that of my colleagues around the nation that illustrate the point that Millennials are sheltered. They have wonderfully close relationships with their families, and feel truly supported, but they have little experience figuring things out for themselves. We all tend to agree that these parents are generally working with what they believe to be their child's best interest at heart and, by being so explicitly involved in their child's life, they are doing precisely what they have always been told is their role and responsibility as a parent. But the ongoing concern is that Millennials and their families perpetuate a sense of arrested development long after they reach young adulthood. We may assume that this is behavior that a young person would grow out of as they leave high school and get adjusted to college, but in fact what we see is that college students are more than willing to cede control or decision-making to their parents (at least around the majority of issues) – and that it doesn't stop at commencement in May four years later.

In interviewing for my book, I spoke with an On-Site Supervisor at a major temporary employment firm who stated: "We are almost in locus parenti. Not only do they look to their employment manager, but they trust almost immediately. What I think happens is that they really get sheltered so much, that they do not realize that it's not about them, it's about business." Another College Relations Manager for a wellness company informed me that, "On numerous occasions I have had parents approach our career booth to drop off their child's résumé and 'pitch' their qualifications. We were surprised when we first started seeing parents show up at career fairs three years ago. Most recently

---

[2] Neil Howe and William Strauss, <u>Millennials Rising: The Next Great Generation</u> (New York: Vintage Books, 2000).

I was surprised when just this fall I had a parent approach me at a master's level career fair!" Perhaps most fascinating was how readily this practice is accepted. "We actually embrace this phenomenon because we understand how important it is for a parent to feel comfortable with the company their child chooses to start or dedicate much of their professional career." I have mixed feelings about this. I can appreciate that this is the way the world is moving, and I truly understand the "investment" parents have made in their children's futures – and I do not simply mean financial, but let's face it, on the most practical level, a job candidate who seems incapable of making a career decision without their parents' input may raise red flags for the prospective employer; these issues also suggest concern about the adult child's professionalism. The message that they are sending is that they aren't really capable of making adult decisions, and who wants an employee with that problem? Work is filled with daily decisions, and we all want employees who are confident and proficient in making them. We need to teach our new Millennial employees how to be more decisive and convey self-efficacy and autonomy. So through intentional supervision and mentorship we effectively endeavor to retrain what more than two decades of parental influence has built.

So what does this seem to mean for today's businesses? We know that it costs any organization a lot to recruit, hire, and train new employees, so if parental involvement in the front-end decision making about taking a particular job minimizes staff turnover, it can advantage the organization as well as the new staff member. We need to mindful of a balance in a developmental approach in the supervision of Millennial employees with the engagement of their parents; and most importantly, we need to provide better training to hiring managers to work in this developmental way with their young employees. Organizations can react to these dynamics with the development of Career Development Seminars for parents, Parent-Liaison Departments, parent newsletters, the enhancement of training for recruiters at the organization, and mentorship programs for new employees. Like it or not, we must adjust to the massive ongoing influence of parents – Helicopter or not – in the lives of their adult children. They have borne this power and authority for more than 20 years, and it and they aren't going anywhere.

Generation RX

The Society for College and University Planning (SCUP) produces a bi-annual report on "Trends to Watch in Higher Education;" the August 2008 report addressed, amidst its discussion of changing demographics in higher education as a trend of import, that the number one issue related to changing demographics is the rise in mental health concerns amongst college students. "The mental health of students attending college is increasingly becoming a cause for concern, in both the US and Canada. The number of students who seek and need mental health services is only likely to rise. Increased awareness and decreased stigmatization for treatment contribute to this trend, but don't explain it all."[3] Citing studies by the American College Health Association—National College Health Assessment and the National Survey of Counseling Center Directors 2007, SCUP discusses a college-age population that is reporting more depression, anxiety, and major psychological disorders. Anecdotally speaking, we find it is sometimes the highest achieving students, under great personal and familial pressure to succeed, who experience the most significant consequences of stress and depression. Young people worry more than ever about their future; we, in turn, worry about what this does to them. It is great that they have drive and determination, but their stress affects them physically. Studies show that many have never learned how to create balance in life and, as a consequence, have trouble sleeping and maintaining a reasonable schedule, staying healthy, and dealing with the normal hurdles of life. Their stress level makes them more prone to anxiety and other emotional concerns, essentially more fragile.

The fact that mental health is being considered in this way by our institutions of higher education certainly suggests that it will play a substantially larger role in other functional areas of society; companies will have to consider this issue in the ways in which they work with their employees. As Millennials graduate from college and take jobs in various organizations, they will continue to face personal and professional stressors, and will now face them without easy access to the resources that are typical on most of today's college campuses. In fact, many of the anxiety issues that impact their personal and academic lives as students will have similar impact on their lives as professionals in the workplace. As one Millennial whom I interviewed told me, "I do believe that I have more personal issues and emotional concerns that are brought to work. I'm not always prepared for certain situations and I find myself getting stressed out easily and sometimes my anxiety gets so bad that I break down in front of my co-workers. On more than one occasion, I've cried at work, which in retrospect is really embarrassing. It's funny because on a few different occasions, when I'm in the midst of having a bad day, I've actually called my family from my desk at work to vent. I do believe that my Millennial peers and I need more guidance on how to deal with stressful workplace issues."

Obviously, we want to have employees who are as effective and productive as possible. This relies to a large degree upon them being able to manage their

---

[3] Society for College and University Planning, Trends in Higher Education, August 2008, 10/18/08 [http://www.scup.org/pdf/SCUP_Trends_8-2008.pdf].

emotional and psychological lives. They need to be "okay" in order to perform at their jobs to the level that we desire, and while we may hold no responsibility to help them to be "okay," we certainly benefit significantly when they are. Organizations may find that in order for their employees to be as productive as possible in the workplace, they need to be responsive to these mental health and other related issues. Effective responses may include providing more flexibility in the work environment, by utilizing technology to allow employees to work more from home, and employing team-based approaches to project management. Other useful tools in addressing staff satisfaction with work environments can include the implementation of generous benefits and professional development programs, and Employee Assistance Programs. Millennials, with all that they have to offer to the workplace, are clearly at their best when their emotional and psychological needs are being met. They have come to expect this and, I might say, even to need this.

The Celebrated Generation

There are those who refer to Millennials as "The Trophy Generation." Certainly we have seen the cumulative effect of the constant outpouring of acknowledgement and reward, where every "non-event" is commended. We have raised a new "celebrated generation" and it has its impact. In June 2008, The New York Times sparked a debate about the merit of elaborate eighth grade graduations, "While some educators are grateful that notice is still being paid to academic achievement, others deride the festivities as overpraising what should be routine accomplishment. Some principals, school superintendents and legislators are trying to scale back the grandeur. But stepping between parents and ever-escalating celebrations of their children's achievements can be dicey, at best."[4] There are many arguments to be made for the benefit and value of acknowledging an accomplishment like finishing middle school, including the fact that for many children coming from unusually challenging home or personal environments, finishing eighth grade is in fact a tremendous accomplishment, but I feel that this is part of a larger picture of excess reward. Even Barack Obama – prior to the completion of his successful run for the Presidency – weighed in on this: "'Now hold on a second — this is just eighth grade,' he said. 'So, let's not go over the top. Let's not have a huge party. Let's just give them a handshake.' He continued: 'You're supposed to graduate from eighth grade.'"[5]

---

[4] Jan Hoffman, "Does 8th-Grade Pomp Fit the Circumstance?",
 The New York Times, June 22, 2008.
[5] Ibid.

The bottom line is that Millennials have been told all of their lives just how special they are. They had activities planned for them, their schedules were a family priority, and their successes were praised and rewarded. They have earned trophies and awards for simply participating in their myriad of activities. And they have been at the forefront of not just the familial agenda, but the societal agenda as well.

It is now "cool" to be smart, and probably because they came into the world at a time when children received new levels of attention and educational reform became a priority, Millennials may be the smartest generation yet. Strauss and Howe noted that "During the 1990s, aptitude test scores have risen within every racial and ethnic group, especially in elementary schools. Eight in ten teenagers say it's 'cool to be smart,' while a record share of teenagers say they 'look forward to school,' take advanced placement tests, and plan to attend college."[6] And they also see themselves as a generation of high achievers, causing significant personal pressure and making them fearful of falling behind their peers; the percentage of tenth graders who expected to graduate from a four-year college or higher went up from 59% in 1990 to 80% in 2002. But there is some conflicting information on this as well. According to the 2006 High School Survey of Student Study of Engagement (over 80,000 students at 110 schools in 26 states), 90% of high school students reported spending five hours/week or less "reading/studying for class." The college counterpart to the high school survey, the 2006 National Survey of Student Study of Engagement reports that 18% of college students reported less than five hours "preparing for class," a statistic that is all the more concerning when paired with the fact that another 26% reported between just six to ten hours.

Further, social media may lend itself to an exaggerated sense of self-importance. Millennials are constantly posting the status of their activities to their Facebook sites and instant messaging profiles, with an audience of friends and family – and even strangers – seeming to want to know what they are doing or thinking at any given moment. This gets internalized over time, and conveys to them that all that they do is of prime importance to most anyone around them. This contributes to a sense of self-importance and grandiosity. And despite difficult economic times, Millennials may still perceive themselves as having lots of professional options, and companies will continue to find themselves "selling" the job to prospective young employees. Their high expectations for their own career advancement will not be subjugated, as they continue to seek out increasingly interesting and gratifying work.

---

[6] Neil Howe and William Strauss, <u>Millennials Go to College</u>, (LifeCourse Associates, 2003).

As organizations address these Millennial characteristics, they will find it helpful to develop more regular evaluation cycles, while additionally assessing the ways in which criticism is delivered. Feedback is key; it bears increasing importance with Millennials, and both the frequency and way in which it is delivered is important. As Ron Alsop writes, "In addition to more frequent and detailed performance assessments, Millennials want companies to nurture their career development."[7] Formal coaching programs can be a useful tool, whereby more seasoned professionals serve as a resource to newer Millennial employees, but recognition of the skill sets and talents that Millennials bring to the workplace will be essential to their professional satisfaction as well. I argue that their lifetime of the combination of exaggerated praise, protection from disappointment and disillusion, and the ubiquitous influence of technology on ego has formed a lot of who this generation is and what they expect from all facets of their lives, most notably their work environs.

The Programmed Generation

Millennials are extraordinarily active, and much of this activity takes place in a group setting of one sort or another, including virtual groups. They have been raised learning, playing, working, and being evaluated in groups, and they are well tuned to team-orientation. There is documented value to all of this teaming, with Millennials listing their top work skills as those relating to working well with others, including those from different races and ethnicities. Further, "there is quite consistent and strong evidence of a positive association between participating in organized activities and a variety of indicators of positive development: those youth who participate demonstrate healthier functioning on such indicators ranging from academic achievement, school completion, post-secondary educational attainment, psychological adjustment, and lowered rates of smoking and drug use, to the quantity and quality of interactions with their parents."[8]

But there seems to be a downside as well. There has been much made over the years of the phenomena of "hyper-scheduling," with evidence on all sides about the positive and negative consequences of so many arranged group-based activities. I have serious concerns about the lack of time for and emphasis on any kind of contemplation, which I strongly believe hinders the development not only of critical thinking and analytical skills, but also of necessary coping

---

[7] Ron Alsop, The Trophy Kids Grow Up: How the Millennial Generation is Shaking Up the Workplace, (California: Jossey-Bass, 2008).

[8] Joseph L. Mahoney, Angel L. Harris, & Jacquelynne S. Eccles, "Organized Activity Participation, Positive Youth Development, and the Over-Scheduling Hypothesis," Social Policy Report: Giving Child and Youth Development Knowledge Away, 2006.

mechanisms. Childhood stress is shown to be a significant factor in young-adult depression; as Madeline Levine writes in The Price of Privilege, "Kids can't find the time, both literal and psychological, to linger in internal exploration; a necessary precursor to a well-developed sense of self."[9]

Yet another consequence of such rigorous structured programming is a lack of creative and leadership development. Millennials are a generation raised in structured activities, always organized, presented, and presided over by adults. As a child, I remember being able to go out after dinner and find other kids playing in the neighborhood; we would come up with our own games, creating rules and structures for them. These activities were not engineered or directed by adults; in fact, rarely were parents present. With this independence and freedom, conflict arose and was then resolved, inquisitiveness was fostered, and true cooperation skills were built. Parents and teachers were not present to intervene and solve, and children had to rely upon their internal skills sets and resiliency. Needless to say, there is a lot of benefit to this autonomy that Millennials lacked in their youth.

On the other hand, Millennials' team-orientation fits in well with organizations that have already placed a high value on this quality, and this can help organizations to evolve further. Consider what I was told when interviewing Julie Wille, a College Recruiting Representative at Hallmark Cards, "Hallmark has a culture of being team-oriented, but everyone is still accountable for their own performance. Most departments are team- oriented and work together to reach common goals. If anything, the Millennials have probably helped to bridge this gap in departments. Many of our interns ask to work with each other on projects and that has happened in a few of our departments, which has been very successful. We also provide some small-scale Millennial training to intern managers so they are prepared if they have not done research. Some managers took it as opportunities to have the interns present to diversity councils on the different generations in the Hallmark workplace and what improvements can be made to achieve the common goals for the company." Organizations can employ different initiatives in that can capitalize on Millennials team-orientation. These can include structured group-based leadership and professional development programs that emulate those that they are used to, which have the additional effect of providing to them a concrete validation of the organization. Further, through the usage of social media technology, virtual workplace teaming may take on a whole new dimension with Millennial employees, and changing the physical layout of work spaces can have posi-

---

[9] Madeline Levine, Ph.D., The Price of Privilege: How Parental Pressure and Material Advantage Are Creating a Generation of Disconnected and Unhappy Kids (New York: HarperCollins Publishers, 2006).

tive impact on the enhancement of a vibrant collaborative environment. Most importantly, Millennials are in need of mentorship and guidance that will help them to further develop skill sets that may need work, and developmental supervision is key to this endeavor.

Generation Optimistic

Millennials are an interesting group; they are generally characterized as being "personally happy" and upbeat about their future. Certainly they were raised with strong messaging about their value and worth for the world around them, and perhaps as a result of this, they want to make a difference in the world. "Students from the Millennial Generation are increasingly interested in jobs where they feel they can make a positive difference – whether that's building solar panels, running a food bank, or making micro-finance loans in Africa."[10] For Millennials, the right job is really about the right fit; consider these data points:[11]

- 79% of Millennials want to work for employers who care about how they impact/contribute to society;

- 44% would actively pursue working for a company after learning about its social commitment;

- 69% of Millennials stated that they are aware of their company's commitment to social causes;

- 30% of Millennials want their job to empower them to make the world a better place;

- 89% are likely or very likely to switch from one brand to another (price and quality being equal) if the second brand is associated with a good cause.

Companies will benefit from overhauling their employee recruitment materials to bring attention to their community service and environmental initiatives, in their efforts to attract the interest of prospective Millennial employees.

---

[10] Geoff Gloeckler, "The Millennials Invade the B-Schools," Business Week, November 13, 2008.

[11] "Cone 2006 Millennial Cause Study," Cause Marketing Forum, October 24, 2006, 11/28/08 [http://www.causemarketingforum.com/page.asp?ID=473].

Of course we worry about the price of the economic downturn for this generation of young people – the proportion of Millennials employed full time fell from 50% in 2006 to 41% in 2010. It is well documented that extended periods of youthful joblessness can significantly depress lifetime income. Interestingly, however, though the recession has been hard on young people, it has not dimmed their optimism. While 68% of Millennials say they are not earning enough money to live the kind of life they want, 88% of those say they expect to earn enough in the future to "live the good life" (this compares to the 76% percentage of Gen Xers and 46% of Baby Boomers with this view).[12]

But what does this mean for us as employers? If we want to attract and retain these employees, what do we do? Perhaps most saliently, a more democratic and consensus-oriented organizational structure holds tremendous appeal to Millennials, who often judge their choices for place of employment around environmental appeal. What Millennial Workers Want: How to Attract and Retain Gen Y Employees reports "those that are just starting their careers want to know that their contributions matter and their skills are improving. To close the revolving door, you may need to restructure the entry level positions, perhaps combining several functions to create a single, more challenging job, or developing a more defined path of advancement out of a routine role."[13] Keep in mind that Millennials are a generation raised on reaction to their needs and wants – at home, school, and society overall, therefore customization from their workplace does not seem to them like an outlandish expectation. We need to be prepared that Millennial employees may want to have their jobs adapted to their specific professional interests and strengths, and with increased teaming on projects and programs, a somewhat natural outcome is the parsing out of responsibilities based on skills, strengths, and interest.

In short, as organizations work to attract and retain Millennial employees, it will be important to maintain and promote a conscientious mission, consider tailoring jobs to the individual, and provide a voice to Millennial employees, so that they feel fully connected to the mission of the organization.

Generation 2.0

"On Sunday, October 26th I decided to put away my iPod, cellular phone, laptop and other devices which pretty much make up my life. Throughout the 24-hours without technology, I felt isolated and out of touch with the outside world, as if I was missing out on some important occurrence that everyone but

---

[12] "Millennials: Confident. Connected. Open to Change." Pew Research Center (2010).
[13] Robert Half International and YAHOO! Hot Jobs, "What Millennial Workers Want: How to Attract and Retain Gen Y Employees," (California, 2007).

me knew of. It never occurred to me how dependent I am on technology. Everything from entertainment to my means of communication revolves around technology, which is not difficult to believe in this day and age." So wrote Amanda, a student of mine who willingly participated in a 24-hour "technology fast" and then wrote an essay about it. Her experience did not surprise me; after all Born Digital describes the impact of technology on today's younger generations, "major aspects of their lives – social interactions, friendships, civic activities – are mediated by digital technologies. ... Most notable, however, is the way the digital era has transformed how people live their lives and relate to one another and the world around them."[14]

There is so much that could be said regarding Millennials and technology – many questions, and even more answers, sometimes sending conflicting messages. *For one, is technology hindering creativity?* Well, perhaps yes, and perhaps no. It is true that as more and more time is spent interfacing with TV and these other forms of media, less and less time is spent doing traditionally creative activities, or engaging in imaginative thought or play. With less time spent being creative, our kids have grown up with less developed creative skills, and maybe that has turned them into less creative young adults. On the other hand, it may be time that we view creativity through a new lens. Look at YouTube, which is just one example of this, but there are so many others – blogging, Wikipedia, their Facebook sites, and so forth. There is some really creative stuff out there on YouTube! There's also a lot of junk, but that doesn't discount the innovation amidst it. Millennials are using digital cameras, cell phones, and video cameras to create their own short movies and other forms of self-expression to post to the web. "The Internet has unleashed an explosion of creativity – and along with it thousands of new forms of creative expression – on a vast scale. These new forms of expression are unlike anything the world has ever seen before. Digital Natives are increasingly engaged in creating information, knowledge, and entertainment in online environments."[15]

Is it a problem that Millennials are reading less? A November 2007 report from the National Endowment for the Arts reports a significant decline in reading in the United States. The study reports that the typical 15- to 24-year-old watches two hours of television a day, and spends only about seven minutes a day reading for leisure. About a third of 13-year-olds read daily, and the percentage of non-readers has more than doubled since 1984, from nine percent

---

[14] John Palfrey and Urs Gasser, Born Digital: Understanding the First Generation of Digital Natives (New York: Basic Books, 2008).
[15] Ibid.

136

to 19 percent in 2004.[16] Singer and Singer discuss the important creative development that occurs with reading. "When we read, a more complicated process occurs than when we view television. We are engaged in the active process of encoding the words on the printed page by combining discrete letters. From strings of words, thoughts are generated, associations are made, and images are constructed."[17] Remember, "nearly two-thirds of employers ranked reading comprehension 'very important' for high school graduates. Yet 38 percent consider most high school graduates deficient in this basic skill."[18]

Is this talent with technology making Millennials more efficient? Millennials grew up working and experimenting on personal computers, and they are exceptionally comfortable continuing to play, figuring things out, designing new programs or websites, and using online communities to enhance the work environment. Companies revel in the efficiencies that Millennials can help to bring to the workplace through the creative employment of technology. As Irene DeNigris, Director of Global University Recruitment at Johnson & Johnson, told me, "The positives are many – they are able to quickly gather and conduct research, they are better able to pull together graphically rich presentations, they are comfortable multi-tasking. Through use of technologies they have been able to reduce project timelines."

But perhaps the biggest concern of all is that of multi-tasking. Do these efficiencies come with a cost? I have long maintained that the Millennial Generation really struggles with exhibiting patience and sitting with uncertainty. As I have discussed, as great multitaskers, Millennials are busy at all times, and technology is a major tool for them as they try to keep up with it all. A colleague recently told me a story of getting a call from a student regarding some academic advising questions. When she remarked that the connection wasn't great and seemed kind of "windy," he told her that he was calling her from the ski slopes, where he was snowboarding! I certainly do my own share of multi-tasking with occasional calls from my cell phone in the car, but I don't think it would ever occur to me, or many of my Generation X or Boomer colleagues, to take care of business from the slopes! But this does raise the obvious question of the efficacy of multitasking. "The human brain literally cannot do two things

---

[16] National Endowment for the Arts News Room, "National Endowment for the Arts Announces New Reading Study," November 19, 2007, 12/14/08 [http://www.nea.gov/news/news07/TRNR.html]..

[17] 49 Dorothy G. and Jerome L. Singer, Imagination and Play in the Electronic Age (Massachusetts: Harvard University Press, 2005).

[18] National Endowment for the Arts News Room, "National Endowment for the Arts Announces New Reading Study," November 19, 2007, 12/14/08 [http://www.nea.gov/news/news07/TRNR.html].

at once, says Sandra Bond Chapman, Ph.D., chief director of the University of Texas at Dallas Center for Brain Health. "It quickly toggles back and forth from one task to the other, taking its toll on our efficiency," she notes."[19]

In fact, recent research conducted at Stanford University elaborates further on this issue. Clifford Nass and his colleagues wanted to understand what made chronic media multitaskers – those who regularly engaged in technology-based multitasking activities – so good at the act of multitasking. What they found was that they actually were not so good at it; and they found a lot more. First of all, this group had experienced a hindering of their cognitive processing skills. Consider this as 'information literacy,' the ability to discern what is important and what is unimportant. These chronic media multitaskers were "suckers for the irrelevant." Secondly, they had greater problems than the control group with the management of working memory. I like to think of memory as a mental file cabinet; the information is not always right there at the ready, but when I think about it, I am able to come up with what drawer within my mental file cabinet, and then what file within that drawer, contains the information that I need. Again, these multitaskers displayed a lesser ability with this. Finally, and most ironically, they demonstrated lesser ability with the one thing at which you'd think they might be better, the ability to shift seamlessly from task to task.[20] Couple this with their challenges with dealing with uncertainty, lack of experience with reflection, and less developed sense of patience, and we see what I consider to be some serious unintended consequences.

I am not indicting Millennials here; I think we all do this – it has become our habituation. The difference here is that Millennials grew up with it. They grew up always being able to reach someone quite quickly, if not immediately, at the other end of their cellphone. They grew up with the immediacy of e-mail. In fact, we are seeing that e-mail may take too long for today's youth; teens who participated in focus groups for a Pew study said that "they view email as something you use to talk to 'old people,' institutions, or to send complex instructions to large groups. When it comes to casual written conversation, particularly when talking with friends, online instant messaging is the clearly the mode of choice for today's online teens."[21] This to me underscores the immediacy issue; Millennial teens are finding and utilizing faster mechanisms for communication, ones that do not require them to wait even a moment for

---

[19] Charlotte Latvala, "De-Stress Your Weeknights," <u>Good Housekeeping Magazine</u>, January 2009.

[20] Eyal Ophir, Clifford Nass, and Anthony D. Wagner "Cognitive Control in Media Multitaskers," Proceedings of the National Academy of Sciences (2009).

[21] Amanda Lenhart, Mary Madden, and Paul Hitlin, "Teens and Technology," July 27, 2005, Pew Internet & American Life Project.

the answer to their question, the exchange of a greeting with a friend, or the gathering of "data" on what others are up to – through their posting of "away messages" that provide detailed information on their comings and goings. And the Millennial teens of that seven-year-old study are today's adult employees, taught by these experiences.

But it is important not to dwell on these negative issues, because the pros – in my opinion – do quite overwhelm the cons. The opportunities to capitalize on the technological skills and savvy of Millennials are endless. There is so much potential for innovation of efficiency and productivity gains; Millennials are great endorsers of "generativity" or "open innovation" – where "innovations let others build yet more innovative things on top of them, from which each party (the platform maker and also the one building upon the platform) can profit."[22] Embracing this Millennial mindset means recognizing the skill sets that are developed by their unique use of technology. It means shifting our paradigms in how we consider the Millennial behavior that we have so long criticized. Take for example the oft-condemned video gaming; The Federation of American Scientists produced a report on video games that cited that "the success of complex video games demonstrates that games can teach higher-order thinking skills such as strategic thinking, interpretive analysis, problem-solving, plan formation and execution, and adaption to rapid change...the skills U.S. employers increasingly seek in workers and new workforce entrants." In essence, Millennials' lifelong experience playing and experimenting with so many forms of technology help them to be exceedingly comfortable figuring things out, designing new programs or websites, and using online communities to enhance their workplaces. Companies have a lot to gain from the efficiencies that Millennials bring to the workplace through the creative employment of technology.

We can get past the technological generation gap by reacting to Millennial learning and work styles, understanding that they are accustomed to collaborative learning environments and the pace of the internet. This means developing interactive training seminars, which are most effective, including presentations with video clips and moving graphics. It especially means capitalizing on social media; when considering employee recruitment, recognize that online recruiting sites now hold 110 million jobs and 20 million unique résumés, with 10 million résumés on Monster.com alone. We're not just talking LinkedIn.com! Try providing uncensored blogs by Millennial employees and HR process FAQ pages in the form of a wiki, make available chat rooms to answer job candidate

---

[22] John Palfrey and Urs Gasser, <u>Born Digital: Understanding the First Generation of Digital Natives</u> (New York: Basic Books, 2008).

questions, post podcasts that express the organizational culture and mission. Don't just ban Facebook or other social networks, exploit them!

But most important is the opportunity for "reverse mentorship," where the knowledge flow is shifted in reverse, from new employee to more seasoned (read: older) employee – even to the boss him or herself. In fact, among the many major organizations utilizing reverse mentorship, General Electric was the first when CEO Jack Welsh recognized the potential to learn from his younger, more technologically savvy new employees. Technology is not the only place where there is room to advantage this opportunity, but it is one where it is most pronounced. Fifty-four percent of Millennials rate themselves as having "top level of expertise" about technology, while only 28% rated their bosses as having similar level of expertise [23] – an opportunity ripe for the taking!

Organizations may be able to respond to all of the issues and opportunities with the enhancement of existing leadership development programs that aim to teach this new generation of employees everything from issues of workplace technology etiquette to proper professional communication. Companies need to be willing to invest in technology upgrades, as the quality of technology within the organization will be a major factor in where the Millennial candidate chooses to go to work. It is evident that Millennial interns and employees have a lot to offer to the organization with their expertise in this area, and this should be capitalized upon by capturing their knowledge base and developing programs that enable Millennials to teach older colleagues how to better utilize technology.

When all is said and done, I continue to find Millennials to be one of the more fascinating groups I've encountered, and the study of them to be among the most fascinating topics. They have a strong community culture, a vibrant group and individual personality, and are poised to make their impact on the world, including the work world. I maintain that they already are making this impact. They have led the way in technology, forcing organizations to amp up their services and equipment, while teaching those of us who are older how to succeed in a digital world. They push us to reconsider how we offer feedback to employees, not just how often, but in what ways. They have encouraged the development of more robust programs and services designed to support employees through difficult personal and professional circumstances. They promote optimistic views of the world and the need for companies to engage in missions and activities that are socially responsible and of benefit to more than just the shareholders.

---

[23] Don Tapscott, Grown Up Digital: How the Net Generation Is Changing Your World (New York: McGraw-Hill, 2009).

In my book, I asked the question "Who are the Millennials?" I concluded then, as I do now, that they are an amalgamation of many complex experiences and characteristics. They have much to offer to our workplaces, and along with that much of which to be mindful. They are shaping the nature of the workplace. They are the future and the future has arrived.

*In a career spanning over 20 years in higher education, **Rachel Reiser** has held positions at several schools where she worked directly with college students, providing her with the opportunity to experience first-hand the changing characteristics of today's late adolescent, and fostering her professional interest in generational studies. Rachel has researched, written, and presented extensively on the demographics and psychographics of the Millennial Generation. She has presented countless programs on this topic to a range of audiences and has served as a consultant to groups and organizations in helping them to consider their work in the age of the Millennial Generation. Her book, <u>Millennials on Board: The Impact of the Rising Generation on the Workplace</u>, was published in February 2010. She can be contacted at rreiser@genspeaks.com.*

THE BUSINESS CASE FOR PAYING INTERNS

Robert Shindell, Ph.D.
President & CEO, Intern Bridge Inc.

"In an economy where companies and organizations often can't afford to hire, bringing an intern on board has become common practice. New graduates often jump at these opportunities, even if the internship doesn't include a paycheck, because paid jobs that offer relevant work experience are few and far between in this struggling economy."
- The Ethics of Unpaid Internships, US News & World Report.
January 19, 2011

As the above quote eludes, internships are still popular with employers despite the economic downturn. However, many of these positions are unpaid as employers try to implement strategies that connect labor needs with mandatory cost-saving measures. In many cases, unpaid internships are simply the norm. In others, human resources professionals implement unpaid programs without fully considering the long-term impact of their decision.

The information in this whitepaper is derived from the most in-depth research into internships available anywhere. All of the data presented are based on the 2011 National Internship and Co-op Study conducted by Intern Bridge. Over 27,000 students from more than 250 universities participated in this research project.

Intern Bridge has always taken the position that all internships, with few exceptions, should offer monetary compensation. This opinion is based on detailed review of economic and business principles, in addition to educational best practices and Intern Bridge data, much of which is outlined in this report. The report seeks to add another layer in the complicated decision of whether or not to offer monetary compensation to interns.

As such, it contains editorial pieces and commentary about the unpaid internship environment. Please continue to visit the Intern Bridge website at www.internbridge.com as we conduct additional research and release new reports regarding the compensation structure of internship programs.

Why Should Interns Earn a Salary?
Before going into any detail about any specific compensation data regarding internships, it is important to first establish why this topic is so important. Why not just make all internship programs unpaid? The broad answer is simple; unpaid internship programs yield employer brands that are less competitive in the job market, prohibit organizations from building a pipeline packed with

talented knowledge workers, widen the gap between the wealthy and the poor, and, in many cases, are simply illegal.

To support the practice of providing intern wages, we must first explore some assumptions about the topic, explore the reasons why students seek internships and then illustrate the host organizations responsibilities and the legalities of providing (or not providing) a wage for interns.

Assumptions

This report offers a few assumptions regarding the reasons organizations host internship programs. The main purpose for-profit companies have historically hosted internship programs is to gain access to highly qualified talent at low cost, something that is especially important given the current state of the economic climate. These are educated individuals who are coming from today's college classrooms beaming with up-to-date information and a desire to hit the ground running - and they arrive at your doorstep at a fraction of the cost of a new hire.

No matter how you slice the numbers, interns simply cost less. The purpose for-profit organizations exist is to turn a profit. Internship programs are a small piece to the puzzle that contribute to their earnings. The main assumption is that for-profit companies have a profit motive in the hiring of interns. If companies lost money in the long-term on interns, they wouldn't hire them.

Not-for-profit organizations and governmental agencies are a bit different, but they too operate as a business. The business of a not-for-profit is to serve a social good or purpose, just like the business of a government agency is to complete specific tasks that ultimately serve their constituents. These entities aren't as concerned about the number on the bottom line of their books at the end of the year. In most cases, these entities hire interns mostly for productivity.

While not-for-profits and government agencies certainly utilize internship programs to build recruiting brands and hire new talent, these motives are typically secondary to getting the work done that allows them to achieve their mission. The assumption with not-for-profit organizations and government agencies is that they want the best and brightest individuals working for them. Better candidates equal stronger employees (either temporary interns or full-time new hires), who can help these entities get closer to achieving their social purpose. The overarching assumption, regardless of for-profit, not-for-profit, or government, is that there is a war for talent and it's heating up.

Economic reports of how disruptive the impending labor shortage will be vary, but it's clear that droves of experienced workers will retire as the recession subsides and recovery begins. During the next decade, there will be a tremendous shift in both the types of jobs available and the talent available to fill these positions. Recent graduates, or "entry level talent", will quickly become the lifeline for human capital needs. There is no better, no cheaper, and no more effective college-recruiting tool than a properly executed internship program. Therefore, the final assumption is that organizations are battling for the best and brightest college graduates, and the battles will only get more heated in the coming years.

It's All About The Pool of Candidates

Every minute, thousands of recruiters are swimming in a sea of highly-qualified and not-so-qualified job candidates on sites like Monster, Experience, NaceLink, etc. The recruiters begin at the surface, pouring through databases, or applicant pools, full of potential new talent. They begin to filter through candidates based on specific criteria such as major, past job experience, and academic performance. The pool continues to get smaller until they're left with a puddle of applicants that the recruiters believe will be a perfect fit for the specific job they are seeking to fill. In the search for a full-time hire, this process makes sense. In the search for an unpaid intern, it defies logic.

Organizations must take into account the financial burdens each college student has incurred. The overall cost of higher education in the United States has continued to rise, and this includes tuition, fees, textbooks and the cost of living. While these costs continue to rise, support for students through financial aid, grants and scholarships are down. This has shifted the burden of the cost of college to the students and their families. More and more students are working while they are attending school just so they can meet their immediate financial obligations. This puts students in a difficult position when it comes to finding a job when they reach graduation and are making the transition from college to the world-of-work.

A college student is not equal to a recent graduate ready to enter the workforce where their professional dedication lies in their job. An intern's primary responsibility is to their academic studies. That only leaves a small amount of time for additional responsibilities. Unfortunately, for many students that means making a choice: accept an unpaid internship, work a part-time job, or attempt to do both (which almost always negatively impacts their studies).

In fact, 64% of students report they would have to work a second job if they accepted an unpaid internship. While that may be possible in the summer, it's difficult during the academic year. Think mom and dad are helping? Think again. Only 35% of students report that their parents could help to support them financially while taking part in an internship. To gain access to the best and brightest talent, organizations must start with the broadest pool of candidates. The cost of providing an intern a modest hourly wage will pay indescribable dividends in the future: lower cost per hire, absent cost of turnover, an incredible recruiting brand, and higher levels of productivity. All that for $10 to $15 per hour.

Why Students Choose to Participate in an Internship

In this current economic climate, many employers have expressed that their organization cannot afford to pay interns a high hourly wage. In some cases, they can only afford to pay minimum wage. Often times, they feel that the gap between what wage they are able to offer and the wage that the competition is paying is so large that it's not even worth it to pay a wage at all.

It is important to note that students do not go into internships looking to become wealthy. In fact, the table below shows a ranked list of the reasons students pursue internships. The top 7 reasons are all experiential based. Students want to convert academic theory to real world experience and build their network.

Times have changed. Inflated internship salaries have become all but extinct. Investment banks, for example, have been notorious for paying interns hourly wages based on first-year entry-level salaries. It was commonplace for interns to be receiving wages upwards of $30/hour. Not anymore. Internship programs (and entry-level talent programs for that matter) have become less about money, and more about content and experience. To illustrate this point, 48% of students would choose a government or not-for-profit internship over a for-profit experience and the latter pay significant less on average. Students today are seeking more than just a high wage for a short period of time. Opportunities to engage in community service, work on green initiatives, network with internal and external clients, participate in group work, meet other interns, and learn about the inner workings of the organization and industry are far more important.

Organizational Responsibility

Unpaid internships create disparate impact towards individuals who can't afford them. An editorial piece in the Chronicle of Higher Education a couple of years ago addressed some of the issues. This concept has been further explored through a series of articles and other resources that can be found on the Intern Bridge website (www.internbridge.com) under the tab entitled "Unpaid Internship Resource Center."

The editor boldly suggested that, in the long-term, unpaid internships contribute to making wealthy students wealthier, and poor students poorer. The point was based on the fact that employers are more likely to hire a graduate with internship experience for a full-time job, and wealthier students are more likely to have that experience on their because they can afford to take part in unpaid internships. There is also something to be said about the skills-gap created between someone with internship experience who gets to practice before getting to the workplace and the student whose first job is also their first practical encounter.

It is important to note that 74% of students whose family's household income is less than $80,000 per year believe earning money is an important consideration when choosing an internship. The numbers suggest organizations that choose to provide monetary compensation often favor their wages towards students of higher socioeconomic status. This practice needs to be further evaluated and will be a topic of future Intern Bridge studies.

Legalities

The questions surrounding intern compensation legalities are numerous, complex, and amongst the most highly debated in the world of experiential education. At the time of the original publication of Total Internship Management, there was virtually no case law when it came to internship programming. In fact, a detailed search of case history throughout the United States over the past several decades yielded only five court cases. None of them are related to intern compensation. Due to the lack of case law, the regulations set forth by the Fair Labor Standards Act are left open to interpretation by labor attorneys, employers, and universities. In 1980, the U.S. Department of Labor published a document to provide clarity to parts of the Fair Labor Standards Act. A major component of this publication was geared towards defining the employment relationship between a college intern and the host organization.

However, this all changed in 2012, when two former interns filed suit again Fox Searchlight Pictures, claiming that they were unpaid for work that they did on the movie set of the film *"The Black Swan."* In this case, *Glatt v. Fox Searchlight Pictures*, 13-4481-cv, or more commonly known as *"The Black Swan Case"*, the decision of the court found that Fox Searchlight Pictures was in violation of the FLSA Wage and Hour Division Rules, and issued a summary judgement.

This was the first time that unpaid interns were granted payment for the work performed during their internship, and it set the tone for a deluge of similar cases. By the end of 2014, more than 45 cases of plaintiffs bringing suit against their internship hosts were filed in courts across the country. The website Pro-Publica has been tracking these cases and has detailed information regarding each one. This information can be found at - https://projects.propublica.org/graphics/intern-suits.

The *"Black Swan"* case was certainly a monumental decision. The ramifications of this case affected students seeking internships, the institutions of higher learning that these students were enrolled and, of course, the employers who provided the internship opportunities. There was some initial backlash from employers around the country to this decision. Many employers stated that they would need to discontinue their internship programs because it was no longer cost effective. However, this was only a certain segment of employers, generally in the media and arts industries. Information gathered by Intern Bridge in a national survey of employers found that 78% of those surveyed were either going to have the same number of interns or increase the number of interns hired for the summer of 2014. Other data collected from The National Association and the Cooperative Education and Internship Association indicated the same.

Although the *"Black Swan"* case delivered a significant blow to those employers who engaged in the practice of unpaid internships, the victory to make sure all interns were paid at least the minimum wage was short-lived. Fox Searchlight Pictures appealed the decision of the lower court and on July 2, 2015 the 2nd Court of Appeals reversed the lower court's decision and set new criteria for deciding where an intern was an "EMPLOYEE."

Contrary to the "Six-Prong Test" that had been used as the rubric for the decision in the lower court in 2012, the 2nd Court of Appeals established a new rubric for determining whether an intern should be compensated under the FLSA Wage & Hour Division rules.

In this decision, the court stated that an intern was not an employee, and the organization hosting the internship was exempt from FLSA if certain criteria were met. The criteria they established are as follows:

An intern shall not be classified as an employee to the extent...

- To which the intern and the employer clearly understand that there is no expectation of compensation. Any promise of compensation, express or implied, suggests that the intern is an employee – and vice-versa.

- To which the internship provides training that would be similar to that which would be given in an educational environment, including the clinical and other hands-on training provided by educational institutions.

- To which the internship is tied to the intern's formal education program by integrated coursework or the receipt of academic credit.

- To which the internship accommodates the intern's academic commitments by corresponding to the academic calendar.

- To which the intern's work complements, rather than displaces, the work of paid employees, while providing significant educational benefits to the intern.

- To which the internship's duration is limited to the period in which the internship provides the intern with beneficial learning.

- To which the intern and the employer understand that the internship is conducted without entitlement to a paid job at the conclusion of the internship.

Even though this new decision by the 2nd Court of Appeals is employer friendly and provides wide latitude in the definition of the difference between "interns" and "employees", employers should remain conscious of the legal environment surrounding internship compensation.

Each year the National Internship and Co-op Study evaluates data collected from interns from across the country. Consistently, we find that those interns who are paid at least minimum wage have significantly higher levels of satisfaction with both their internship and the host organization, compared to those interns who are unpaid.

If your organization chooses not to pay interns at least minimum wage for the time they spend with you in their internship, you may be doing more damage to your organization's reputation than you may be aware.

As employers and business owners, challenge yourself to stop thinking about what it will cost you to start paying your interns, and consider what it's costing you today in terms of service, cost, and quality to NOT pay your interns. What undiscovered opportunities to improve your business are awaiting discovery by that paid intern? What special projects that could retain more clients, increase your margins, and drive down errors, never get started because your full-time staff is too busy and you've yet to benefit from the contributions of a paid intern? The choice is certainly yours to make and if you are motivated by improving your business in a manner that leverages the inputs of a flexible, cost-effective, and highly talented workforce, you will make the decision to pay your interns now and in the future.

INTERNSHIP PROGRAMS FROM A DIVERSITY RECRUITING PERSPECTIVE

Shay M. Lawson, Esq.
Director of Diversity Education and Recruiting Initiatives, Intern Bridge, Inc.

The ability to attract, train, and retain diverse talent is key to the survival of any organization large or small; and the first step is attracting diverse talent to internship programs. As technology connects our world in ways never imagined, organizations must realize the importance of diversifying the workplace to remain competitive in today's global economy. A 2009 study found that organizations that boasted diversity in both race and gender fared better than their competitors in market share, customer influence, and revenue.[1] A Deloitte Human Capital report citing this same study states that some organizations saw as much as a 9% increase in sales revenue when racial diversity was increased, and a 3% increase in the same when gender diversity was increased.[2]

GOLDEN NUGGET: No one department can be charged with diversity. HR, Management, and Recruiting must all work together to successfully execute diversity recruiting efforts.

Example:

> *Organization X is in the finance industry. Management at "X" have noticed women are largely underrepresented and would like to make an effort to increase gender diversity. HR does a departmental survey on the current needs of "X" and determines there is a need for additional personnel within the mortgage sector. A recruitment strategy is created to focus summer internship recruiting at campuses with high female populations, therefore increasing its desired talent pool. Management focuses internship programming around the mortgage sector of the organization. At the end of the summer "X" is able to extend offers to several female interns who have the skills to immediately contribute to organization goals in the mortgage sector.*

Although interns are temporary, organizations must focus on the type of candidates they eventually would like to onboard when determining internship level

---

[1] Cedric Herring, Diversity Does It Pay, Race, Gender, and the Business Case for Diversity. American Sociological Review (2009) p. 208-224.

[2] Deloitte. Only Skin Deep? Re-examining the Business Case for Diversity. Deloitte Human Capital Australia (2011) p. 9

talent. In this example, management, human resources, and recruiting worked together to increase diversity at an internship level, while maintaining focus on organizational goals. This kind of future thinking will require your organization to conduct an internal evaluation of what the company needs will be in the coming year or years. Once this evaluation is complete, the organization can now narrowly tailor a recruiting strategy that moves past bringing diverse bodies in the door, forward to one that prepares intern talent to ultimately drive organizational goals. All together the steps "X" took look like this:

1. Human Resources determined the needs of the company using a "Organizational Needs Survey" (notice the survey is not a "Diversity Survey" but one that asks questions to measure company needs); then

2. Recruitment increased the desired talent pool by focusing efforts to female dominated campuses; then

3. Management tailored internship programming to meet the needs of the company as determined in the survey done by HR; and so the

4. Organization was in a direct position to hire talent that drives bottom line and meets diversity objectives.

This same four step approach to diversity recruiting will ensure your organization attracts the kind and quality of talent that is prepared to contribute to the bottom line upon hire.

Step One: Determining Your Target Candidate Pool

In the earlier example Organization X's management recognized the need for diversity specifically in terms of gender. However, many organizations are at square one trying to understand how to best diversify the workforce. In both cases departmental/function surveys are the best compass to determine what direction diversity efforts should take. Those with clearly identified diversity objectives can use the surveys to determine basic skills desired, diagnose current skill deficiencies among the current pool, and work with internship coordinators to strengthen those skills during the internship process. Those looking to identify the direction of its diversity efforts can use surveys to find organizational weaknesses, identify communities whose unique talents can strengthen the organization, and work with recruiters to narrow program recruiting efforts towards those communities.

GOLDEN NUGGET: Redefine diversity to focus on the unique talents, experiences, and perspectives offered by a particular group that can drive organizational goals.

Example:

> *Organization "Y" has identified diversity as a goal in the coming year. It decides to launch its first diversity initiative in the form of a diversity internship program. Recruiting works with Human Resources to do a survey by job function and determines the greatest need within "Y" is for a uniform procedure and record keeping method organization wide. Based on this information Recruiting focuses its efforts on attracting interns with prior military experience for their knowledge of complex systems and procedures unifying varying functions. Information sessions are held in conjunction with the Veterans Administration and Wounded Warriors in addition to its normal internship recruiting efforts. "Y" receives ten applications from young Veterans and is able to extend offers to three. Internship coordinators ensure shadowing opportunities in each department so interns can grasp the duties and responsibilities of the entire organization. Two of the interns are offered positions upon program completion and are able to lead a formal procedure creation program.*

In this example, "Y' considered the unique knowledge set regarding organization and procedure candidates with prior military experience bring to the table. The desired candidate pool was increased through linking existing recruiting efforts in conjunction with affinity organizations. Internship programming was crafted with future contribution in mind to provide foundational knowledge. "Y" was then positioned to hire candidates whose diversity drives an identified organizational goal rather than filling a quota. How could a first generation American student bring insight to niche markets? How can older students contribute towards fostering team work and peer mentorship among an intern group? These are the types of considerations that must be taken into account when seeking to move beyond the quotas and into how diverse groups can add to an internship program and eventually company bottom lines.

Step Two: Attracting Diverse Candidates

Diverse candidates want to know they are genuinely desired within an organization, and not merely the faces of executive lip service to its dedication to inclusion. The two biggest mistakes organizations make are believing diverse candidates will be attracted to a company (1) because a diversity internship program is in place; and (2) because the internship recruiter is a member of a diverse group. In the examples of "X" and "Y" recruiting efforts were specifically tailored to attract diverse talent. In the 2007 edition of "Total Internship Management," diversity consultant Debora Bloom briefly outlines some key questions organizations can ask as they look to tailor their recruiting efforts:

"Does your organization host meetings of National Association of Hispanic MBAs (NSHMBA) or the National Association of Asian American Professionals, the Black Nurses Association or similar organizations? Does someone from your organization actively participate in the professional and civic associations of people of color or people with disabilities? Do you recruit from historically black colleges, from colleges that have high populations of Native Americans, or from geographic areas with a large number of people from Spanish speaking backgrounds?"

Are you recruiting at community colleges, online programs, or other nontraditional programs? Are you including first generation college students, first generation Americans, LGBT communities, and young veterans in your search? It is easy to see how quickly this list expands when considering the definition of diversity provided above. However, identifying where you can recruit diverse talent is only the first half. The second half is how recruiting is done.

GOLDEN NUGGET: In order to attract diverse talent organizations must be visible, relatable, and consistent. Attracting talent starts before recruiting season begins and requires real thought into effectively marketing your internship program to a target demographic. By sending representatives to target populations often, relationships are forged and, interest touch points can be easily gauged to adjust recruiting methods.

Example:

> *Organization Z is looking to recruit students with disabilities to its summer internship program. Before school starts in the fall semester, "Z" sponsors a new student social for students with disabilities to get to know the campus, student services staff members, and familiarize themselves with ADA accommodations. During the fall semester, "Z" cohosts an event with Delta Alpha Pi (an honor society with a mission to educate others regarding disability issues). At the Delta Alpha Pi event, a representative from "Z" engages in conversation with a member and is told a major concern among students with disabilities is flexibility in scheduling for therapy and doctor appointments. During fall and spring recruiting events, "Z" updates its internship marketing materials to include information about its flexible scheduling and leave options. "Z" increases its number of applicants with disabilities by 30%.*

As a result of being active and visible far before recruiting season, "Z" was able to show its interest in the population, make connections, readjust marketing materials, and highlight organizational policies that appeal to the target demographic. Consistency is king when it comes to attracting diverse talent, and is best demonstrated through being visible and relatable early on. The least amount of work is done in identifying what affinity group your organization can partner with. The real work begins in strategizing how to make best use of those partnerships to attract the target talent well before formal recruiting beings.

Steps Three and Four: Getting the Internship Program Right

By now, the obvious common theme of this chapter is future thinking. If the internship program itself is a failure, buy-in may be lost on multiple levels of the organization, and the work you have done to identify and attract diverse talent will be a waste. Accordingly, the third step may be the most important step of the diversity recruiting process. Go back to the organizational surveys conducted and use the data to make an honest assessment of what the company needs. Combine those results with insights gained from student engagement to tailor your internship program to make a meaningful impact on the interns and ultimately prepare them to make an immediate contribution should the organization decide to hire.

Recall in the example of Organization "X" the company did a survey and found a need for more personnel in the mortgage sector. The internship program was then tailored to focus experiential learning around the mortgage sector, so interns who received offers at the end of the program were able to address an immediate company need. In the example of Organization "Y" the company survey found a need to improve organization wide procedures and record keeping methods. The internship program was then tailored to give an organization wide experience, so interns who received offers at the end of the program were equipped to use their military experience with procedures to make an immediate impact on the company need.

Tailoring of this sort creates a shift in thinking of diversity as something that is the 'right thing', to something that makes business sense because it drives the organization forward. Consequently, an internship program with a view towards attracting diverse talent is a necessary molding ground of future employees who are able to merge their unique talents with organization specific experience to bring quantifiable results.

FINAL GOLDEN NUGGET: When you prepare individuals with unique talent/experience at the internship level to create solutions that boost bottom line factors, such as revenue and market share, diversity recruiting becomes a necessity instead of an initiative.

Shay M. Lawson, Esq., is the Director of Diversity Recruiting Initiatives and Education for Intern Bridge Inc, where she works with HR and Recruiting professionals from around the country to recruit, retain, and train diverse talent within an organization. She can be reached at shay@ internbridge.com or shay@shaymlawson.com

HARNESSING THE POWER OF SOCIAL MEDIA FOR YOUR INTERNSHIP PROGRAM

Kim Brown and Dan Klamm, Syracuse University

Social media. No doubt you've heard the term. Perhaps you consider your employees "power users." Perhaps your company is just dabbling in Facebook and maybe Twitter, too. Or perhaps the use of social media is entirely foreign to you. Regardless of your level of prowess, this chapter will address:

- Why social media matters to employers who hire interns

- The role social media plays in recruiting and hiring interns

- How social media can help or hinder the internship itself

- Ways to use social media to maintain professional relationships with your interns long after the internship has ended

What IS social media?

Social media is a term that refers to *forms of communication (as Web sites for social networking and microblogging) through which users create online communities to share information, ideas, personal messages, and other content.* (http://www.merriam-webster.com/dictionary/social%20media)

Who uses social media? That depends on the platform. In general, 67% of all Internet users are using some form of social media, according to the Pew Research Center.

So as not to be overwhelming, let's look at some of the main social media platforms where we – as career services professionals in a college environment – see our students most actively engaged: LinkedIn, Facebook, Twitter, Instagram, Pinterest, YouTube and Google +.

LinkedIn

At Syracuse University, we encourage all students to build LinkedIn profiles and to say – in their headlines or summaries – that they are looking for an internship. This can be an ideal way for you to identify potential candidates. A basic LinkedIn account gives you open access to millions of prospective interns.

Facebook

With more than one billion monthly users, Facebook can be a great tool to share information about internship opportunities within your company.

You want to be where your target audience is; often, companies will build brand pages, and we've found that prospective interns will interact with those pages. Those interactions can help you to identify strong candidates for your program.

Twitter

Twitter is a microblogging site that limits messages to just 140 characters. As we'll discuss later in this chapter, a quick search of #internship yields thousands of results. Many students are using Twitter to actively engage with employers they're interested in working for – and employers are responding. Some have even devoted Twitter accounts to their internship hiring process.

Instagram

This photo-sharing service can be a great tool, especially for identifying creative candidates. Searching #internship on Instagram also reveals hundreds of results. Some companies have even made job offers on Instagram! Recently, Eprize extended a full-time offer to a former intern via an Instagram photo - a story that was documented by social media blog Mashable.
http://mashable.com/2013/05/18/instagram-job-offer/

Pinterest

More and more companies are exploring Pinterest and creating boards to showcase their brands. Pinterest provides a huge opportunity for you to give interns an insider's look at your company and also to identify potential candidates. Did you know that many people post their résumés on Pinterest? It's not just for arts and crafts or wedding planning!

YouTube

Many students are creating YouTube channels or, at the very least, YouTube videos, to express their interest in certain companies and internship/job opportunities. YouTube can also be a great resource for companies to post videos about available opportunities and what you might be looking for in candidates. Videos are attention grabbers - and they don't require hours of editing.

Google+

This is relatively new territory - and very exciting! As the chapter progresses, we'll discuss how you can utilize Google+ Hangouts to stay in touch with your interns and even to run a remote internship program. All you need is a Gmail address and a webcam!

How can you use social media to develop your internship program?

Now that we've laid out the main social media platforms - and you've thought about how you have already been or might consider using them at your company - how will you utilize the platforms to develop a successful internship program?

One of the best things you can do as you start to develop and grow your internship program is to follow companies who are actively using social media to recruit interns. Take their lead and see how they are able to actively engage college students. We'll share some of our favorite companies already doing this a little later on in the chapter.

An attractive aspect of using social media is the ability to crowdsource and to learn best practices from others. Remember that this is new territory for a lot of companies. You can use social media to learn what has worked and what has failed for them. One active gathering place for professionals in the college recruiting industry in the College Recruiting Central group on LinkedIn. The group feature discussions and tips/tricks to successfully recruit a college-aged audience. You'll find the group here: http://www.linkedin.com/groups?home=&gid=135722

What role does social media play in recruiting and hiring interns?

Social media changed the game of recruiting and hiring interns. Long gone are the days of displaying glossy brochures in campus career centers as the main means of advertising an internship program, or using the once-a-year campus career fair as the sole touchpoint with prospective interns. Now, forward-thinking organizations build awareness of their internships and showcase their workplace culture every day through the platforms students naturally inhabit. Social media has created an unprecedented opportunity to get in front of large swaths of diverse students on a regular basis -- and some of the most effective work can be done at a low cost, without expensive ad budgets or campus travel.

Many organizations have social media channels dedicated to the HR function, such as Starbucks (@StarbucksJobs) or the Department of State (@DOScareers). In some cases, companies dedicate specific accounts to college recruiting, like Google Students (@GoogleStudents) or Macy's College Recruiting (@MacysCollege). What are the goals of these accounts? How do these organizations effectively use these accounts, and how can YOU use social media to support your recruiting process?

Effectively leveraging social media starts with branding your organization as an attractive place to work. Millennials are naturally suspect of conventional branding efforts, such as sleek marketing videos, so social media efforts should feel more organic. It could be as simple as posting a Facebook photo gallery of the company holiday party (a la creative agency MRY) or sharing employees' unscripted, six-second Vine videos about why they love working for the organization. Ernst & Young even has a junior-level employee live-tweeting his work-day. Regardless of your chosen tactics, the key is to provide a sneak peek into the culture of the workplace so that college students can see what it would be like to intern with your organization.

The next step is publicizing internship opportunities. Streamline all of your internship postings to be "social media friendly," which means doing away with PDFs and other attachments, and opting instead to display internship information via easily shareable online links. Instead of letting internship postings just sit on your website awaiting discovery, proactively send out the links via your organization's social media channels. Post jobs on your company's LinkedIn page. Ask college career centers (many of which have large and engaged student followings on their respective campuses) to publicize the links as well. Better yet, empower your current interns to act as brand advocates and spread awareness of future internship opportunities via their networks – consider offering them incentives for doing so.

Then, once students are aware of internship opportunities at your organization, give them a chance to ask questions of hiring managers, employees... even current interns! Social media makes it easy to open a dialogue. Host a Twitter chat for prospective interns, or even schedule a Google+ Hangout to give interested candidates an opportunity to hear directly from current interns and ask questions. Social media has raised the bar of expectations among students – they have come to expect transparent, two-way communication with companies; those that don't deliver may find themselves struggling to attract top-notch intern talent.

HELPFUL LINKS

Tweetchat
Google+ Hangout
Bit.ly
LinkedIn Advanced Search

It's not all about wooing candidates, though. When it comes to sourcing internship candidates, social media can play a role. Look at who your organization interacts with on a regular basis – are there any particularly enthusiastic college students? They might be a natural fit for an internship. Likewise, encourage your employees (particularly recruiters) to be active on LinkedIn – not just to have up-to-date profiles for themselves, but to proactively spread awareness of job opportunities among their various networks and groups, and to be visible in the space as a champion for your brand. Tap into LinkedIn's advanced search and Recruiter tools to pinpoint students who might be qualified and interested in your internship opportunities.

You've brought on an intern…so now what?

The role of social media in the internship itself
The next step is publicizing internship opportunities. Streamline all of your
The role of social media in the internship will depend on the nature of the
internship. You may have used social media to spread awareness of your opportunities, but doing social media may have nothing to do with the internship itself. Clearly, hiring an intern to handle your company's social media is
different than hiring an intern who will have little to no interaction on your
company's social media channels.

Regardless of what you've hired the intern to do, be very clear about your
expectations for what he/she can/can not do on his/her personal social media
channels while at work. Set clear guidelines: can the intern be on Facebook/
Twitter/etc. during the day while at the internship? If so, are you comfortable
with him/her tweeting about what the internship entails and what some of his/
her duties are? These are questions to think about prior to having an intern
join your team. Many companies will include these guidelines in an intern
handbook or guide that they distribute prior to the start of the internship.

If you plan to have your intern do some or all of the social media for
your company, we recommend that you hire students who have demonstrated
knowledge of social media. These interns can act as reverse mentors to company employees who may be looking to gain experience in that realm. A smart
intern can improve your company's presence by leaps and bounds. Just ask
Matt, who owns several coffee shops in Syracuse and was just getting the social
media presence for those shops off the ground. He hired an intern to help and
later described intern Hailey as "a rockstar" and "irreplaceable." He wanted to
clone her because of the profound impact she had on boosting the social media
presence of each cafe and – with that – boosting foot traffic and sales at his
various locations.

You can also think about using social media to facilitate the internship
itself. If you are doing orientations with interns across the country, or assem-
bling a remote team of interns from different locations, consider using a tool
such as the Google+ Hangout. If you're familiar with Skype, you'll have no
problem adjusting to Google+. Even those who are not Skype-savvy will find
Google+ easy and efficient when it comes to connecting with interns - even before you've brought them on board! You can even offer weekly Hangouts with
remote interns to ensure effective communication and collaboration across the
intern team.

Your intern as brand ambassador

Just as you can empower brand ambassadors in the recruiting process for your internships, you also want to give your interns to ability to be brand ambassadors for your company once they're on board. Just as employees are a reflection of your company, interns also represent you and your company's brand. They are incredibly influential among their peers – and can help you to reach an audience that you may not have been able to connect with in the past. Think about whether you want your intern to mention your company's name in his/her LinkedIn profile or Twitter bio.

On LinkedIn, encourage your intern to post relevant discussions within their own circles of influence - whether those might be in a college group on LinkedIn or in a group devoted to internship best practices. On Twitter, you can encourage your intern to participate in Twitter chats that may help to build recognition of your company. A chat such as #InternPro gathers an audience of people who are sharing what works for them and are also trying to learn new ways to improve internship programs. Think of the positive attention your intern can bring to your company if he/she shares a particularly innovative initiative.

What role does social media play after the internship is over?

When an intern leaves your organization and goes out into the world – whether to return to school for another year, or to pursue full-time employment – social media can be used in several ways: to offer your intern a lasting "thank you" for his/her contributions, to keep in touch with him/her for future opportunities, and to empower him/her to act as an advocate for your internship program. After all, if you worked with an all-star intern, you may want to bring him/her back as a full-time employee some day (or hire one of his/her talented contacts).

Assuming that the internship was successful and that you would vouch for your intern's skills, write him/her a LinkedIn recommendation! Millennials crave recognition for a job well done, and LinkedIn is the perfect way to validate your intern's contributions and to publicly reaffirm his/her unique talents. The recommendation can be short and sweet, touching on a major project that the intern oversaw or his/her key strengths, but this recommendation will help your intern remember your organization fondly. Further, it gives the added benefit of exposing your internship program to all of the other people in your intern's LinkedIn network – professors, advisors, mentors, and other students who might be seeking internships the next season.

As your intern goes onto his/her next steps, be sure to keep in touch. LinkedIn makes it easy to keep on top of his/her professional moves and accomplishments, while Twitter (or even Facebook, if the nature of the supervisor/intern relationship was more casual) allows for a more personal look at the latest happenings in his/her life. It's always been a best practice to stay in touch with former employees and interns, and social media just makes it all so much easier to do. Instead of an e-mail to check-in every three months, you can occasionally comment on a photo or remark on a tweet to keep the relationship warm.

Finally, perhaps the most powerful use of social media after an internship is to empower your former interns to spread the word about your internship program! Former interns who had great experiences with your organization are – in many ways – your ideal marketing and recruiting agents. Encourage them to publicize internship opportunities among their social (media) circles. Consider involving them in recruiting processes – for instance, having former interns host a Twitter chat for prospective interns about what it's like working for your organization, or having them serve as resources in a Google+ Hangout during on-boarding for your next crop of interns.

Tying it all together

As with any new effort, you'll want to evaluate the role social media played in your internship program. Did you learn new ideas from other employers? Was your applicant pool better qualified than in previous years? Talk to your interns: how did they learn about the internship and would they recommend new/different ways for you to spread awareness of what's available at your company?

With social media ever-changing, you'll likely be building on our suggestions in this chapter and learning new tools in addition to the ones we shared. One thing is certain: social media is now an integral part of the world of work and the most effective organizations will be the ones embracing its full potential.

CONSIDERING INTERNS THAT REPRESENT SPECIAL POPULATIONS: NON-TRADITIONAL STUDENTS, VETERANS, AND PERSONS WITH DISABILITIES

Amanda L. Walker, Ed.D., CDF
Director of Career Services
Austin Peay State University

As an employer, by now you understand the importance of funding or adding funding for an internship program. An internship program provides a valuable resource for filling fulltime openings with little to no additional money spent on recruitment or on-boarding. Have you considered how valuable a diversified pool of candidates could be to your internship program? For instance, have you thought about what a non-traditional student, a veteran, or a person with disabilities may bring to the table for your company? Most of you may have said no to this question. But can you explain why you should consider these special populations of students? Simply put, they offer skills, abilities, and experiences that other traditional students may not be able to understand or bring to the table. Let us present to you why you should consider a non-traditional, veteran, or person with disabilities as a student intern.

Non-Traditional Students as Interns

Non-traditional students are the new norm at most college campuses (Ely, 1997). Non-traditional students fall into one or more of the following categories:

• They have delayed enrollment (does not enter college the same year they graduate high school).

• They may have to attend college part-time.

• They may work 35 hours or more while enrolled in college.

• They are considered financially independent of their parents.

• They have dependents other than a spouse (usually children).

• They are a single parent.

• They are over the age of 25.

It is estimated that more than 73 percent of all college students meet one or more of this criteria (National Center of Education Statistics, 2015). Chances are you have already interviewed a non-traditional student and may not have known it. Employers often believe that non-traditional students are older adult students, but this may not be the case.

Why consider hiring non-traditional students? Non-traditional students offer experience that was gained outside the classroom. Most non-traditional students have worked part-time or full-time positions prior to attending college. This experience allows them to better understand how the academics relate to the world of work. Essentially, because of the likelihood of prior work experience, they are more familiar with company procedures and understand the protocols. In addition, non-traditional students can quickly acclimate to a new work environment. Most are accustomed to changing roles and multitasking in the work and home environment. Because of their non-traditional work and life experiences, they can often step into leadership opportunities sooner and with little oversight. Furthermore, most non-traditional students are very goal oriented (often they enroll in college to create a better life for themselves and their families). They often want or desire a need to get ahead in life to create more opportunities for themselves. Non-traditional students also represent a diverse workforce. Lastly, non-traditional students can handle the demands of work and school. They are used to juggling work and home life and understand it is something that is required to reach their goals.

Veterans Students as Interns

There are more than 820,000 veterans pursing post-secondary degrees in the United States and receiving GI Bill tuition dollars to cover the cost of tuition. Veterans are eligible to receive benefits for up to 36 months in most degree areas and up to 48 months in STEM degree programs. Veterans are determined to complete their degree programs. They want to gain on the job experience that they may not have received on the battlefield if they are entering a different path than their military role. They are a trainable population of workers who are mission driven. They desire employers that provide them with directions, goals, and expectations on how to carry out the job (or mission as they know it).

Why consider hiring veterans? Veterans that are converted into full time hires often come with federal benefits, such as employer tax credits (with certain restrictions) and exemptions from paying employee health benefits which veterans receive as a part of service to the armed forces. Veterans offer leadership and teamwork skills as well as the ability to work under high-pressure situations. They are trustworthy and often hold themselves to higher expectations than non-military employees. Their outlook on life may have a much different perspective after the military experience thus allow them to recognize what values they want for themselves and an employer. Veterans are highly organized. Because they are used to procedures and protocols they like structured work environments to help them make sense of why and how to carry out the goals and objectives for projects/assignments they are assigned. Veterans are dependable. Often in their previous line of work they were forced to depend on their team members, and because of this they are accustomed to making sure they follow through with their assignment or assigned duties. Additionally, veterans are trained to communicate well. Their communication skills were highly important to all missions (big and small), thus veterans tend to communicate well with others. And as if these qualities were not enough, veterans have a relentless attention to detail. They often review and re-review all work, projects, and assignments simply out of habit. They are able to see that one task builds on another and that allows them to get a better understanding of the big picture.

Veterans are ideal candidates for internship and full-time entry-level employment opportunities. They are often looking for opportunities to grow within a company and want opportunities to take on leadership roles. As interns, they will often step into mentor roles for other interns because of their life experience and skills they often display quickly while on the job. Considering a vet for an internship could lead to a possible conversion to a full-time hire, which then could in return provide the company with tax incentives for hiring a veteran. Another added benefit that may be overlooked is that veterans have lifetime health care coverage from the Department of Veteran Affairs (if minimum service requirements met), thus there would be no additional monies to support an employer-paid portion of benefits for vets in an internship or full-time position.

Students with Disabilities as Interns

Nearly 1 in 5 people in the United States have some type of recognized disability according to the US Census Bureau (2012), which is about 56.7 million people or 19 percent of the population. It is important to know what is considered a disability in the workplace. First, not everyone with a medical condition is protected under the disability law statutes. In order to be protected, a person must be qualified for the position, and have a disability as defined by the law. The following are ways a person that can show they have a disability and can request reasonable accommodations (as outlined by U.S. Equal Employment Opportunity Commission, 2015):

1. A person may be disabled if he or she has a physical or mental condition that substantially limits a major life activity (such as walking, talking, seeing, hearing or learning).

2. A person may be disabled if he or she has a history of a disability (such as cancer that is in remission).

3. A person may be disabled if he or she is believed to have a physical or mental impairment that is not transitory (lasting or expected to last six months or less) and minor (even if he does not have such impairment).

Why consider hiring persons with disabilities? Persons with disabilities make up a considerable number of our population. It is impossible to consider not having a disabled person in several different roles within a company. Being disabled does not mean they are not a valuable team member or not a hard worker. Simple and affordable accommodations that often are less than $500 (and even sometimes at no cost) can be made so that the employee can be successful. As any other worker we have discussed in this chapter, they will bring diverse life experiences that have built their values, work ethic, and adaptive skills. Persons with disabilities have not had things come easy to them. They are accustomed to hard work; often doing more to learn how to do the same tasks as their peers. Persons with disabilities are open to new challenges and often bring a different perspective to the table when discussing new projects or company initiatives. They want to be recognized as equals among their peers who are capable of doing similar tasks. Persons with disabilities want to prove they are valuable and will work hard to show employers, themselves, and family members they can make a difference in how society views them, whether its in the workforce, community, or in the classroom.

Conclusion

Once overlooked student populations offer new options to engage and retain a new workforce through internship opportunities. Employers that are willing to consider any of these once overlooked student populations are taking advantage of workers that have specialized skills, come from diverse backgrounds, and have a desire to create a life full of opportunities for themselves. At the end of the day, employers are challenged to not only meet the needs of their ever-changing workforce but also retain and engage new employees that "represent a new model of employment, which is one of a multi-generational, diverse workforce" (Gladwell & Dorwart et al., 2010). And what better way to engage students from one or more of these populations of workers than with internship opportunities to represent the new norm in the workplace environment? Life experiences, as well as diverse backgrounds, allow for employers to embrace the opportunities with interns and ultimately convert them to full-time positions as a way of expanding staffing needs and creating a new company norm.

Disability Discrimination. (n.d.). Retrieved August 9, 2015, from www.eeoc.gov

Ely, E. E. (1997). The Non-Traditional Student.

Gladwell, N. J., Dorwart, C. E., Stone, C. F. & Hammond, C. A. (2010). Importance of and satisfaction with organizational benefits for a multigenerational workforce. Journal Of Park And Recreation Administration, 28 (2), pp. 1--19.

Stats on Disability. (n.d.). Retrieved August 8, 2015, from www.census.gov

Non-traditional Student Definition. (n.d.) Retrieved August 8, 2015, from www.nces.ed.gov/pubs/webs/97578e.asp

Dr. Amanda L. Walker is currently serving as the Director of Career Services for Austin Peay State University. Dr. Walker is also a certified Career Development Facilitator.

Dr. Walker is an active leader in various organizations such as, the Clarksville and Middle Tennessee SHRM associations, National Career Development Association (NCDA), National Association of Colleges and Employers (NACE), Southern Association of Colleges and Employers (SoACE), Tennessee Association of Colleges and Employers (TACE), and Clarksville Chamber of Commerce. Most recently, Dr. Walker was chosen to participate in Leadership Clarksville which recognizes rising leaders in the Clarksville-Montgomery region.

Since 2013, Dr. Walker has presented at five professional conferences within career services. Her knowledge and passion for experiential education shines through with each presentation that she facilitates. In addition, Dr. Walker has had the opportunity to publish a book chapter, analyze and report on a national research project, as well as, contribute to textbook chapters over the past two years. Dr. Walker devotes much of her time to experiential education research and engages students in the process of experiential learning by promoting participation and assisting employers in developing internship programs.

Dr. Walker has earned a Bachelor of Arts in Political Science and Master of Arts degree in Higher Education from The University of Mississippi and her Doctorate of Education from Delta State University in Professional Studies in Higher Education. Her dissertation focused on experiential education opportunities and the need for curricular change.

EMPLOYMENT LAW ISSUES FOR INTERNSHIPS

Michael R. Brown, Partner, Seyfarth Shaw LLP, as revised by
Joanne Seltzer, Shareholder, Jackson Lewis P.C.[1]

Internships have become a rite of passage for college and university students. They are often viewed as the gateway to admission into more prestigious graduate schools and more financially rewarding employment. Many institutions of higher learning have incorporated internships into their undergraduate curriculum.[2] These internships provide students with practical experience and enhance the educational process. The explosion of student internships, closely followed by an equally explosive number of lawsuits brought by interns against their sponsoring companies, however, has created a perilous legal condition for both employers and educational institutions who sponsor or host internship programs.

This Section will discuss employment law issues for organizations that host student interns or internship programs. Its analysis will focus primarily on federal employment law issues, but will contain references to state law where applicable. It will highlight potential issues that organizations should be aware of and how they should structure their internship programs in such a fashion so as to decrease the potential likelihood for violating federal or state employment laws. Finally, this section will examine the conflict among courts and governmental agencies regarding the test to be applied in determining whether an intern is, in fact, an employee, eligible to receive the protections afforded him or her under federal, state and local laws.

Employee v. Volunteer

Is a paid student intern an "employee" of the organization hosting an internship program? Is an unpaid student intern a "volunteer" or a "trainee"? Does the intern attain a different status by virtue of the educational component of an internship program? It should be emphasized that the analysis of employee status varies depending upon the particular facts and circumstances of each potential situation. Also, the ultimate determination will depend in large part upon what federal or statute employment law is being applied to the particular intern and the internship program.

---

[1] This chapter was prepared by Michael R. Brown, a Partner in the Boston office of Seyfarth Shaw LLP, who gratefully acknowledges the invaluable assistance of Vincent Domestico, a legal intern from Northeastern University Law School.

[2] For instance, both Northeastern University and Endicott College in the Boston, MA area condition graduation upon the successful completion of internships of varying lengths.

Although the U.S. Supreme Court has declined to rule on the issue to date, the U.S. Department of Labor ("DOL"), in Fact Sheet #71, published in April 2010, has established a six-part test to determine whether a student intern is an employee for the purposes of the Fair Labor Standards Act ("FLSA").[3] Under this test, a student intern will not be considered employee unless all of the following six factors are satisfied. The factors are as follows: (1) the internship, even though it includes actual operation of the facilities of the employer, is similar to that which would be given in an educational environment; (2) the internship experience is for the benefit of the intern; (3) the interns do not displace regular employees, but work under their close supervision of existing staff; (4) the employer that provides the training receives no immediate advantage from the activities of the intern; and on occasion its operations may actually be impeded; (5) the intern is not necessarily entitled to a job at the conclusion of the internship; and (6) the employer and the intern understand the intern is not entitled to wages for the time spent in the internship.

As noted earlier, the DOL has taken an all or nothing approach with respect to the application of its six-part test. Thus, a student intern is an employee of the host organization unless the student satisfies each of the six criteria. The DOL has consistently stated (and some courts have agreed), that no single prong of the test is by itself dispositive. For example, the fact that a student intern and the host organization have an understanding that he is not entitled to a job at the completion of the internship does not preclude a finding of employee status. An employer must determine whether an internship satisfies each and every prong of the test. A finding of "employee" status means, at the very least, that the intern must be paid minimum wage and overtime pay for hours worked over forty in any workweek.

Paid interns are almost always considered to be employees of the host organization because paid employment would not satisfy the sixth prong of the DOL's six-part test (that the intern understands that he/she is not entitled to wages for the time spent in training). In contrast to the unpaid intern, the paid student intern accepts and works at the internship with the explicit understanding that he or she will be compensated for the time spent working for the host organization.

The fourth prong of the DOL test provides that an intern cannot provide an employer with any immediate advantage or benefit. For instance, the DOL was asked in 1994 about an internship program assisting in the daily

---

[3] While this test has been consistently applied by the DOL in its opinion letters and utilized by courts in wage and hour actions, it holds no precedential value. Moreover, this test is applicable to the employee status of an intern under the FLSA, and does not address state wage and hour claims, workers' compensation claims or other state employment issues.

management of hostels. The DOL was asked whether the arrangement whereby students received a free room (approximately $15 a night) in exchange for 25 hours of work per week would violate the FLSA for failure to pay minimum wage to the students. The DOL stated that "[b]ased on the information in your letter, it is our opinion that criterion number 4 discussed above would not be met since it is apparent the employer derives an immediate advantage from the duties performed by the interns in question. Therefore, such interns would be considered employees under the FLSA and subject to its minimum wage and overtime pay provisions."

A corollary to the fourth prong of the test is the third prong which precludes the intern from displacing regular employees. This prong of the test can be particularly troublesome for a host organization that relies heavily on its interns to do tasks that otherwise would fall to regular employees. An organization should be particularly careful if it readily admits or states that, without its interns, it would have to hire regular employees to do the jobs undertaken by interns. Such statements or actions will be sufficient to fail the fourth prong of the DOL test and therefore expose the employer to liability for violations of the FLSA.

Thus, an organization should pay particular attention to the third and fourth prongs of the DOL test. If it can be demonstrated that the employer gains an immediate benefit from the activities of the students, or if the intern displaces regular employees, the student will be considered an employee under the FLSA and thus subject to the wage and overtime laws contained therein. As discussed more fully below, it would be good practice to have the student intern sign an agreement acknowledging satisfaction of each prong of the DOL test. While this practice will not necessarily shield the hosting organization from liability under the FLSA, it will certainly strengthen the organization's defense against a potential FLSA violation assuming the acknowledgement is truthful. Additionally, the organization should emphasize to prospective interns in any application materials that they are not employees of the organization. Such language would serve to put the student on notice of the internship status, and including such language in solicitation materials would alert the school about the classification.

Companies who are hosting internship programs and are uncertain whether such programs would create a potential liability under wage and hour laws, may want to consider asking the DOL for guidance regarding their particular programs by requesting an opinion letter from the agency. Although the opinion letters issued by the DOL on such subjects are not considered to be persuasive authority by courts, they are given deference in determining the question of whether the employer willfully violated wage hour law. In May 2013, for example, the President of the American Bar Association ("ABA"), Laurel G. Bellows, appealed to the DOL to allow law firms to offer unpaid internships to law school students in order to provide them with hands-on experience to successfully compete in the dwindling legal job market. In September 2013, the DOL advised that: if the tasks involved in the internship provide training similar to what would be received in an educational environment; if the internship doesn't displace regular employees; and if the intern does not provide the law firm with an immediate advantage, the internship is permissible. The DOL stressed that, in order for the legal internship to pass muster, the firm must provide the law students with written assurances that they would receive educational experience related to the practice of law in a clinical program and be assigned exclusively to pro bono matters that don't generate a fee for the firm. This clarification, however, has limited value to most for-profit host organizations whose internships do not allow for the segregation of tasks in the same efficient and well-documented manner as hours worked in a law firm. In a 2010 *New York Times* article regarding internships, the acting director of the DOL's Wage and Hour Division, Nancy J. Leppink, stated: "If you're a for-profit employer or you want to pursue an internship with a for-profit employer, there aren't going to be many circumstances where you can have an internship and not be paid and still be in compliance with the law."

There is currently an ongoing dispute among the federal circuits relating to the amount of deference to be paid to the DOL's six-factor analysis, with the Supreme Court refusing to weigh in on the question. In *Kaplan v. Code Blue Billing and Coding, Inc.*, an FLSA claim brought in Florida's Southern District by former interns placed into externships by MedVance Institute's medical billing program, the court dismissed the intern's claims, finding them to be non-employees and not eligible for the FLSA's protection. The Court of Appeals for the Eleventh Circuit affirmed the dismissal. The interns subsequently petitioned the U.S. Supreme Court to offer guidance on the proper test to be applied in evaluating whether interns should be classified as employees for the purposes of state and federal wage and hour laws and the amount of deference to be given the DOL's six-factor analysis. On November 12, 2013, the Supreme Court denied the certiorari petition, leaving the federal circuits free to continue to apply different, and often conflicting standards to the intern/employee analysis.

Wage Issues

In light of the startling increase in the number of lawsuits brought by unpaid interns, both employers and educational institutions should be aware that student internship programs could raise a number of issues regarding potential violations of wage and hour laws. The FLSA mandates employers to pay their employees a regular wage that is at least equivalent to the federal minimum wage. If the state minimum wage is higher than the federal minimum, the higher wage must be paid. In direct contrast to this requirement, a significant percentage of student internships are unpaid. Does having student interns work without receiving pay constitute a violation of the FLSA and other state wage and hour laws? Also, even if the host organization does not pay the student intern, are they nevertheless employees? Even if an unpaid student intern clearly understands that he or she is not entitled to wages for the time spent in training, does the work provided to the host organization provide more benefit to the host organization than training to the intern, thereby allowing the unpaid student intern to acquire employee status under the FLSA and state wage and hour laws?

The Second Circuit Court of Appeals has become the most recent battleground for the conflict among federal courts in evaluating the protections to be afforded interns under wage and hour statutes. In June 11, 2013, Judge William H. Pauley of the Southern District of New York granted the motion to certify a class of unpaid interns in *Eric Glatt v. Fox Searchlight Pictures*. The unpaid interns, who had worked on production of the film *Black Swan*, claimed that they did not fall under the trainee exception promulgated by the DOL, because they were asked to perform routine tasks that would otherwise have been performed by regular employees. Noting the conflict among courts with respect to the interpretation of the trainee exception to the FLSA, the court chose to apply a "totality of the circumstances" standard to its evaluation of whether the interns would be considered covered employees under the FLSA. Weighing all of the factors, and giving clear deference to the DOL's six-factor test, the court denied the defendant's motion to dismiss the class, thereby allowing the interns to proceed as a class under the FLSA as "employees."

Prior to the court's decision in *Glatt*, however, Judge Harold Baer of the Southern District of New York had reached an entirely opposite result in *Wang v. The Hearst Corporation*, a lawsuit brought by a class of unpaid interns working for the magazine publisher. Like the interns in *Glatt*, the *Wang* interns contended that they were required to perform routine tasks that could have been performed by regular employees, a contention that was supported by internal emails that instructed the staff to use unpaid interns rather than paid messengers to save costs. Contrary to Judge Pauley's admonition about the irrelevance of the interns' understanding that they would not be paid for their labor, Judge Baer considered, as an important factor, that the interns "understood prior to their internship that the position was unpaid." With facts that were almost identical to those in *Glatt* and giving limited deference to the DOL's six-factor test, Judge Baer ruled that the interns could not, as a matter of law, prove that they were employees under the FLSA and the New York Labor Law ("NYLL") and denied the interns' motion for class certification under the NYLL.

The attorneys representing the intern classes both in *Glatt* and in *Wang* appealed to the Second Circuit for an interlocutory order for clarification as to how cases brought by interns should be evaluated since the recent trend of interns filing suits began. On November 27, 2013, the Second Circuit granted the motions to pursue the interlocutory appeals of the two cases, acknowledging the confusion over the test for evaluating whether interns should be more properly classified as employees.

The confusion reigning in the federal courts is similarly found in state court cases. Due to the differing tests for determining employee status under state wage and hour laws, it is crucial that an organization evaluate its jurisdiction's statutory and common law to determine whether interns are considered employees and thus subject to state minimum wage and hour laws. For example, the Massachusetts Department of Labor ("Mass. DOL") was called on to answer a related question.[4] The Mass. DOL stated that "employment through the NU [Northeastern University] co-op program is work under a training program in an educational institution, therefore, it is not an 'occupation' covered by the Massachusetts Fair Wage Law." Unfortunately, the Mass. DOL did not on its own initiative answer the more important question for our purposes; i.e. is a student intern an employee for purposes of Massachusetts wage and hours laws. Nonetheless, the Mass. DOL's analysis appears to lean towards a finding of non-employee status for student interns. Thus, it is possible that the Mass. DOL (or other state DOL), would find that a school sponsored program such as Northeastern's co-op program precludes a student intern from seeking protection under the Massachusetts wage and hour laws. Additionally, the Mass. DOL opinion letter does not address the impact of compensation in its analysis. The Mass. DOL's failure to address this issue does not clarify whether student interns are entitled to be paid minimum wage. As a result, it appears possible that an organization may compensate its student interns working under a school-sponsored internship program at a rate less than the Massachusetts minimum wage.

---

[4] Unfortunately the requesting organization asked the wrong question. Rather than asking whether co-op students were employees under Massachusetts wage and hour laws, it asked whether the student interns were professionals, and as such whether they were exempt from the Massachusetts Minimum Fair Wage Act.

Will an Agreement Protect the Employer?

Employers often require employees to sign an employment agreement. This agreement establishes the particulars of employment including compensation, sick pay, vacation pay, and duration of employment. Employees are often hired with the expectation that they will remain employed for an indefinite period of time. In contrast, student interns are usually engaged for a discrete, well defined period of time. These periods may range from a few weeks to many months and are often tied to the university's academic calendar. Must these employers have the school (if school sponsored) or the intern sign an agreement establishing the terms and conditions of his/her engagement?

While departmental agencies and courts have not spoken directly to this specific issue, it would appear to be good practice for an organization to have an agreement with the student intern and with a school (if a school sponsored internship) to document the understanding among all three parties relating to the academic content of the internship. This agreement should establish the parameters of the internship, including its measurable goals. It should establish the degree of supervision the organization will have over the training and work of the student intern and, most importantly, it should establish the expectation, or lack thereof, regarding the payment of wages and/or the availability of permanent employment.

School sponsored internships and externships have become increasingly common and popular in recent years. As mentioned earlier, some undergraduate and graduate institutions condition graduation upon the successful completion of multiple internships of varying lengths. It is likely that these internships will require greater supervision and evaluation than non-school sponsored internships. Moreover, these agreements may specify the minimum number of hours a student is required to work and minimum amount of wages a student intern must be paid.

Despite the benefits of a well-designated internship agreement, however, neither an educational institution nor an employer should lull itself into believing that an internship agreement will effectively immunize it from legal challenge. In *Glatt v. Searchlight Pictures Inc.*, the court rejected the employer's argument that the interns had a clear understanding that they would not be paid. The court concluded that the Fair Labor Standards Act ("FLSA") does not allow employees to waive their entitlement to wages and that "[T]he purposes of the Act require that it be applied even to those who decline its protections." Even a well-constructed internship agreement, willingly signed by an intern, may not adequately protect an employer from liability for unpaid wages under the FLSA and under most state wage and hour laws.

Workers Compensation

Another potential employment law issue involving interns is whether they are employees for purposes of a state workers' compensation act.[5] For example, the New York Workers Compensation Act governs all workers' compensation claims and is the exclusive remedy for employees who suffer work related injuries. Thus, if under New York law the interns are employees, then they are covered under the Worker's Compensation Act. However, much as the employee/volunteer distinction was important under the FLSA, it is likewise crucial in determining the applicability of a state workers' compensation statute. If the interns are deemed to be volunteers, then they are not covered under a workers' compensation scheme and are not precluded from suing the organization for tort claims arising from their injuries sustained at work. This presents serious potential liability issues to host organizations who may be faced with claims for damages far in excess of the state's workers' compensation scheme.

For interns earning college credit or fulfilling graduation requirements, does the school's workers' compensation plan cover the student? While there is little case law and authority addressing this issue, a few courts have addressed the applicability of a workers' compensation statute to an intern for school credit. For example, in a case arising in Colorado, the court had to determine whether a paid student intern in a university-sponsored program was deemed an employee of the hosting organization for purposes of workers' compensation. The court held that the student was an employee of the organization for workers' compensation purposes and moreover that unpaid interns were also covered under the school's workers' compensation plan.

In a New York case, the court addressed whether an unpaid student intern was covered under the school's workers' compensation plan. This court also held that the unpaid student intern was covered under the school's workers' compensation coverage, stating that where "necessary training and experience gained ... is required for graduation and licensure, training is a thing of value and the equivalent of wages." While these cases are not dispositive on this issue, they do represent one avenue available to courts when confronted with these situations. As school sponsored internships become more common this issue will attract more court attention. While the answer is not fully clear, it is likely that a paid student intern will qualify as an employee under the various state

---

[5] Workers' compensation is a matter of state law, and therefore this section will address selected workers' compensation statutes and cases involving student interns as examples only. This section should not be considered exhaustive and it is encouraged that an organization determine whether an intern is covered under its workers' compensation policy or if an intern is covered under the school's policy.

workers' compensation acts and that even unpaid interns may qualify under their schools' policies.

Vicarious Liability

May the actions of a student intern expose a host organization to liability? Vicarious liability may be imposed for the illegal acts of a company's employees committed within the course of their employment. Vicarious liability hinges on whether the individual is an employee or independent contractor. While the law of each jurisdiction will vary, the law in Massachusetts, for example, would render most interns employees for the purposes of employer liability because an internship tends to be highly supervised relationship. Thus, although an intern may not be considered an employee under the FLSA and Massachusetts Wage and Hour Laws, that intern may nonetheless be considered an employee for liability purposes under state law.

Even if the interns are not considered to be employees, an organization may be still be vicariously liable for negligence in selecting the intern or in directing the intern's work. For example, if an organization does not perform a background check for an intern, it may be vicariously liable for its negligence in selection. This can be a particularly worrisome situation for financial institutions, healthcare providers, or educational institutions hosting interns. Given the prevalence of student internship programs, it is likely that an issue involving vicarious liability will arise in the near future. As of now, it is yet another unresolved area in the law involving student interns.

Discrimination Statutes

In light of the uncertain employment status of interns, may an intern nevertheless assert a federal or state discrimination claim against the host organization? The answer to this question may depend on the jurisdiction in which the internship is located.

On October 3, 2013, Judge P. Kevin Castel of the Southern District of New York ruled on state law claims of hostile work environment, quid pro quo sexual harassment and retaliation brought by a former unpaid intern working for a satellite television company. In *Wang v. Phoenix Satellite Television, Inc.*, the plaintiff, Lihuan Wang brought claims under the New York State Human Rights Law ("NYSHRL") and the New York City Human Rights Law ("NYCHRL"), claiming that her supervisor subjected her to a sexually hostile environment by making unwanted advances during a business trip and failed to hire her for full-time employment when she refused his advances. In an issue of first impression in the Second Circuit and in New York courts, the court concluded that an intern is not eligible for the protections provided under either the city or state anti-discrimination statutes. Citing the Second Circuit's decision in *O'Connor v. Davis*, where the court dismissed a Title VII gender discrimination claim brought by an intern, the court concluded that, as under federal law, "compensation is a threshold issue in determining the existence of an employment relationship" under New York State and City law as well. The court firmly rejected Ms. Wang's contention that the NYCHRL, which affords claimants broader protections than both its federal and state counterparts, would recognize an unpaid intern as an employee for the purposes of anti-discrimination protection.[6]

The result would have been quite different if Ms. Wang's internship had been located in Oregon rather than in New York. On June 13, 2013, Oregon Governor John Kitzhaber signed into law a bill extending employment discrimination protection to interns under Oregon's employment discrimination laws for workplace violations including sexual harassment, unlawful discrimination and retaliation for whistle-blowing. The definition of "intern" for the purposes of eligibility for this extended protection tracks the test for unpaid interns who are exempt from the FLSA, thereby providing protections to those individuals who are expressly excluded from federal protection.

Because of the unsettled state of both federal and state law and responding to the sustained increase in intern lawsuits, a number of corporations, including publishing giant Conde Nast, have announced their decision to eliminate internship programs for 2014.

Summary

While internships of all kinds have become more popular, there are many legal issues that are still unanswered. Until we have more answers, a hosting organization should be aware of the distinct likelihood that an intern will be considered an employee under federal law and thus should be paid minimum wage and overtime, will most likely be eligible for workers' compensation if injured on the job and could impose vicarious liability on the host organization. As noted, these issues, and others, are subject to both federal law and the law of the state of the host organization. Hopefully, there will be more definitive answers in the years to come.

---

[6] The court did, however, allow Ms. Wang to pursue her claim that she had been denied full time employment in retaliation for her rejection of her supervisor's advances under a "failure to hire" theory that can be brought by both employees and applicants under both New York state and city laws.

Michael Brown is a Senior Partner in the Boston office of Seyfarth Shaw LLP. His telephone number is 617-946-4907 and his email address is mrbrown@seyfarth.com. Joanne Seltzer is a Shareholder with Jackson Lewis P.C. Her telephone number is 212-545-4070 and her email address is joanne.seltzer@jacksonlewis.com.

Addendum

In 2012, Glatt v. Fox Searchlight Pictures, *more commonly known as* "The Black Swan Case", *was filed as the first amended class complaint of former interns seeking redress for violation of the FLSA and Wage & Hour Division rules citing the "Six-Prong Test" that was established as a metric for deciding if interns were employees and required to be paid at least minimum wage.*

In June 2013, the district court concluded that the plaintiffs in the case were improperly classified as "unpaid interns" and should have been paid as employees for the hours they worked performed and were granted summary judgment.

THE MANAGER'S GUIDE TO COACHING AND DELIVERING FEEDBACK TO INTERNS

Joseph R. Weintraub, Ph.D. and James Hunt, DBA
Division of Management, Babson College

Introduction

The internship experience provides students with the opportunity to get grounded in the "real world" while, hopefully, adding value to the organization or person sponsoring the internship itself. In this regard, sponsors can play a significant role in shaping the interns' personal and professional development. A key ingredient in providing this learning opportunity is the sponsor's willingness and ability to deliver quality coaching and feedback to the student interns. We recognize that finding time to coach and deliver feedback is an issue in most organizations; and since interns will generally leave the organization in a relatively short period of time, coaching and feedback are often more of a challenge to do, and do well. However, since most companies also want to benefit from the internship experience, we would argue that the business case for providing coaching and feedback to interns is quite compelling.

While the principles of coaching and delivering feedback to college interns are based on the same principles that would be used in other organizational settings, it is important to understand that college interns are not the same as other employees. The interns are typically students who may or may not end up working in their internship organization or even in the same field as their internship after they complete their education. Because many of these students are relatively young and inexperienced with the world of work, the host organizations and the people who supervise and work with these students have the opportunity to provide a meaningful and developmental experience for the students. In fact, the early boss-employee (i.e. boss-intern) experiences often have the most impact in shaping how students will see future work experiences, including the students' attitudes about work and even their eventual leadership approach.

Approaches to Coaching

Our own research and the research of others shows that coaching is one of the lowest rated competencies for managers—it just doesn't happen as often as it should. In this section, we will discuss a few approaches to coaching, including our recommendation of one coaching strategy that can help maximize the internship experience for the intern, supervisor and company.

There are many organizational approaches and models of coaching. One commonly used approach is the "sports coach" model where coaches impart their specific knowledge to the coachee so the coachee can then start doing things "right." In sports, this approach is used frequently in teaching new or enhanced skills (i.e., how to kick a ball with more power). This model also may bring forth images of a well known basketball coach noted for his fiery temper who yells at his young charges in front of the masses.

Another frequently used coaching method is the parental model where, once again, the "coach" is often found delivering a list of "do's and don'ts," much like how loving parents might tell their three-year-old about the importance of safety while crossing a busy street. In both of the above approaches, the coaches deliver their instructions in a one-way format, with no input from the coachee (intern). The intent is often well-meaning, but the impact on the student learner is frequently viewed as negative. Below, we discuss a developmental model to coaching that we strongly recommend when dealing with college interns.

The Weintraub-Hunt Model for Coaching College Interns: A Developmental Approach

In the work that we have done on effective coaching in organizations, we presented a developmental approach to coaching that effective managers have used successfully to develop employees and to create coaching-friendly organizations (see The Coaching Manager: Developing Top Talent in Business by James Hunt and Joseph Weintraub, Sage Publications, 2002, and The Coaching Organization: A Strategy for Developing Leaders, also written by James Hunt and Joseph Weintraub Sage Publications, 2007). The modification of our original "Coaching Manager" model is presented here as The Weintraub-Hunt Model for Coaching College Interns, which integrates our approach to organizational coaching with the current research efforts of Richard Bottner (2007) who examined college internship experiences.

The Weintraub-Hunt Model for Coaching College Interns (see chart below) offers an opportunity for companies and the people who manage college internship programs and interns to increase the growth and learning of the interns within their respective organizations.

The utility of our developmental approach has been demonstrated consistently in our organizational work and through our research, with over 7,500 students and coaches at Babson College in Wellesley, Massachusetts studied since 1997 in the Babson College Coaching for Leadership and Teamwork Program (www.babson.edu/coach). The developmental approach used in our model is learner focused – coaching is targeted at what the learner hopes to learn.

The approach is oriented toward learning and change rather than on compliance (i.e., do it or else). The model also helps the intern/learner to capitalize on existing strengths as much or more than on overcoming weaknesses.

Selecting "Coachable" Interns

No coaching program can be successful unless the students who are selected for internships have been carefully screened and chosen. Part of this selection process should also screen for the "coachability" of the interns – do they have a desire to learn and to be coached? Southwest Airlines is one example of a good organization that selects people at all levels who possess both the "attitude and ability" to do the job. With interns, it is important for them to realize that they will be coached and be active participants in what we would hope will be a positive learning experience.

Defining Successful Performance

If you have the right talent, the intern's supervisor needs to define what success would look like for the intern and the organization. Defining success can be done by clearly outlining roles and responsibilities and/or describing the results that would constitute success both during the internship, as well as at the internship's conclusion.

This step is often missed, leaving the intern and the organization confused and disappointed. It becomes very difficult to provide appropriate coaching if there isn't a clear set of expectations about the criteria for success. Not understanding the culture is one of the major reasons people at all levels fail in organizations – so, be sure to spend the upfront time to define the job, as well as how things get done in your company's corporate culture.

One simple strategy to define success is to create what we call the company "success manual" which describes the three most important reasons we want this intern, and spells out the ways to succeed (and fail!) in this internship. The time you spend in the beginning is indeed time well spent.

Creating a Coaching-Friendly Context

Interns can often feel lost or set apart if they are not properly introduced to people within the organization. Letting interns know that they don't have to have all the answers and that it is okay to ask questions if they don't know something are key concepts in creating an environment where the intern can feel that it is okay to ask for help.

Assuming a "Helpful" Mindset

One of the ways to maximize success and to provide a solid learning experience for the intern is to have the supervisors and others who work with college interns look for ways to be helpful and to have conversations with them, when appropriate, about the internship experience.

Stopping the Action: Creating Coaching Moments

At different intervals, perhaps once a week or once every two weeks, it is important to check in with the interns to see how things are going. These scheduled check-ins give the boss/coach relationship an important structure and sends a powerful message about the value of the interns and their importance to the organization's learning. There are also unscheduled coaching moments that occur when something has happened where the reflection about the experience would add great value to the internship experience.

The Coaching Dialogue: Asking Good Questions

Of all the strategies for working with interns, sitting down with the intern and asking questions about them is essential if development of the intern is a goal of the internship experience. Our coaching model has, at its core, the use of effective questioning as a fundamental process. We strongly recommend that interns receive frequent coaching and that coaches are doing more questioning than they are lecturing. For example, after a project was completed, you might ask questions such as "How did that go?" "What was it like?" "How did it feel?" "What were you trying to accomplish?" "What did you learn?" and "How do you plan to use the knowledge gained from this internship?"

Observing Effectively

In order to do a good job coaching an intern, it is essential that you see them at work and/or have access to good observational data from others. Otherwise, the coaching and feedback processes are more limited in their ability to effect change. Be clear on the difference between behavioral observation where you have specific examples of what somebody did versus hearsay or inference of what you think may be going on.

Providing Balanced Feedback

Student interns are in a learning mode. They are not necessarily, at this stage of their development, polished and knowledgeable about the job or the organization. So, be sure to balance the need to deliver good feedback with the understanding that we want to help them to become better. This is where the marriage between coaching and feedback makes a difference. Blending a developmental coaching orientation along with good feedback often works best when dealing with interns.

Creating a Developmental Plan with the Coachee/Intern

Most interns don't get a lot of time to interact with their internship managers. But to get the most out of the internship experience, we recommend that part of the coaching process include the creation of a developmental plan during the internship itself that focuses on defining goals for the internship itself, as well as for the personal/professional goals of the intern. This conversation is one of the best ones that interns will have and sends a strong message that the organization cares about its interns, both during and after their internship experience. This conversation lasts from 30-60 minutes but returns huge dividends to the intern and the organization.

Follow-up

In spite of good intentions to develop interns, the use of follow-up strategies to check in on the organization's goals, as well as on the intern's developmental plan, is highly recommended. The follow-up should happen as part of the internship assignment itself and/or after they have completed their internship assignment, to see how they are doing after life as an intern. This latter approach takes time and is certainly more challenging, but it sends a powerful message that the organization cares about them and their personal development. The informal network of student interns then spreads the word about how good the organization is where they had their internship.

Providing Feedback to College Interns

Good coaching typically involves the use of feedback. But one distinction is critical to remember: feedback by itself is not necessarily coaching. Telling an intern that he blew it in delivering a presentation at the weekly staff meeting is feedback, but certainly not developmental coaching. In this section, we will discuss the components needed to deliver the type of feedback that is clear, developmental in nature and where the possibility of personal change can be achieved.

Coaching and delivering feedback to college interns is a key part of the internship experience. After all, an internship is generally selected by students to provide an experience that they could not ordinarily receive in a traditional classroom. We recognize that finding time to deliver feedback is an issue in most organizations; and since interns will generally leave the organization in a relatively short period of time, feedback is often more of a challenge to do and do well. Since most companies also want to benefit from the internship experience, we would argue that the business case for feedback and coaching is quite compelling. According to most research on learning, feedback offered without the support of coaching may not be all that helpful to the student intern.

Feedback should be delivered to the intern in a "helpful" way and, perhaps most importantly, feedback must be delivered by a coaching manager who is aware of (a) the powerful emotional impact that can accompany feedback, and (b) how the intern's reactions can shape his or her ability to learn from feedback.

The Benefits of Feedback

The benefits of feedback, especially when combined with appropriate levels of coaching, can be enormous for both organizations and interns alike.

As such, developing skill in effectively providing feedback to employees should be considered an important goal for all managers of interns. Research on the benefits of employee feedback (London, 1997) can also, in most instances, be applied to student interns:

- Feedback helps to keep goal-directed behavior on course. Keeping interns informed about progress as they attempt to change or pursue any goal helps them see how far they have come and how far they have to go.

- Feedback helps interns set appropriate goals for themselves and the internship itself. On the basis of the feedback that interns receive, they see what they have accomplished. Those who are motivated will want to push further.

- Positive feedback, when appropriate, can help interns feel that they have achieved something even when their achievement doesn't lead to a tangible result (such as project completion). Unavoidably, some projects will be completed after the intern has returned to school.

- Motivation theory and research also show that feedback can serve to enhance motivation since interns will understand what it takes to be successful. They will know the rules of the road. The intern who can say, "Now I know how to get there" is more likely to make the attempt.

- Feedback can help interns develop a greater ability to detect errors on their own. When coupled with self-assessment, feedback helps us better judge our own actions because our ability to observe ourselves has been calibrated by comparison with the feedback of others.

- Related to the last point, feedback can also help interns see what they need to learn. They have a clearer sense of their own weaknesses or learning gaps. Their ability to take charge of their own development is enhanced.

- People who are accustomed to getting feedback tend to seek it out. The effective provisioning of feedback by a manager is one of the most important tactics for creating a coaching-friendly context, and should be the goal of every intern's director.

The Basics of Providing Balanced Feedback

In describing the basic components of feedback, we will also report on what the coaching managers we have studied have told us works and doesn't work. We'll also try to fit the various components more directly to the model of coaching described in our book <u>The Coaching Manager: Developing Top Talent in Business</u>. In this section, we'll also rely heavily on work by Buron and McDonald-Mann (1999).

Before giving feedback, we make the assumption that you and the intern have discussed what he or she is working on and that you have given the intern an opportunity to reflect on his or her own performance. We also assume that you were clear on what aspects of the intern's performance you were trying to observe and what was important in the situation. Finally, we assume that you have had a chance to get some solid data about the performance of the intern, data that you trust.

We also assume that you have decided what your goal is in giving the feedback. In addition to learning, is your goal to help appraise or celebrate the intern's previous actions? Or is your goal to encourage the intern or provide helpful information as he or she looks forward to the next challenge in your organization and/or in their future career? Either way, the basic structure of feedback is the same, and the suggestions for how to manage the process are similar. Having said that, the art of coaching, an art that one learns only with practice, is in knowing how to offer feedback in a way that conveys as much useful information as possible.

Feedback: The Basic Requirements

Feedback content should include the following:

- The situation in which your observations were made.
- Your observations of the intern in action.
- The impact of the intern's behavior or actions, on you and others as appropriate.

Total Internship Management

Before offering feedback, be sure to do the following:

- Set the stage for your feedback discussion in a way that will encourage the maximum degree of openness, which is essential to learning. Make sure that the location, degree of confidentiality, and timing are appropriate to the individual and the situation.

Effective feedback is:

- Focused on what the intern is trying to accomplish or has told you that he or she wants to learn.

- Given frequently.

- Given, whenever possible, right after an action along with the intern's reflection on his or her action.

- Given, whenever possible, with a helpful, not an angry, attitude.

- Focused on behaviors that have a reasonable probability for change.

- Specific, using behavioral terminology.

- Focuses on the task, action, or behavior, not on the person.

- Is direct and usually begins with "I" statements.

- Delivered without interpretation.

- Checked by the coaching manager to make sure that the intern heard the message the manager wanted to deliver

- Followed by the question: "What do you plan on doing with this feedback?"

- Followed by the suggestion of a follow-up meeting, particularly if the feedback to the intern has been negative.

The Coaching Manager

Feedback represents a form of communication, or a message. What should the message include? Feedback content usually includes the following: a description of the situation in which you observed the intern; a description of the behavior of, or actions taken by, the intern you observed; and finally, a description of the impact of the behavior or actions of the intern on others or on a relevant business outcome. "Here is what I saw, and here is what I think was the impact of what I saw" is the basic structure of a feedback message.

Note what is included and not included in the message. What is included is factual information, to the highest degree possible. What is not included is an interpretation. You may have to climb the ladder of inference a bit when describing what you "think" is the impact of a particular action or behavior; but oftentimes, you'll know. You'll know because you can describe the impact of the employee's behavior on you: "I don't know what others might have thought about your approach to this, but I liked it. It really addressed my concerns." If you describe the impact from your vantage point, you're making very few inferences. After all, an individual's manager is a key stakeholder in the actions of that individual. The impact on you as manager of the intern does count; and the impact you experience from the actions of an intern may be similar to the impact experienced by others. You can therefore state, "This was the impact on me," with real authority.

On the basis of our own research and review of the writing to date on personal learning, we encourage you to always consider the importance of the intern's goals while delivering feedback. If you focus on what the intern is trying to accomplish or has told you he or she wants to learn, you have been given license by the intern to be clear and direct.

Setting The Stage For Feedback

Setting the stage for feedback is important. In some situations, the scheduled individual setting is most appropriate. You may have been asked to go out and gather a significant amount of performance data for the intern, or the issues may be quite sensitive. Structure (a scheduled meeting) and confidentiality (away from everyone else) may help the intern focus on what is being said rather than on the reactions of others. In other instances, the stage may have been set by your working understanding with the intern. Perhaps the intern expects to meet with you in the hall, right after the big meeting. Once you and your intern are used to the give-and-take of feedback, you may find yourself providing more of it in informal settings. The point we are making with regard to setting the stage is to be sensitive to the intern's needs. When in doubt, ask. If you're not satisfied with the answer, the old rule "praise in public, criticize in private" should serve as your guide. We encourage you to always set the stage in such a way that the self-esteem of your intern will be minimally threatened.

Setting the stage also involves a consideration of timing. Feedback, particularly if it is based on substantial data collected by the coaching manager, perhaps involving others, may be eagerly sought but anxiously anticipated by the employee. Substantial feedback takes time to absorb. If you are going to engage in a major feedback intervention, make sure you and the intern have sufficient time to thoroughly discuss the issues raised by the feedback.

If feedback is being given to enhance an intern's learning and the intern is trying to build effectiveness in addressing a challenging goal, then feedback from multiple observations will be useful. Your intent should be to give the intern enough data to build a "video" of his or her performance over time.

Likewise, feedback that is given right after an action and the individual's reflection on that action is more likely to result in learning. The events are fresh in everyone's mind. Feedback that is timely is thus important as well. It may be necessary for you to take a few minutes to figure out what you want to say, but don't delay too long.

The feedback you provide should be specific and focused on the task, action, or behavior. By specific, we mean descriptive. It is important to gather data that accurately reflect the intern's performance. Feedback involves delivering that data in a way that is helpful.

For the receiver of feedback to be able to make use of the data provided by the coaching manager, the information must be presented clearly and simply. The language and style of the presentation should be appropriate to the audience. Avoid non descriptive or technical terms unless you are sure that the receiver of the feedback can work with those terms and can understand what they mean.

The best feedback is also usually quite direct. Directness usually requires the use of "I" statements. "This is what I saw." Some of us have experienced, and probably all of us have heard about, feedback statements that begin, "We don't think…" The reality is that unless the intern knows who you are talking about when you use the word "we," such a feedback statement may have very little credibility. "We" statements can also make the intern feel "ganged-up on" or attacked. If the coaching manager has to provide feedback on behalf of several individuals, it is much more effective to be specific about who said what. We also feel strongly that feedback directed to interns and to all employees should always be intended to maintain or enhance the individual's self-esteem. So, the way we deliver feedback is critical to the intern's ability to learn and reflect.

Avoid interpretations drawn from the second, or above, levels of the ladder of inference. Such interpretations are likely to generate defensiveness – and worse yet, are likely to be wrong. Interpretation occurs during the coaching dialogue through the use of questions. Our favorite example of inference masquerading as feedback is "You have a bad attitude." Such a statement is actually devoid of data and represents a pure interpretation. A descriptive statement that would support such an interpretation might be something like "You told the last three customers who walked in the door that you hated working here and that you can't wait to go back to school." Note that such a descriptive statement is in some ways even more hard-hitting than the interpretation. Data almost always carry more weight than the inappropriate use of inference.

Finally, ask the intern what he or she can or will do with the feedback. Ideally, feedback leads to additional reflection, and then action. Having delivered the feedback, or after delivering each point of the feedback, the coaching manager should stop, make sure that he or she was understood, and ask for the intern's thoughts on how the feedback can help. Remember that the coaching process begins with a coaching dialogue. It is important to keep the dialogue going by providing plenty of opportunity for the employee to reflect on the feedback you have provided. A little silence during these periods is okay. It is far better to offer some feedback, ask for the employee's reactions, and then wait, rather than hurry on to the next point. Indeed, if the feedback has any real substance to it, it is natural for the employee to need a few minutes to digest what has been said. Make sure you, the coaching manager, don't do all the talking!

After the feedback is given, the intern may move ahead with future reflection and action. If the feedback is particularly negative or problematic, however, it may be wise to schedule another meeting to follow up soon after the meeting at which the feedback was given. Even under the best of circumstances, critical feedback can be difficult for some interns to manage, so don't try to overdo the giving of feedback. Keep your list short, except in the case of delivering positive feedback where, in most cases, interns will not be as uncomfortable in receiving good news! Follow-up meetings show concern for the intern and symbolize the coaching manager's commitment to the intern's ongoing learning.

The Lack of Feedback

We know from our consulting work in organizations that most people do not receive feedback or, if they do, they don't receive feedback that is perceived as helpful. It is critical that interns receive feedback. The old adage that "some feedback, even negative, is better than no feedback at all" is generally true. It is also true that missing or incomplete spoken feedback does not mean that the intern gets no feedback at all. Inaction on the part of the manager is also feedback. The intern will often fill in the gaps. The intern will particularly wonder, "Did I do a good job?" and/or "Does the manager think I can really handle this?" Ultimately, like it or not, the intern will be thinking about questions such as "Does she like me?" "Am I doing a good job/" "Does anyone here care about me?" and "Is this a good manager to be working for?"

The lesson here is to look for opportunities to deliver feedback to interns that is constructive and helpful; but don't feel that you have to give a daily report card – after all, the interns wanted a departure from the grading of their work at school!

" PROVIDE CONSTRUCTIVE CRITICISM when you do something wrong. Have the patience to teach you to do it right."

"I LEARNED SO MUCH from my mentors and it really opened my eyes to some of the things I could expect in the field."

"AN ORGANIZATION CAN GREATLY augment the meaningful experience of an internship by using coaching and learning techniques."

"HAVE A MENTOR GUIDE INTERNS through the experience. The mentor should give constructive criticism. That will make the internship worthwhile because students will learn from their mistakes."

"TO MAKE AN INTERNSHIP MEANINGFUL, I think they should have a mentor, someone the intern can go to when they have problems."

"PROVIDE EACH INTERN with a successful mentor who will be there to answer questions and lead them through their journey."

"HAVING A MENTOR would be key; someone who could help an individual through tasks and give advice on future career goals and how to attain them."

The Manager's Guide to Coaching and Delivering Feedback to Interns

Dr. Weintraub is an Organizational Psychologist who focuses in the areas of individual and organizational effectiveness. He teaches and consults in the areas of leadership development, coaching, team effectiveness, human resources, and performance management. Dr. Weintraub is the Founder and Faculty Director of the Babson Coaching for Leadership and Teamwork Program. His work on coaching has received several awards including the "Management Development Paper of the Year" from the Academy of Management and recognition for innovative practices in business education from the Carnegie Foundation. He is the co-author of the books The Coaching Manager: Developing Top Talent in Business (Sage Publications, 2nd Edition, 2011) and The Coaching Organization: A Strategy for Developing Leaders (Sage Publications, 2007).

James M. Hunt is an Associate Professor of Management at Babson College, where he teaches leadership, entrepreneurship and career management and development. He is a Faculty Director of Babson Executive Educations Leadership and Influence Program. He lead the design team for Babson's Managerial Assessment and Development Course in the Fast Track MBA Program, he designed and co-founded Babson's Coaching Inside the Organization Program at Babson Executive Education and also co-founded and co-Faculty Directed Babson's Coaching for Leadership and Teamwork Program. James has held the Charles Barton and Charles McCarthy Term Chairs during his career at Babson. In 2009 James was awarded the Dean's Prize for Teaching in All Programs. In 2003 he was a co-recipient of the first Alumni Association Award for Distinguished Teaching and Service.

MY NOTES

MY NOTES

MY NOTES

APPENDIX

APPENDIX A
LIST OF MAJORS

Agriculture & Related Sciences

Agribusiness Operations

Agricultural Business

Agricultural Business Technology

Agricultural Communications

Agricultural Economics

Agricultural Education Services

Agricultural Equipment Technology

Agricultural Mechanization

Agricultural Power Machinery

Agricultural Production

Agricultural Supplies

Agricultural/Food Processing

Agriculture - General

Agronomy/Crop Science

Animal Breeding

Animal Grooming

Animal Health

Animal Husbandry

Animal Nutrition

Animal Sciences

Animal Training

Aquaculture

Crop Production

Dairy Husbandry/Production

Dairy Science

Equestrian/Equine Studies

Farm/Ranch Management

Floristry/Floriculture

Food Science

Food Technology/Processing

Greenhouse Management

Horse Husbandry/Equine Science

Horticultural Services

Horticulture Science

Horticulture, Ornamental

International Agriculture

Landscaping

Livestock Management

Pest Management

Plant Breeding

Plant Sciences

Plant/Nursery Operations

Poultry Science

Range Science/Management

Soil Science and Agronomy

Taxidermy

Turf Management

Architecture & Related Programs

Architectural History/Criticism

Architectural Technology

Architecture

Architecture &
   Related Programs - General

City/Community/Regional Planning

Environmental Design

Interior Architecture

Landscape Architecture

**Area, Ethnic, Cultural,
   & Gender Studies**

African Studies

African-American Studies

American Studies

Area Studies

Asian American Studies

Asian Studies

Canadian Studies

Caribbean Studies

Central/Eastern European Studies

Chinese Studies

East Asian Studies

European Studies

French Studies

Gay/Lesbian Studies

German Studies

Hispanic-American Studies

Italian Studies

Japanese Studies

Korean Studies

Latin American Studies

Native American Studies

Near/Middle Eastern Studies

Pacific Area/Near Rim Studies

Polish Studies

Regional Studies

Russian/Slavic Area Studies

Scandinavian Area Studies

Slavic Studies

South Asian Studies

Southeast Asian Studies

Spanish/Iberian Studies

Ural-Altaic/Central Asian Studies

Western European Studies

Women's Studies

Arts, Visual & Performing

Acting

Art - General

Art History/Criticism/Conservation

Arts - General

Arts Management

Ballet

Ceramics

Commercial Photography

Commercial/Advertising Art

Crafts/Folk Art/Artisanry

Dance

Design/Visual Communications

Total Internship Management

Directing/Theatrical Production

Drama/Theater Arts

Drawing

Fashion Design

Fiber/Textile/Weaving Arts

Film Production/Cinematography

Film Studies

Fine/Studio Arts

Graphic Design

Illustration

Industrial Design

Interior Design

Jazz Studies

Metal/Jewelry Arts

Multimedia

Music - General

Music - General Performance

Music - Piano/Organ

Music - Voice/Opera

Music Conducting

Music History/Literature

Music Management/Merchandising

Music Pedagogy

Music Theory/Composition

Musicology/Ethnomusicology

Painting

Photography

Playwriting/Screenwriting

Printmaking

Sculpture

Stringed Instruments

Theater Design/Stagecraft

Theater Literature/History/Criticism

Theatre Arts Management

Biological & Biomedical Sciences

Anatomy

Animal Behavior/Ethology

Animal Genetics

Animal Physiology

Aquatic Biology/Limnology

Bacteriology

Biochemistry

Bioinformatics

Biological Immunology

Biology

Biomedical Sciences

Biometrics

Biophysics

Biostatistics

Biotechnology

Botany

Cellular Biology/Histology

Cellular/Anatomical Biology

Cellular/Molecular Biology

Chemical/Physical/
    Molecular Biology

Conservation Biology

Developmental Biology/Embryology

Ecology

Entomology

Environmental Biology

Environmental Toxicology

Epidemiology

Evolutionary Biology

Exercise Physiology

Genetics

Genetics - Human/Medical

Marine/Aquatic Biology

Microbiology

Molecular Biochemistry

Molecular Biology

Molecular Genetics

Molecular Pharmacology

Neuroanatomy

Neurobiology/Physiology

Oncology

Parasitology

Pathology - Human/Animal

Pharmacology

Pharmacology/Toxicology

Physiology

Plant Genetics

Plant Molecular Biology

Plant Pathology

Plant Physiology

Radiation Biology

Reproductive Biology

Systematic Biology

Toxicology

Wildlife Biology

Zoology

**Business, Management,
& Marketing**

Accounting

Accounting Technology

Accounting/Business Management

Accounting/Finance

Actuarial Science

Administrative/Secretarial Services

Apparel/Accessories Marketing

Auctioneering

Auditing

Banking/Financial Services

Business - General

Business Administration/
Management

Business Communications

Business Statistics

Business/Managerial Economics

Construction Management

Credit Management

Customer Service Management

Customer Service Support

E-Commerce

Total Internship Management

Entrepreneurial Studies

Executive Assistant

Fashion Merchandising

Finance/Banking

Financial Planning

Financial Services Marketing

Franchising Operations

Hospitality Administration/
  Management

Hospitality/Recreation Marketing

Hotel/Motel Management

Human Resources Development

Human Resources Management

Information Processing/Data Entry

Information Resources Management

Insurance/Risk Management

International Business

International Finance

International Marketing

Investments/Securities

Knowledge Management

Labor Studies

Labor/Personnel Relations

Logistics/Materials Management

Management Information Systems

Management Science

Marketing Management

Marketing Research

Merchandising

Nonprofit Management

Office Clerical Services

Office Management

Operations Management

Organizational Behavior Studies

Personal/Financial Services
  Marketing

Public Finance

Purchasing/Procurement/Contracts

Real Estate

Reception

Resort Management

Restaurant/Food Services
  Management

Retailing

Sales and Distribution

Sales/Selling Skills

Small Business Administration

Special Products Marketing

Taxation

Tourism/Travel Marketing

Tourism/Travel Services

Transportation/Transportation
  Management

Travel/Tourism Management

Vehicle Parts/Accessories Marketing

Warehousing/Inventory
  Management

Communications & Journalism

Advertising

Broadcast Journalism

Communications/Rhetoric

Digital Communications/Multimedia

Health Communications

Journalism

Mass Communications/Media Studies

Organizational Communication

Photojournalism

Political Communications

Public Relations

Publishing

Radio/Television

Communications Technologies

Animation/Special Effects

Communications Technologies - General

Computer Typography

Desktop Publishing

Graphic Communications

Graphic/Printing Equipment Operation

Photographic/Film Technology

Platemaking

Printing Management

Printing Press Operations

Radio/Television Broadcasting

Recording Arts Technology

Computer & Information Sciences

Artificial Intelligence/Robotics

Computer Graphics

Computer Networking/ Telecommunications

Computer Programming - General

Computer Programming - Specific Applications

Computer Programming - Vendor/Product Certification

Computer Science

Computer Systems Analysis

Computer/Information Sciences - General

Computer/Systems Security

Data Entry Applications

Data Processing Technology

Database Management

Information Sciences/Systems

Information Technology

Networking/LAN/WAN Management

System Administration

Web/Multimedia Design

Web/Multimedia Management

Word Processing

Construction Trades

Building Construction Inspection

Building/Property Maintenance

Carpentry

Concrete Finishing

Construction Site Management

Construction Trades - General

Drywall Installation

Electrician

Glaziery

Lineworker

Masonry/Tile Setting

Metal Building Assembly

Painting/Wall Covering

Pipefitting

Plumbing

Power/Electric Transmission

Roofing

Well Drilling

Education

Adult Literacy Instruction

Adult/Continuing Education
    Administration

Adult/Continuing Teacher Education

Agricultural Education

Art Teacher Education

Bilingual/Bicultural Education

Biology Teacher Education

Business Teacher Education

Chemistry Teacher Education

College Counseling

Computer Teacher Education

Counselor Education

Curriculum/Instruction

Drama/Dance Teacher Education

Driver/Safety Education

ESL Teacher Education

Early Childhood Education

Early Childhood Special Education

Education - General

Education Administration/
    Supervision

Education of Blind/Visually
    Handicapped

Education of Brain Injured

Education of Deaf/Hearing
    Impaired

Education of Developmentally
    Delayed

Education of Emotionally
    Handicapped

Education of Gifted/Talented

Education of Learning Disabled

Education of Mentally Handicapped

Education of Multiple Handicapped

Education of Physically
    Handicapped

Education of Speech Impaired

Education of the Autistic

Educational Assessment/Testing

Educational Evaluation/Research

Educational Statistics/Research
Methods

Elementary Education

English Teacher Education

Family/Consumer Sciences -
Education

Foreign Language Teacher Education

French Teacher Education

French as Second/Foreign Language

Geography Teacher Education

German Teacher Education

Health Occupations Teacher
Education

Health Teacher Education

History Teacher Education

Instructional Media

International/Comparative Education

Junior High Education

Kindergarten/Preschool Education

Latin Teacher Education

Mathematics Education

Montessori Teacher Education

Multicultural Education

Music Teacher Education

Native American Education

Physical Education

Physics Teacher Education

Psychology Teacher Education

Reading Teacher Education

Sales/Marketing Education

School Librarian Education

Science Teacher Education

Secondary Education

Social Science Teacher Education

Social Studies Teacher Education

Social/Philosophical Foundations
of Education

Spanish Language Teacher
Education

Special Education

Speech Teacher Education

Teacher Assistance

Teacher Education, Multiple Levels

Technology/Industrial
Arts Education

Trade/Industrial Education

Waldorf/Steiner Teacher Education

Engineering

Aeronautical/Aerospace Engineering

Agricultural Engineering

Architectural Engineering

Biomedical Engineering

Ceramic Sciences/Engineering

Total Internship Management

Chemical Engineering

Civil Engineering

Computer Engineering - General

Computer Hardware Engineering

Construction Engineering

Electrical/Communications
    Engineering

Engineering - General

Engineering Mechanics

Engineering Physics

Engineering Science

Environmental Engineering

Forest Engineering

Geological Engineering

Geotechnical Engineering

Industrial Engineering

Manufacturing Engineering

Marine Engineering/Naval
    Architecture

Materials Engineering

Materials Science

Mechanical Engineering

Metallurgical Engineering

Mining/Mineral Engineering

Nuclear Engineering

Ocean Engineering

Operations Research

Petroleum

Polymer/Plastics

Software Engineering

Structural Engineering

Surveying Engineering

Systems Engineering

Textile Sciences/Engineering

Water Resource Engineering

Engineering Technologies

Aeronautical/Aerospace Engineering

Architectural Drafting

Architectural Engineering
    Technology

Automotive Engineering Technology

Biomedical Engineering Technology

CAD/CADD Drafting/Design

Civil Drafting/Civil Engineering

Civil Engineering/Technology

Computer Engineering

Computer Hardware

Computer Software

Computer Systems

Construction/Building Technologies

Drafting and Design Technology

Electrical Engineering Technologies

Electrical/Electronics Drafting

Electromechanical Technologies

Energy Systems

Engineering Technology - General

Engineering/Industrial Management

Environmental Engineering
   Technology

Hazardous Materials Management

Heating/A.C./Refrigeration

Hydraulics/Fluid Power

Industrial Safety

Industrial Technology

Instrumentation Technology

Laser/Optical Technology

Manufacturing Technologies

Mechanical Drafting

Metallurgical Technology

Mining

Nuclear

Occupational Safety

Petroleum Technology

Plastics

Quality Control

Robotics

Solar Energy

Surveying Technology

Telecommunications

Water Quality/Treatment

English Language & Literature

American Literature

American Literature (Canadian)

Creative Writing

English

English Composition

English Language; Literature -
   General

English Literature (British)

Speech/Rhetorical Studies

Technical/Business Writing

Family & Consumer Sciences

Adult Development/Aging

Apparel/Textile Manufacturing

Apparel/Textile Marketing
   Management

Child Care Management

Child Care Service

Child Development

Clothing/Apparel/Textile Studies

Consumer Economics

Consumer Merchandising

Consumer Services/Advocacy

Facilities/Event Planning

Family Resource Management
   Studies

Family Systems

Family/Community Services

Fashion/Fabric Consultant

Foods/Nutrition Studies

Family/Consumer Sciences -
   General

Family/Consumer Sciences - Business

Home Furnishings

Housing Studies

Human Development/Family Studies

Human Nutrition

Human Sciences Communication

Institutional Food Production

Textile Science

Work/Family Studies

Foreign Language & Literature

African

American Sign Language (ASL)

Ancient Near Eastern/
    Biblical Languages

Arabic

Celtic

Chinese

Classics

Comparative Literature

Czech

Danish

Dutch/Flemish

East Asian

Filipino/Tagalog

Foreign Language; Literature -
    General

French

German

Germanic Languages

Greek, Ancient

Greek, Modern

Hebrew

Iranian/Persian

Italian

Japanese

Korean

Language Interpretation/Translation

Latin

Linguistics

Native American

Norwegian

Polish

Portuguese

Romance Languages

Russian

Sanskrit/Classical Indian

Scandinavian

Semitic

Sign Language Interpretation

Slavic

South Asian

Southeast Asian

Spanish

Swedish

Turkish

Ukrainian

Urdu

Health Professions
& Clinical Sciences

Acupuncture

Anesthesiologist Assistant

Art Therapy

Asian Bodywork Therapy

Athletic Training/Sports Medicine

Audiology/Hearing Sciences

Bioethics/Medical Ethics

Cardiopulmonary Technology

Cardiovascular Technology

Chinese Medicine/Herbology

Chiropractic Assistant

Clinical Laboratory Science

Clinical Nutrition

Clinical Pastoral Counseling

Clinical/Medical Laboratory
    Technology

Clinical/Medical Social Work

Communication Disorders

Community Health Services

Community Health/Preventative
Medicine

Cytogenetics Technology

Cytotechnology

Dance Therapy

Dental Assistance

Dental Hygiene

Dental Laboratory Technology

Diagnostic Medical Sonography

Dietetic Technician

Dietician Assistant

EMT Ambulance Attendant

Electrocardiograph Technology

Electroencephalograph Technology

Emergency Medical Technology

Environmental Health

Gene Therapy

Genetic Counseling

Health Aide

Health Facilities Administration

Health Physics/Radiologic Health

Health Services - General

Health Services Administration

Health System Administration

Hematology Technology

Herbalism

Histologic Technician

Histologic Technology

Home Attendant

Homeopathic Medicine

Kinesiotherapy

Management/Clinical Assistant

Marriage/Family Therapy

Massage Therapy

Maternal/Child Health

Medical Administrative Assistance

Medical Assistance

Medical Claims Examiner

Medical Dietetics

Medical Illustrating

Medical Informatics

Medical Insurance Billing

Medical Insurance Coding

Medical Laboratory Assistance

Medical Office Administration

Medical Office Assistant

Medical Office Computer Specialist

Medical Radiologic Technology

Medical Reception

Medical Records Administration

Medical Records Technology

Medical Staff Services Technology

Medical Transcription

Medication Aide

Medicinal/Pharmaceutical Chemistry

Mental Health Counseling

Mental Health Services Technology

Midwifery

Movement Therapy/Education

Music Therapy

Nuclear Medical Technology

Nursing (RN)

Nursing - Adult Health

Nursing - Critical Care

Nursing - Family Practice

Nursing - Maternal/Child Health

Nursing - Occupational/
    Environmental Health

Nursing - Pediatric

Nursing - Practical

Nursing - Preoperative/Surgical

Nursing - Psychiatric

Nursing - Public Health

Nursing Administration

Nursing Anesthesiology

Nursing Assistance

Nursing Midwifery

Nursing Science

Occupational Health/
    Industrial Hygiene

Occupational Therapy

Occupational Therapy Assistance

Ophthalmic Laboratory Technology

Ophthalmic Technology

Opticianry/Opthalmic
    Dispensing Services

Optometric Technician/Assistant

Orthotics/Prosthetics

Pathology Assistant

Perfusion Technology

Pharmacy Assistance

Phlebotomy

Physical Therapy

Physical Therapy Assistance

Physician Assistance

Pre-Dentistry

Pre-Medicine

Pre-Nursing

Pre-Pharmacy

Pre-Veterinary Medicine

Public Health

Public Health Education

Radiation Protection Technician

Radiologic Technology/
  Medical Imaging

Recreational Therapy

Renal/Dialysis Technology

Respiratory Therapy

Respiratory Therapy Technician

Speech-Language Pathology

Speech-Language Pathology/
  Audiology

Substance Abuse Counseling

Surgical Technology

Veterinarian Assistance

Vocational Rehabilitation Counseling

Ward Clerk

Yoga Therapy/Teacher Training

History

American History (U.S.)

Asian History

Canadian History

European History

History - General

History of Science/Technology

Public History/Archives

Law & Legal Studies

Court Reporting

Legal Administrative Assistance

Paralegal/Legal Assistance

Pre-Law

Liberal Arts & Sciences

General Studies

Humanities

Liberal Arts; Sciences

Library Science

Library Assistance

Library Science

Mathematics

Algebra/Number Theory

Analysis/Functional Analysis

Applied Mathematics

Computational Mathematics

Mathematics - General

Statistics

Statistics/Probability

Mechanic & Repair Technologies

Aircraft Mechanics

Aircraft Powerplant Technology

Alternative Fuel Vehicle Technology

Appliance Installation/Repair

Auto Body Repair

Automotive Technology

Avionics Maintenance/Technology

Business Machine Repair

Communications Systems

Computer Installation/Repair

Diesel Mechanics

Electrical/Electronics Equipment Repair

Engine Machinist

Gunsmithing

Heating/A.C./Refrigeration Mechanics

Heavy Equipment Maintenance

Industrial Electronics

Industrial Equipment Maintenance/Repair

Locksmithing

Marine Maintenance/Ship Repair

Mechanics; Repair - General

Medium/Heavy Vehicle Technology

Motorcycle Maintenance/Repair

Musical Instrument Fabrication/Repair

Security Systems

Small Engine Mechanics/Repair

Vehicle Emissions Inspection/Maintenance

Watchmaking/Jewelrymaking

Multi/Interdisciplinary Studies

Accounting/Computer Science

Ancient Studies/Civilization

Behavioral Sciences

Biological/Physical Sciences

Biopsychology

Classical/Ancient Mediterranean/Near Eastern Studies

Cognitive Science

Cultural Resource Management

Gerontology

Global Studies

Historic Preservation/Conservation

Intercultural/Multicultural/Diversity Studies

Mathematics/Computer Science

Medieval/Renaissance Studies

Museum Studies

Natural Sciences

Neuroscience

Nutrition Sciences

Peace/Conflict Resolution Studies

Science, Technology;
  Society Systems Science/Theory

Natural Resources & Conservation

Environmental Science

Environmental Studies

Fishing/Fisheries

Forest Management

Forest Resources Production

Forest Sciences/Biology

Forest Technology

Forestry - General

Land Use Planning

Natural Resource Economics

Natural Resources; Conservation -
General

Natural Resources Management/
  Policy

Urban Forestry

Water/Wetlands/Marine Management

Wildlife/Wilderness Management

Wood Science/Paper Technology

Parks, Recreation & Fitness

Exercise Sciences

Health/Physical Fitness

Parks, Recreation, Fitness - General

Parks/Leisure Facilities Management

Sport/Fitness Administration

Personal & Culinary Services

Aesthetics/Skin Care

Baking/Pastry Arts

Barbering

Bartending

Beauty Salon Management

Cosmetic Services

Cosmetology

Culinary Arts/Chef Training

Culinary Arts/Related Services

Facial Treatments

Food Prep/Professional Cooking

Food Service

Funeral Direction

Funeral Services/Mortuary Science

Hair Styling/Design

Institutional Food Service

Make-up

Manicure/Nails

Mortuary Science/Embalming

Personal; Culinary Services - General

Restaurant/Catering Management

Philosophy & Religion

Buddhist Studies

Christian Studies

Ethics

Islamic Studies

Jewish/Judaic Studies

Logic

Philosophy

Philosophy; Religion - General

Religion/Religious Studies

Physical Sciences

Acoustics

Analytical Chemistry

Astronomy

Astrophysics

Atmospheric Physics Dynamics

Atmospheric Sciences

Atomic/Molecular Physics

Chemical Physics

Chemistry

Geochemistry

Geology

Geophysics Seismology

Hydrology Water Resources

Inorganic Chemistry

Meteorology

Oceanography

Optics

Organic Chemistry

Paleontology

Physical Sciences - General

Physical Theoretical Chemistry

Physics

Planetary Sciences

Polymer Chemistry

Theoretical Mathematical Physics

Precision Production Trades

Boilermaking

Cabinetmaking Millwork

Furniture Design Manufacturing

Ironworking

Machine Shop Technology

Machine Tool Technology

Precision Production Trades -
    General

Sheet Metal Technology

Shoe/Boot/Leather Repair

Tool/Die Technology

Upholstery

Welding Technology

Woodworking

Psychology

Clinical Psychology

Community Psychology

Counseling Psychology

Developmental/Child Psychology

Educational Psychology

Experimental Psychology

Family Psychology

Forensic Psychology

Industrial/Organizational Psychology

Personality Psychology

Psychobiology/Physiological
 Psychology

Psychology - General

Social Psychology

Public Administration & Services

Community Organization/Advocacy

Human Services

Public Administration

Public Policy Analysis

Public Services

Social Work

Youth Services

Science Technologies

Biology Technician

Chemical Technology

Industrial Radiologic Technology

Nuclear Power Technology

Science Technologies

Security & Protective Services

Correctional Facilities Administration

Corrections

Criminal Justice Studies

Criminalistics/Criminal Science

Fire Protection/Safety Technology

Fire Science/Firefighting

Fire Services Administration

Forensic Technologies

Juvenile Corrections

Law Enforcement Administration

Police Science

Protective Services

Security Services Management

Security/Loss Prevention

Social Sciences

American Government/Politics

Anthropology

Applied Economics

Archaeology

Canadian Government/Politics

Cartography

Criminology

Demography/Population Studies

Development Economics

Econometrics

Economics

Geography

International Economics

International Relations

Political Science/Government

Social Sciences - General

Sociology

Urban Studies

Total Internship Management

Theological Studies
   & Religious Vocations

Bible Studies

Ministry

Missionary Studies

Pastoral Counseling

Pre-Ministerial Studies

Religious Education

Religious/Sacred Music

Talmudic Studies

Theology

Youth Ministry

Transportation & Materials Moving

Air Traffic Control

Air Transportation

Airline - Commercial Pilot/Flight Crew

Aviation Management

Commercial Fishing

Construction/Earthmoving Equipment

Diving - Professional/Instruction

Flight Attendance

Flight Instruction

Marine Science/Merchant Marines

Transportation & Materials Moving - General

Truck/Bus/Commercial Vehicle Operation

Source: "Major and Career Profiles" Copyright (c) 2007 The College Board, www.collegeboard.com. Reproduced with permission.

APPENDIX B
SAMPLE LIST OF CAMPUS STUDENT ORGANIZATIONS

The list below represents a collection of clubs and organizations at Boston University. Not all of the clubs listed here are available at all institutions. Likewise, most institutions will have organizations not listed here. This section of the appendix provides a preliminary resource in building a foundational understanding of the vast number, and different types, of student organizations on today's college campuses

Community Service Organizations

Alpha Phi Omega

AWARE

Building Tomorrow

Campus Girl Scouts

Child at Heart

China Care Fund

COM Champions

Dance Marathon

Darfur Coalition

Engineers Without Borders

Environmental Student Organization

Exposure Initiative

Fight JPA

First Book Campus Advisory Board

Foundation of International Medical Relief of Children

Free The Children Campus Initiative

Global Alliance to Immunize Against Aids

Global Medical Brigades

H.A.V.E.
(Hunger Affects Virtually Everyone)

Habitat for Humanity International

Heartbeat Africa

Hug Don't Hate

International Student Volunteers

ONE

Peer Health Exchange

Red Cross Volunteers

Rotaract

Silver Wings

Speak Easy

Students for Camp Heartland

Students Infecting the Community with Kindness

UNICEF Campus Initiative

Unite for Sight

Culture Organizations

African Students Organization

Albanian Club

Total Internship Management

Arab Students Association

Armenian Students Association

Asian Student Union

Asian Studies Initiative

Asociacion de Estudiantes
Graduados de Espanol

Bangladeshi Students' Association

Bhangra

Brazilian Association

BU PorColombia

Chinese Student and
Scholar Association

Chinese Students Association

Cuban-American Student
Association

Danzon

Filipino Student Association

French Cultural Society

Hawaii Cultural Association

Hellenic Association

Hillel Students Organization

Hong Kong Student Association

India Club

Indonesian Society

International Student Hospitality
Association

International Students Consortium

Italian Students Association

Japanese Student Association

Kalaniot

Korean Student Association

La Fuerza

Latinos Unidos

Lebanese Club

Mexican Student Association

Organization of Pakistani Students

Palestinian - Israeli Peace Alliance

Persian Student Cultural Club

Polish Society

Preservation of Endangered
Cultures Project

Russian Cultural Society

Singapore Society

Spectrum

Spice

Students for Israel

Taiwanese American
Student Association

Taiwanese Student Association

TARANG Indian
Student's Association

Thai Students Association

Turkish Student Association

Undergraduate Chinese Society

UMOJA

Vietnamese Student Association

Law Organizations

American Civil Liberties Union - LAW

American Constitution Society

Asian Pacific American Law Students Association

Black Law Students Association

BUSL Coffeehouse

Children and the Law

Communication, Entertainment, Sports Law Assn.

Earthrights International - LAW

Environmental Law Society

Federalist Society

Health Law Association

Intellectual Property Law Society

International Law Society

IP Society Student Bar Association

J. Reuben Clark Law Society

Jewish Law Students Association

Labor & Employment Law

Latin American Law Student Association

LAW Softball Team

Law Students for Choice

Legal Follies

Older Wiser Law Students

OutLaw

Phi Alpha Delta

Public Interest Project

Shelter Legal Services

South Asian American Law Students Association

Student Government LAW School

Women's Law Association

Performance Organizations

Allegrettos

Athena's Players

Aural Fixation

Ballroom Dance

Barbershop Sweethearts

Boston Lindy Kats

BosTones, The

BU Band

BU On Tap

Bulletproof Funk

Capoeira Club

Chankaar

Choral Society

Chordially Yours

Composers and Musicians

Concert Band

Dance Theatre Group

Dear Abbeys

Dheem: Classical Indian Dance Association

Edge, The

Total Internship Management

Encore!

Exhibition Drill Team

Fusion

Garba/Raas Club

Giddha

In Achord

Jalwa

Jazz Band

Liquid Fun

Marching Band

On Broadway

Orchestra

Outtakes, The

Pep Band

Record Label

Shakespeare Society

Slow Children At Play

Soulstice

Speak for Yourself

Stage Troupe

Step About Boston

Suno (Hindi A Cappella)

Sweet Liberty Dance Team

Terpsichore

TFE (Theater for Engineers)

Treblemakers

Trú Sole

Underground Music Appreciation

Unofficial Project

Vibes

Wandering Minds

Willing Suspension

Political Organizations

American Civil Liberties Union -
    Undergraduate

Americans for Informed Democracy

Amnesty International

College Democrats

College Republicans

Debate Society

Friends of Spartacus Youth

International Relations Organization

Libertarian Society

Liberty in North Korea

Model United Nations

NAACP

Right to Life

Students Against Human Trafficking

Students for a Democratic Society

Students for MASS PIRG

Unity 08 College Team

US India Political
    Action Committee

VOX: Voices for Choices

Women's Center

World Affairs Forum

Professional Organizations

Ad Club

Alpha Epsilon Delta

Alpha Eta Mu Beta Honor Society

Alpha Kappa Psi

Alpha Sigma Lambda

American Institute of Aeronautics
    & Astronautics

American Marketing Association

American Society of Mechanical
    Engineers (ASME)

Anthro Works

Archaeology Club

Arnold Air Society

Art History Association

Art League

Arts Administration Student
    Association

Astronomical Society

Beta Alpha Psi

Bioethics Society

Biomedical Engineers Society

Biotechnology Association

BSBA Finance Club

BSBA Private Equity

CAS Dean's Host

Chemia

Club Managers of America

Creative Writing Club

Deaf Studies Club

Delta Sigma Pi

Diner's Club

Diversity in Management

Early Childhood Educators Club

Editorial Society

Elementary Education

Entrepreneurship Club

Environmental Examiner

Eta Kappa Nu

Exceptional Educators

Fashion and Retail Association

Fine Arts Management
    & Education Society

First Draft

FIRST Robotics

Geological Society

Golden Key Honor Society

Growling Dog Productions

Health Science Club

Human Physiology Society

Institute of Electrical
    & Electronics Engineers

Institute of Industrial Engineers

International Management
    Organization

Kappa Kappa Psi

Korean Business Club

Total Internship Management

Leaders for Corporate
 Social Responsibility

Linguistics Association

Lock Honorary Service Society

Management Consulting Association

Management of Information
 Systems Club

Marine Science Association

Mathletic Association

Mathematical Association of America

Media and Entertainment Club

Minorities in Law

Minority Association of
 Pre-Health Students

Minority Engineers Society

Mock Trial Organization

Motion Picture Association

Music Educators National Conference

National Society for
 Minorities in Hospitality

National Society of
 Collegiate Scholars

National Student Speech Language
Hearing Assn

Nutrition Club

Occupational Therapy Club

Operations Management

Physical Therapy Association

Pi Sigma Alpha

Pi Tau Sigma

Pre Dental Society

Pre Law Review

Pre Law Society

Pre Medical Society

Pre Veterinary Society

Pre-Med Study Assistance

Pre-Optometry Professional
 Society

Psi Chi

Public Health Initiative

Public Relations Student
 Society of America

Real Estate Club

Rehabilitation Counselors
 Organization

Rocket Team

Sargent College Honor Society

Sigma Alpha Lambda

SMG Pre Law Society

Society of Athletic Training Students

Society of Automotive Engineers

Society of Hispanic
 Professional Engineers

Society of Manufacturing Engineers

Society of Professional Journalists

Society of Women Engineers

Sports Management Association

Students for the Development &
    Advancement of Higher Education

Tau Beta Pi Association

Tau Beta Sigma

Undergraduate Classics Association

Undergraduate Economics Association

Undergraduate History Association

Undergraduate Mathematics
    Association

Undergraduate Philosophy Association

Undergraduate Psychology Association

Undergraduate Religion Association

Venture Capital Private Equity

Writer's Workshop

Recreation Organizations

Alpine Ski Team

Badminton Club

Baseball Club

Cheerleading Squad

Cycling

Dance Team

Equestrian Team

Fencing Club

Gymnastics Club

Inline Hockey Team

Kung Fu Club

Men's Lacrosse

Men's Rugby Club

Men's Volleyball Club

Men's Water Polo

Shotokan Karate Club

Snowboard Team

Submission Grappling

Synchronized Skating Team

Synchronized Swimming

Table Tennis Association

Ultimate Frisbee

Women's Rugby Club

Women's Volleyball Club

Religious Organizations

Asian American Christian
    Fellowship

Asian Baptist Student Koinonia

Baha'i Association

Buddhist Association

Chabad Jewish Student
    Organization

Chi Alpha Christian Fellowship

Christians on Campus

Episcopal Student Organization

Hindu Students Council

Hong Kong Students Christian
    Fellowship

Inner Strength Gospel Choir

Intervarsity Christian Fellowship

Islamic Society

Total Internship Management

Latter-day Saint Student Association

Lotus: Buddhist Club

Lutheran Campus Ministry

Milahl: Korean Christian Fellowship

Mustard Seed

Navigators Christian Fellowship

Nemeton: Wiccan Student Alliance

Orthodox Christian Fellowship

Real Life: Campus Crusade for
Christ

Sikh Association

Unitarian Universalist
    Campus Organization

Victory Campus Ministry

Vita Novis Christian Fellowship

Women's Interfaith Action Group

Social Organizations

Ages 8 & Up

Anime Group

Art Proliferation Society

Billiards Club

Boston Scholars Club

Bowling Association

Brownstone Journal

BURN Magazine

Chess Club

Cigar Aficionado Society

Club Domestique

College Bowl

Cricket Club

Crud

Curling Club

DDR

Drink Responsibly

Film Society

Flintknapping Club

Holocaust Education Committee

Juggling Association

Knitting Club

Literary Society

Mac Users Group

Massively-Multiplayer Online
    Gaming Society

Medieval Recreation Society

Organic Gardening Club

Origami Club

Outing Club

Photography Club

Role-Playing Society

SAR: Class of 2007

SAR: Class of 2008

Scuba Divers

Ski & Snowboard Club

Students for Sensible Drug Policy

Students in Free Enterprise

Tennis Club

Transitional Mentor Program

Triathletes and Beyond	Society
Video Game	Zen Society

Printed with permission from the Boston University Student Activities Office.

APPENDIX C
SAMPLE INTERVIEW QUESTIONS

Although the same steps used to hire full-time employees can be followed to hire interns, employers may find that they need to adjust the interview format in order to fit the nature of the internship and the candidate's experiences.

Because students generally lack professional experiences, internship interview questions should focus on goals. Throughout the interview, ask questions that will help you determine if the internship you are offering will be an appropriate experience for the candidate to meet his or her career goals.

When hiring an intern, place as much effort into the selection process as you would hiring a full-time employee. An intern may become a future employee. You will be spend time and money to train the intern, so choose someone you believe would be a good fit in your organization in the future.

Focus on future goals in place of professional experience:

- How do you think this internship experience will prepare you for your career?

- What are your plans for after graduation?

- Where do you see yourself in five/ten years?

- What are your long term and short term goals?

Look for: Answers that indicate that the student has thoughtfully considered his or her career path and is planning to pursue a career related to your industry after graduation. In addition, an ideal internship candidate will express a strong interest in the educational and learning value of the opportunity rather than to simply to fulfill a requirement.

Inquire about academic experiences rather than professional:

- Tell me about a time when you had a heavy course load. How did you manage your time?

- How do you feel your campus involvement (if any) relates to the professional workplace?

- What has been your most rewarding college experience thus far?

- Why/how did you choose your major?

- What was your greatest achievement?

- What courses in your major have you completed thus far?

Look for: Answers that highlight the student's decision-making skills as well as his or her ability to manage deadlines and academic coursework. Also, look for a student who can transfer the skills gained via campus involvement into the professional workplace. It is also important to make sure that the student has completed sufficient coursework and has the knowledge necessary to work at an internship level.

Ask questions to determine the candidate's work ethic:

- Tell me about a time when you had to work as a member of a team to complete a task. What role did you fulfill?

- What was your favorite summer or part-time job? Why?

- What have you learned from your part-time or student jobs (if listed on résumé)?

- Why did you choose the career field you would like to work in?

- What will motivate you in this position?

- Why do you think you will be successful in your chosen field?

- What do you believe is an intern's role in an organization/company?

Look for: Answers that show a student has found value in past experiences, including part-time or temporary jobs. Look also for student responses that express responsibility, dedication, and a willingness to learn by experience.

Analytical & Problem-Solving:

- Describe a situation when there seemed to be no way to complete a project and yet you found a way. What happened?

- How do you handle projects with short deadlines that require precise calculations and analysis? What is your approach?

- What kinds of problems have people recently called on you to solve? Tell me about your contribution to solving the problem.

Look for: Answers that illustrate that the student knows the steps to effective and efficient problem solving, that they understand and can work within timelines and deadlines, as well as the essential communication skills needed to engage with others. Look also for student responses that express their ability to take responsibility for projects and problem resolution.

Leadership & Interpersonal:

- What do you do differently from your classmates? What will you bring to the position that other candidates with similar academic and work experience may not offer?

- Give an example of a situation when you had to compromise your own goals/objectives for the sake of the team.

- Please describe a time when your work was harshly criticized? How did you react to this feedback?

- Talk about a group project when a team member was not fulfilling their commitments. How did you deal with the person? What were the end results?

Look for: Answers that show a student has the fundamental understanding of their own leadership styles and how they interact with others. You may also want to look for answers that illustrate the students' ability to recognize and understand ethical behavior and decision making. This may also be a good opportunity to learn how the student handles feedback and criticism and their ability to be a productive member of a team.

APPENDIX D
SAMPLE INTERVIEW EVALUATION RUBRIC

Question	Correct 5-4	Somewhat 3-2	Incorrect 1		Score
How do you think this internship experience will prepare you for your career?				X 2	
What are your plans for after graduation?				X 2	
What are your long term and short term goals?				X 2	

Listen For:
Answers that indicate that the student has thoughtfully considered his or her career path and is planning to pursue a career related to your industry after graduation. In addition, an ideal internship candidate will express a strong interest in the educational and learning value of the opportunity rather than to simply to fulfill a requirement.

Question	Correct 5-4	Somewhat 3-2	Incorrect 1		Score
Tell me about a time when you had a heavy course load. How did you manage your time?				X 2	
What has been your most rewarding college experience thus far?				X 2	
Why/how did you choose your major?				X 2	

Listen For:
Answers that highlight the student's decision-making skills as well as his or her ability to manage deadlines and academic coursework. Also, look for a student who can transfer the skills gained via campus involvement into the professional workplace. It is also important to make sure that the student has completed sufficient coursework and has the knowledge necessary to work at an internship level.

continued on page 232

Total Internship Management

Question	Correct 5-4	Somewhat 3-2	Incorrect 1		Score
Tell me about a time when you had to work as a member of a team to complete a task. What role did you fulfill?				___ X 2	
Why do you think you will be successful in your chosen field?				___ X 2	
Additional Question				___ X 2	
Additional Question				___ X 2	
Listen For: *Answers that show a student has found value in past experiences, including part-time or temporary jobs. Look also for student responses that express responsibility, dedication, and a willingness to learn by experience.*					

APPENDIX E
POSSIBLE INTERN TASKS

Consider having an intern...

- Research the viability of a new program, campaign, or initiative; compile and present statistics.

- Complete a backburner project that has been bogging down permanent staff.

- Create a proposal on a potential social media strategy, evaluate various social media platforms, or come up with suggestions for how your current social media strategy might be improved.

- Critique your company's website...from a user perspective; brainstorm ideas for boosting usability.

- Propose solutions for a mid-level problem that no one has had time to address.

- Research and identify the most influential blogs in your industry. Follow them and provide weekly reports.

- Scan industry media for news items; provide regularly scheduled updates.

- Accompany employees to client, sales, or other outside meetings; have them take an observer role, but ask for their input and ideas and answer any questions they have after you've left.

- Evaluate some area of IT functionality for tech-savvy interns; ask if they see a way to improve efficiency, streamline programs, or cut costs.

- Take responsibility for some regular task. Even if it's as simple as taking, and placing, the weekly supply order, it will demonstrate follow-through and an ability to take ownership.

- Prepare a budget.

Total Internship Management

- Create support materials, such as charts, graphs, or other visuals.

- Plan and coordinate an event or meeting.

- Generate a marketing plan, financial forecast, or other report.

- Produce a video or slide presentation.

- Perform a study or survey; analyze and present results.

- Write internal communications.

- Compile employee manuals or develop process directions for tasks with high employee turnover.

- Source goods or search for lower-cost sources for high-volume materials.

- Clean up a database.

- Serve as a liaison between the company and clients or vendors while freeing up staff members for more crucial issues.

- Aid in the modification or enhancement of your internship program.

- Help screen and train replacement interns prior to their departure.

- When assigning tasks, try to strike a balance between those activities that provide a meaningful learning experience for the intern, and those activities that increase productivity in the organization.

Below, please find specific tasks that help students gain real-world work experience in the following areas:

Arts/Design
- Schedule/attend client meetings
- Brainstorm project ideas
- Create artwork/client communication
- Proofread client communications
- Create mood boards
- Create portfolio of projects

Medicine
- Conduct/participate in research projects
- Maintain files
- Create spreadsheets for information
- Attend staff meetings with medical office staff
- Attend patient consultations

Business/Finance
- Create documents/spreadsheets
- Attend client and staff meetings
- Review financial information
- Attend/participate in performance reviews
- Provide customer service
- Participate in training sessions

Education
- Decorate/organize classroom
- Assist students with projects
- Create/modify lesson plans
- Attend/participate in teacher/staff meetings
- Monitor student progress
- Create communication to parents

Government
- Attend committee meetings
- Prepare meeting minutes
- Maintain blogs/social media
- Create/modify documents

Total Internship Management

Government (continued)
- Work with lobbyists
- Assist with research projects

High Tech
- Perform equipment maintenance
- Create reports/maintain files
- Organize/maintain documents on equipment
- Maintain social media
- Troubleshoot equipment issues

Law
- Conduct legal research
- Attend staff/client meetings
- Organize files/notes
- Type legal documents

Marketing/Advertising
- Maintain a blog
- Update/revise website information
- Attend/schedule client meetings
- Create/edit marketing plans
- Maintain social media

Media/Journalism
- Create newsletters/client communication
- Distribute promotional material
- Maintain blog
- Monitor social media
- Prepare news releases

Non Profit
- Create fund-raiser invitations/communications
- Contact/schedule volunteers
- Work on budgets
- Prepare news releases
- Type minutes from committee meetings

Science/Engineering
- Clean/maintain laboratory space
- Develop/report on test plans
- Create reports
- Set up test equipment
- Assist in conducting tests

APPENDIX F
SAMPLE INTERN POSITION DESCRIPTIONS

1. MARKETING INTERNSHIP: INSURANCE COMPANY

STUDENT INTERN - MARKETING DEPARTMENT

Internship Description:

Our Company has more than a century of experience as a personal lines insurance carrier. Consistently ranked highest in customer satisfaction by its policyholders, our company is strong, stable and financially secure.

Our office located in Lincoln, RI, is seeking an intern for our Marketing Department. This is a paid internship, and the working hours are 37.50 hours per week during the summer months. The selected candidate will be responsible for assisting and supporting the Marketing Department with a variety of social media and marketing initiatives.

Job Functions and Responsibilities:

Social Media focus includes:
- Assist with social media engagement by helping manage social channels.
- Drafting and editing copy for social channels.
- Monitoring social media web analytics on a weekly basis
  (e.g. page views, twitter followers), and provide reports of growth
  and other activity.

Marketing/advertising focus includes:
- Engaging with marketing teams on a regular basis to brainstorm ideas for new and innovative marketing and social media campaigns.
- Assist with gathering data for marketing reports and supporting a variety of marketing and advertising programs.

General responsibilities include, but are not limited to:
- Researching industry specific sites (blogs, forums, etc.) for product reviews, customer comments, and other relevant marketing information.
- Maintaining marketing program files.

Job Requirements:

- Must have excellent written and verbal communication skills.
- Knowledge and experience with Facebook, Twitter, YouTube and other social media platforms.
- Strong attention to detail and organizational skills.
- Our internship is designed for individuals who are currently enrolled at an accredited college/university and who will be continuing their undergraduate studies in the fall. Candidates should be seeking a Bachelor's degree in Marketing, Public Relations, Communications or Journalism.
- All applicants must submit a cover letter.
- Transportation to and from the internship environment.

Hours Per Week: 37.5 • **Wage/ Salary:** hourly

2. MARKETING INTERNSHIP: PUBLIC RELATIONS

CORPORATE PUBLIC RELATIONS COMPANY: PUBLIC RELATIONS INTERN

Internship Description:

Are you the next PR Superstar? If so, you're going to need the skills and relevant work experience to get your foot in the door of your first public relations job.

We take great pride in nurturing the up-and-coming public relations stars of tomorrow. Through our hands-on, year-round corporate public relations internship program, students compete for a unique opportunity to work alongside an award-winning public relations team that develops innovative global programs to help support the organization's organization growth, client retention and profitability.

Work With A Global Leader

Established in Rhode Island 175 years ago, we are a $4.6 billion organization that insures more than one out of every three FORTUNE 1000 organizations and similar-sized organizations in nearly 200 countries. The organization, ranked 766 among FORTUNE Magazine's largest organizations in America, employs more than 5,100 people in 62 offices worldwide.

Experience You Will Gain

Unlike internships at other organizations, our public relations interns gain meaningful, real-world experience in the four key areas that the most astute public relations practitioners demonstrate competency in research, planning, implementation and evaluation. You can expect to develop confidence and marketable skills by engaging in or assisting with many of the following activities:

- Preparing news releases, bylined articles, award nominations, fact sheets, executive biographies;
- Enhancing the organization's social media presence, corporate Web site, corporate Intranet;
- Participating in strategy meetings, conference calls, media interviews;
- Monitoring earned media coverage using the latest research tools;
- Publishing the organization's quarterly media coverage report;
- Supporting special events and site tours; and much more!

Qualifications

Only the best and brightest need apply. To be considered for the public relations Summer/Fall or Winter/Spring internship, you must:

- Maintain an overall GPA of 3.0 or higher;
- Major in public relations, communications, English, journalism or marketing;
- Plan to pursue a career in public relations; and
- Be a junior or senior in college.
- Applicants are responsible for transportation to and from the internship experience.

Hours are flexible and depend on the student's class schedule, course requirements (if applicable) and availability.

Hours Per Week: 40 • **Wage/ Salary:** paid

Application Instructions:

The chosen candidate can expect to work full-time during summer 2012 and part-time (12-15 hours per week) during fall 2012.

3. COMMUNICATIONS / EDITORIAL INTERNSHIP

MULTI-MEDIA NEWS ORGANIZATION: EDITORIAL INTERNSHIPS

Internship Description:

We are a local multi-media news organization serving communities throughout Eastern Massachusetts. From more than 160 hyper-local websites, to magazines and specialty products, to 100 plus weekly and daily newspapers, we offer advertising solutions to both large and small organizations.

Internship opportunities exist at our locations throughout eastern Massachusetts in all areas of our organization. The internships offered provides an opportunity to experience a reporter's role and be part of a news team working both in print and online. An intern is assigned to an editor and during the course of the internship works closely with that editor to gather news, conduct interviews, write articles, and take photographs and video. Interns can expect to have their work published in print and online on a regular basis. An intern's hours are mutually agreed upon by the interns and his or her supervising editor, and should be between 15 and 20 hours per week for a period of four to twelve plus weeks.

Internships are unpaid. There is a weekly minimum hour's requirement of 8 hours for college students, but flexible schedules are available. Internships must be a requirement of the school for academic credits. Before you begin your internship, documentation from the school will be required stating how many credits you will receive, how many hours are you required to work per week, start and end dates of internship, and if your supervisor is required to fill out an evaluation.

You will need to provide a résumé and cover letter which outlines your goals for an internship.

Qualifications:

Journalism, English, Communication or Media Major in a Bachelor's Degree Program, Transportation

Hours Per Week: 8+ Flexible • **Wage/ Salary:** Unpaid

4. PSYCHOLOGY INTERNSHIP

YOUTH AND FAMILY SERVICES CORPORATION: BEHAVIOR SPECIALIST

Internship Description:
We believe that every child has the right - and should have the opportunity - for full inclusion in life. In 1997, we established a Youth and Family Services Program to help children with disabilities learn the skills they need to become active, participating members of the larger community.

To support a child's development, we create individualized programs that are family-centered, recognizing that parents or guardians are a critical part of the implementation team. We bring together an interdisciplinary team that supports and works with families to fins positive ways to deal with the many challenges posed by a child's disabilities. Depending upon what services and expertise are needed, this support team can be comprised of an administrator, treatment consultant, clinical supervisor, treatment coordinator, and behavioral specialist.

Our Youth and Family Services Program is designed for eligible children ages 3-21 with special health care needs or who are at risk for chronic physical, developmental or behavioral conditions.

Our Home-Based Therapeutic Services include:

* Behavior Management
* Social & Daily Living Skills
* Community Integration
* Parenting Skills Training

Qualifications:

* Must be 19 years old
* Must have an Associate Degree in human services or currently be enrolled in at least 6 semester hours of relevant undergraduate coursework at an accredited college/university
* Must have a favorable criminal background check

- Must have a valid driver's license and access to an insured vehicle
- Must have a favorable driving record

Hours Per Week: 20 • **Wage/ Salary: Competitive**

5. ENGINEERING INTERNSHIP

TECHNICAL CAREER EDUCATION
TEST ENGINEERING INTERN

Internship Description:

The Test Engineering Intern will be responsible for developing and executing physical and electrical performance testing to have more comprehensive characterization of fluid dispensing equipment. Essential job duties and responsibilities include:

- Developing test plans to effectively evaluate dispense equipment (valve, dispenser, barrel) performances,
- Selecting the test methodology and instrumentation required,
- Setup the test equipment, execute tests,
- Summarize their test results and conclude in a formal report format.
- Any other duties will be assigned.

Qualifications:

- Pursuit of a mechanical, industrial or electrical engineering bachelor's degree at least a junior in standing
- Self-directed and motivated
- Technical Report Writing skills
- Proficient in Microsoft Office Preferred Skills and Abilities
- Familiar with Labview
- Knowledge of physical and electrical measuring methods Working Conditions and Physical Demands Mixed Environment of office, laboratory and manufacturing. To perform this job successfully, an individual must be able to perform each essential duty satisfactorily. Must be able to lift up to 20lbs daily and 40lbs on occasion.
- 10-15 hours per week availability, $17/hour
- Transportation to and from internship experience

Total Internship Management

Reasonable accommodations may be made to enable individuals with disabilities to perform the essential functions.

Employment is contingent upon passing a post offer drug screening and background check. We are fully committed to Equal Employment Opportunity and to attracting, retaining, developing and promoting the most qualified employees without regard to their race, gender, gender identity or expression, color, religion, sexual orientation, national origin, age, physical or mental disability, citizenship status, veteran status, or any other characteristic prohibited by state or local law.

APPENDIX G
INTERN GOALS & OBJECTIVES

Please take a moment to summarize below the top 5 objectives, outcomes, and/ or areas of responsibility established for your intern as part of their internship experience.

OBJECTIVE #1:
Measure of Success: 1. 2. 3. 4. 5.
OBJECTIVE #2:
Measure of Success: 1. 2. 3. 4. 5.
OBJECTIVE #3:
Measure of Success: 1. 2. 3. 4. 5.
OBJECTIVE #4:
Measure of Success: 1. 2. 3. 4. 5.
OBJECTIVE #5:
Measure of Success: 1. 2. 3. 4. 5.

APPENDIX H
INTERN WORK PLAN

Intern Name:
Supervisor Name:
Final Version Y/N:
Date Prepared:
Date Reviewed with Supervisor:
If Yes, Date Finalized:

Purpose for Pursuing	Related Sub-Tasks	Owners(s)	Partners (s)	Planned Completion	Actual Completion	Task Complete	Related Notes/ Accomplishments

Repeat this process for as many objectives as you have for the intern.

APPENDIX I
COMPENSATION DATA

This section of the appendix provides detailed compensation data based on Intern Bridge research. The compensation data listed here has been sorted by the student's academic major, the position they held within a host organization, and the various industries in which they interned. The compensation data is unique in that it is "as reported by students," as opposed to most compensation data, which is "as reported by organizations."

COMPENSATION DATA BY MAJOR

Major	Average Hourly Salary
Agriculture, Agriculture Operations, And Related Sciences	$11.35
Architecture And Related Services	$11.11
Area, Ethnic, Cultural, And Gender Studies	$10.50
Biological And Biomedical Sciences	$10.61
Business, Management, Marketing, And Related Support Service	$13.66
Communication, Journalism And Related Programs	$10.18
Communications Technologies/Technicians And Support Services	$10.60
Computer And Information Sciences And Support Services	$16.16
Construction Trades	$14.00
Culinary Arts	$8.33
Education	$10.36
Engineering	$17.92
Engineering Technologies/Technicians	$14.00
English Language And Literature/Letters	$9.13
Family And Consumer Sciences/Human Sciences	$10.00
Foreign Languages, Literatures, And Linguistics	$10.53
Health Professions And Related Clinical Sciences	$11.37
History	$11.08
Legal Professions And Studies	$9.20
Liberal Arts And Sciences, General Studies And Humanities	$11.17

COMPENSATION DATA BY MAJOR (CONTINUED)

Major	Average Hourly Salary
Library Science	$18.00
Mathematics And Statistics	$12.45
Mechanic And Repair Technologies/Technicians	$9.00
Military Technologies	NDR
Multi/Interdisciplinary Studies	$12.06
Natural Resources And Conservation	$10.66
Parks, Recreation, Leisure And Fitness Studies	$8.08
Philosophy And Religious Studies	$11.14
Physical Sciences	$12.56
Psychology	$10.03
Public Administration And Social Service Professions	$12.81
Science Technologies/Technicians	$14.30
Security And Protective Services	$11.50
Social Sciences	$10.84
Technology Education/Industrial Arts	$10.20
Theology And Religious Vocations	$11.67
Transportation And Materials Moving	$9.33
Visual And Performing Arts	$10.58

COMPENSATION DATA BY INDUSTRY

Industry	Average Hourly Salary
Agriculture (Support Services, Natural Resources, Environmental Resources, etc.)	$11.72
Arts And Entertainment	$9.82
Construction	$13.71
Educational Services	$9.91
Financial Services (Banking, Financial Planning, Asset Management, etc.)	$15.47
Food And Lodging Services	$10.17
Government: Federal Agencies	$13.47
Government: State And Local Agencies	$11.46
Health Sciences	$12.11

COMPENSATION DATA BY INDUSTRY (CONTINUED)

Industry	Average Hourly Salary
Information Services (Publishing, Broadcasting, Telecommunications)	$13.16
Manufacturing	$16.65
Not-For-Profit Organization	$10.01
Oil, Gas, and Coal Extraction/Transport	$20.74
Professional And Scientific Services (Accounting, Engineering, Computer/IT Services, Consulting Services, Human Resources, Scientific Research, Marketing, Advertising, Legal Services, etc.)	$14.57
Real Estate/Leasing Companies	$11.86
Retail/Merchandising	$12.94
Transportation (Airlines, Railroads, Trucking, Logistics)	$15.05
Utilities/Energy Provider	$17.15
Wholesale	$15.22

COMPENSATION DATA BY POSITION

Position	Average Hourly Salary
Accounting/Auditing	$15.94
Actuarial	$15.58
Administrative/Support Services	$10.98
Analyst	$15.33
Brand Management	$20.00
Broadcasting	$8.74
Business Development	$10.69
Buying/Purchasing	$13.17
Computer Drafting and Design	$11.73
Consulting	$13.48
Counseling	$9.92
Customer Service	$9.59
Cyber Security	$19.00
Database Management	$12.20
Education	$9.47

COMPENSATION DATA BY POSITION (CONTINUED)

Position	Average Hourly Salary
Engineering	$17.99
Event Planning	$8.95
Farming/Agriculture	$10.37
Finance	$13.92
Fundraising/Development	$12.00
Game Design	$12.43
Hotel/Restaurant/Hospitality	$9.90
Human Resources	$11.75
Information Management/MIS	$14.47
Investigation	$10.50
IT/Systems	$15.84
Law	$11.07
Law Enforcement/Security	$11.67
Library Science	$14.00
Management	$12.35
Marketing	$11.39
Medicine	$11.24
Operations	$13.94
Political Organization/Lobbying	$10.26
Product Management	$14.18
Programming/Software Development	$19.20
Project Management	$11.95
Public Relations	$9.65
Research	$11.90
Sales	$11.52
Supply Chain Management/Logistics	$17.31
Tax	$21.50
Technical Support	$15.18
Web Development	$11.06

COMPENSATION DATA BY STATE WHERE INTERN WORKED

State	Average Hourly Salary
Alabama	$14.62
Alaska	$17.00
Arizona	$13.10
Arkansas	$11.67
California	$14.85
Colorado	$14.85
Connecticut	$13.83
Delaware	$24.00
District of Columbia	$12.02
Florida	$9.97
Georgia	$13.67
Hawaii	$12.00
Idaho	$17.00
Illinois	$14.44
Indiana	$15.57
Iowa	$12.08
Kansas	$14.18
Kentucky	$12.00
Louisiana	$14.40
Maine	$10.57
Maryland	$12.43
Massachusetts	$13.39
Michigan	$12.00
Minnesota	$12.33
Mississippi	$21.00
Missouri	$12.75
Montana	$13.82
Nebraska	$10.29
Nevada	$21.00
New Hampshire	$17.67
New Jersey	$13.84
New Mexico	$21.44
New York	$12.18

COMPENSATION DATA BY STATE WHERE INTERN WORKED (cont.)

State	Average Hourly Salary
North Carolina	$13.66
North Dakota	$14.00
Ohio	$12.92
Oklahoma	$15.63
Oregon	$15.50
Pennsylvania	$13.34
Rhode Island	$9.57
South Carolina	$12.30
South Dakota	$9.50
Tennessee	$12.32
Texas	$16.36
Utah	$19.67
Vermont	$11.50
Virginia	$14.31
Washington	$15.66
West Virginia	NDR
Wisconsin	$12.10
Wyoming	$16.50
International Internships	NDR

APPENDIX J
LIST OF RELEVANT ASSOCIATIONS

The following is a list of organizations that you should know about if you are serious about experiential education in your organization.

Cooperative Education and Internship Association
www.CEIA.org

Council for the Advancement of Standards
http://www.cas.edu/

Eastern Association of Colleges and Employers
www.eace.org

Midwest Association of Colleges and Employers
www.MWACE.org

Mountain Pacific Association of Colleges and Employers
www.MPACE.org

National Association of Colleges and Employers
www.naceweb.org

National Commission for Cooperative Education
www.NCCE.org

National Society for Experiential Education
www.NSEE.org

Southern Association of Colleges and Employers
www.SOACE.org

World Association for Cooperative Education
www.WACEINC.org

Please note that it is highly likely that your state has its own internship association. An internet search should yield the contact information for the folks who manage the group.

APPENDIX K: PARTICIPATING ORGANIZATIONS

The following is a partial list of organizations who participated in this landmark research.

AAA Southern New England

AstraZeneca Pharmaceuticals

Blue Cross & Blue Shield
   of Rhode Island

Bose

Boston Public Schools

Citizens Financial Group

Ecco USA, Inc.

Federal Aviation Administration

Girl Scouts of Rhode Island

Hannaford Bros. Co.

John Hancock

Lycos

MA Medical Society

Massachusetts Hospital Association

MetLife

National Lumber

New Balance Athletic Shoe, Inc.

Ocean Spray Cranberries, Inc.

Osram Sylvania, Inc, a Siemens Co.

Papa Ginos

PUMA North America, Inc.

Staples

Sun Life Financial

Target Stores

Wyeth Biotech

Aigner Associates

Alkermes

Altus

Atlantic Resource Group

Avecia Biotechnology Inc.

BAO Inc.

Battenfeld Gloucester Engineering

Celerant Consulting

Chestnut Hill Realty

Coley Pharmaceutical Group

Compensation Consulting Resources

Conquest Business Media

Corporate Technologies

Eagle Tribune Publishing

Earthwatch Institute

ENSR

Equinox Group

Facing History and Ourselves

FM Global

Foster-Miller

Fuld & Company, Inc

Gazelle Strategic Partners, LLC

Gentle Giant Moving Company

Getronics

Granite Telecommunications

Harpoon Brewery

Hartford Courant

HCPro

Hexagon Metrology, Inc

Hollingsworth & Vose Co.

Horn Group

Hudson Lock, LLC

Inanovate, Inc

Intellagents

Invensys Process Systems

JCSI

John Snow, Incorporated

KGA, INC.

Kirkland Albrecht & Fredrickson

Lexington Business Solutions

Lightbridge, Inc.

Looney & Grossman LLP

Madison Floral, Inc.

Marrakech, Inc.

May Institute, Inc.

Medical Information Technology, Inc.
   (MEDITECH)

Mettler-Toledo Process Analytics

MSPCA-Angell

NESI

New England Research Institute, Inc.

Noresco

NorthEast/Eagle Electric

Occupational and Environmental
   Health Network (OEHN)

OmniSonics Medical Technologies, Inc.

Parkland Medical Center

Permabit

Phoenix Marketing International

Pine Street Inn

Pioneer

Pivot Solutions, Inc

Portland Press Herald Maine
   Sunday Telegram

PSG

Rainbow Worldwide Relocation
   & Logistics

Randstand

Redcats USA

Reynolds Resources

sdg Management Intelligence

SEPATON

Sepracor

Springwell

Staffing Solutions, Inc.

Stanley Bostitch

Strategic Resource Solutions, LLC

Taco, Inc.

TERI (The Educational
   Resource Institute)

The Village Bank

TNCI

UHY Advisors, NE, LLC

United Plastic Fabricating

Total Internship Management

ValleyWorks Career Center

Vega & Associates, Inc

Vermont Mutual Insurance Group

Vion Pharmaceuticals Group

Vitale Caturano & Company Ltd.

Wheelabrator Technologies Inc.

William Arthur

World Energy Solutions, Inc.

World Travel Holdings

Only organizations that provided advance permission have been listed.

The preceding is a list of participating organizations only,
and does not imply endorsement of this, or any other, Intern Bridge publication or service.

APPENDIX L
PARTICIPATING UNIVERSITIES

The following is a list of universities who participated in this research.

Adelphi University

Albertus Magnus College

Albright College

Alfred University

Aquinas College

Arizona State University

Ashland University

Augustana College

Athens State University

Babson College

Ball State University

Baruch College

Becker College

Bellarmine University

Benedictine College

Beloit College

Berry College

Biola University

Brandeis University

Brown University

Bucknell University

Buffalo State College

Butler University

California State University, Fresno

California State University, Sacramento

California State University San Marcos

Calvin College

Canisius College

Capital University

Carroll College

Catholic University of America

Cazenovia College

Central Michigan University

Christian Brothers University

Cincinnati State Technical and Community College

Claremont Graduate University

Clark Atlanta University

Clarke College

Cleveland State University

Coe College

Colgate University

College for Creative Studies

College of the Atlantic

College of the Holy Cross

College of St. Scholastica

Columbus State University

Converse College

Creighton University

Curry College

Davidson College

Defiance College

Delaware Valley College

Delta College

Drury University

Duquesne University

Eastern Connecticut State University

Eckerd College

Elmhurst College

Embry-Riddle Aeronautical University

Emory & Henry College

Ferris State University

Ferrum College

Florida Institute of Technology

Florida International University,
    College of Business

Fort Scott Community College

Framingham State College

Franklin W Olin
    College of Engineering

Gallaudet University

Gannon University

George Mason University

Georgia College & State University

Georgia Southern University

Goodwin College

Grinnell College

Gustavus Adolphus College

Hamline University

Hampshire College

Hampden-Sydney College

Hardin-Simmons University

Harris-Stowe State University

Heidelberg University

Hendrix College

Hope College

Hostos Community College CUNY

Howard University

Huston-Tillotson University

Idaho State University

Indiana State University

Indiana Tech

Indiana University

Indiana University Northwest

Indiana University Purdue
    University Fort Wayne

Indiana University - School of
    Informatics - IUPUI

Indiana University Southeast

Indiana Wesleyan University

Iowa Lakes Community College

IUPUI

James Madison University

John Carroll University

John Jay College

Johnson C. Smith University

Kalamazoo College

Kansas Wesleyan University

Kaplan University

Kendall College of Art and Design
of Ferris State University

Kettering University

Kutztown University

Lafayette College

LaGuardia Community College/
CUNY

Lake Erie College

Lakeland College

Lakeland Community College

Lawrence University

Lehigh University

Liberty University

Linfield College

Loras College

Loyola University Chicago

Loyola University New Orleans

Luther College

Lynchburg College

Macalester College

Malone University

Manhattan College

Marian University

Marietta College

Marist College

Maryville University

Massachusetts Bay
Community College

Massachusetts College of Art
and Design

Mayville State University

McPherson College

Messiah College

MIAD - Milwaukee Institute of
Art & Design

Michigan state University

Michigan Technological University

Middle Tennessee State University

Middlebury College

MiraCosta College

Minneapolis College of
Art and Design

Minnesota State University,
Mankato

Monmouth University

Monroe College

Montana Tech

Montserrat College of Art

Moore College of Art & Design

Moravian College

Morehead State University

Mount Ida College

Mount St. Mary's University

Murray State University

New York Institute of Technology

Nichols College

North Carolina A&T State University

North Dakota State University

Northern Essex Community College

Northern Illinois University

Northland College

Northwest Missouri State University

Northwestern Oklahoma State
University

Northwood University

Norwich University

Oklahoma State University

Olivet Nazarene University

Our Lady of the Lake University

Pace University

Pacific Northwest College of Art

Paul Smith's College

Penn State Erie, The Behrend College

Point Loma Nazarene University

Pomona College

Presbyterian College

Principia

Purdue University

Radford University

Ramapo College of New Jersey

Randolph - Macon College

Rensselaer Polytechnic Institute

Rhode Island College

Roanoke College

Robinson College of Business, GSU

Rockhurst University

Rocky Mountain College

Roosevelt University

Rose-Hulman Institute
of Technology

Rosemont College

Sacred Heart University

Saint Joseph's University

Saint Louis University, John Cook
School of Business

Saint Mary-of-the-Woods College

Samford University

Santa Clara University

Savannah College of Art and Design

Shorter College

Seattle Pacific Universtiy

Seton Hall University

Seton Hill University

Shippensburg University

Sierra College

Simmons College

Sinclair Community College

Skidmore College

Southern Catholic College

Southern Illinois University
Carbondale

Southern Illinois University
Edwardsville

Southern New Hampshire University

Southern Vermont College

Springfield College

St. Edward's University

St. Lawrence University

St. Norbert College

St. Olaf College

Stony Brook University

SUNY College of Technology -
Alfred State College

SUNY Fredonia

Syracuse University

Texas A&M International University

Texas Christian University

Texas State University

The Ohio State University,
Fisher College of Business

The University of Akron

The University of Iowa

The University of Montana

The University of Tampa

The University of Texas at Dallas

The University of Texas at El Paso

The University of Texas at
San Antonio

The University of Texas at Tyler

The University of West Alabama

The Washington Center for
Internships &
Academic Seminars

Union College

Upper Iowa University

University of Alabama at
Birmingham

University of Arkansas at Pine Bluff

University of California, Irvine

University of California, Riverside

University of California, San Diego

University of California,
Santa Barbara

University of Central Florida

University of Colorado, Leeds
School of Business

University of Connecticut

University of Dayton

University of Evansville

University of Houston Bauer
College of Business

University of Illinois at Springfield

University of Illinois at
Urbana-Champaign

University of Louisiana at Monroe

University of Mary Washington

University of Maryland, Baltimore
County (UMBC)

University of Maryland - College Park

Total Internship Management

University of Memphis

University of Michigan, Ann Arbor

University of Michigan - Dearborn

University of Minnesota - Twin Cities

University of Minnesota Duluth

University of Missouri,
      Trulaske College of Business

University of Missouri - St. Louis

University of Nevada Las Vegas

University of New Haven

University of North Carolina Wilmington

University of North Dakota

University of Northern Colorado

University of Oklahoma -
      Career Services

University of Saint Francis

University of South Alabama

University of South Carolina

University of South Carolina Upstate

University of South Florida

University of the Pacific

University of Vansville

University of Virginia

University of West Florida

University of Wisconsin - Milwaukee,
      Lubar School of Business

University of Wisconsin Oshkosh

University of Wisconsin- Green Bay

University of Wisconsin - Madison

University of Wisconsin - River Falls

University of Wyoming

Wake Forest University

Walsh College

Washburn University

Washington and Lee University

Washington State University

Wentworth Institute of Technology

Western Michgian Unviersity

Westminster College

Whittier College

Wichita State University

William Jewell College

Winona State University

Winthrop University

Wittenberg University

Woodbury University

Xavier University

APPENDIX M
BIBLIOGRAPHY AND RESOURCES

Alex-Assensoh, Y., & Ryan, M. (2008). Value-added learning. *Peer Review*, 10(2/3), 34-36.

Beard, D.F. (2007). Assessment of internship experiences and accounting core competencies. *Accounting Education*, 16, 207-220.

Beck, J.E. & Halim, H. (2008). Undergraduate internships in accounting: What and how do Singapore interns learn from experience? *Accounting Education*, 17, 151-172. doi:10.1080/09639280701220277

Beenen, G. (2007). Learning fast: Understanding MBA internship effectiveness. *Academy of Management Annual Meeting Proceedings*, 1-6.

Burgstahler, S. & Bellman, S. (2009). Difference in perceived benefits of internships for subgroups of students with disabilities. *Journal of Vocational Rehabilitation*, 32, 155-165. doi:10.3233/JVR-2009-0485

Cedercreutz, K., & Cates, C. (2010). Cooperative education at the University of Cincinnati: A Strategic asset in evolution. *Peer Review*, 12(4), 20-23.

Chambliss, C., Rinde, C., & Miller, J. (1996). *The liberal arts and applied learning: Reflections about the internship experience.* (Report No. HE029552). (ERIC Document Reproduction Service No. ED399916)

Chatzsky, J. & McGrath, M. (2011, November 28). The great American internship swindle. *Newsweek*, p. 22.

Coco, M. (2000). Internships: A try before you buy arrangement. *SAM Advanced Management Journal*, 65(2), 41-47

Cook, S.J., Parker, R.S., & Pettijohn, S.E. (2004). The perceptions of interns: A longitudinal case study. Journal of Education for Business, 79, 179-185.

Cross, K. (1994[a]). "The Coming of Age of Experiential Education."
NSEE Quarterly 19(4): 1, 22-23

D'Abate, C.P., Youndt, M.A., & Wenzel, K.E. (2009). Making the most of
an internship: An empirical study of internship satisfaction.
Academy of Management Learning & Education, 8, 527-539.

Divine, R.L., Linrud, J.K., Miller, R.H., & Wilson, J.H. (2007).
Required internship programs in marketing: Benefits, challenges
and determinants of fit. *Marketing Education Review*, 17(2), 45-52.

Eyler, J. (2009). The Power of Experiential Education.
Liberal Education, 95(4), 24-31.

Gault, J., Redington, J., & Schlager, T. (2000). Undergraduate business
internships and career success: Are they related? *Journal of
Marketing Education*, 22(1), 45–53.

Gavigan, L. (2010). Connecting the Classroom with real-world experiences
through summer internships. *Peer Review*, 12(4), 15-19.

Gordon, David, "Tracking Internship Outcomes through Comparative
Quantitative Assessment." *NACE Journal*, Winter 2002, 28 – 32.

Govekar, M.A. & Rishi, M. (2007). Service learning: Bringing real-world
education into the B-school classroom. *Journal of Education for Business*,
83, 3-10.

Greenberg, Robert and Harris, Marcia B., "Measuring Up: Assessment
in Career Services." *NACE Journal*, December 2006, 18 – 24.

Hindmoor, A. (2010). Internships within political science.
Australian Journal of Political Science, 45, 483-490.

Horn, L., Peter, K., & Rooney, K. (2002). *Profile of undergraduates in U.S.
postsecondary institutions: 1999-2000*. (No. NCES 2002-168).
U.S. Department of Education, National Center for Education Statistics.
Washington D.C.: U.S. Government Printing Office.

Jaarsma, D.A.D.C., Muijtjens, A.M.M., Dolmans, D.H.J.M., Schuurmans, E.M., Van Beukelen, P., & Scherpbier, A.J.J.A. (2009). Undergraduate research internships: Veterinary students' experiences and the relation with internship quality. *Medical Teacher*, 31, e178-e184.

Kardash, C.M. (2000). Evaluation of an undergraduate research experience: Perceptions of undergraduate interns and their faculty mentors. *Journal of Educational Psychology*, 92, 191-201.

Kazis, R., Callahan, A., Davidson, C, Mcleod, A., Bosworth, B., Choitz, V., & Hoops, J. (2007). Adult learners in Higher Education: Barriers to Success and Strategies to improve results. Washington, DC: U.S. Department of Labor, Employment and Training Administration, Office of Policy Development and Research by Jobs for the Future. (Publication No. DOL AF125370000230)

Keller, G. "Comparing The Five Factors of Production in Southeast Wisconsin", The Monarch Management Review, UGSM-Monarch Business School, Vol. 1, Num. 1, Oct. 2011

Knemeyer, A.M. & Murphy, P.R. (2001). Logistics internships: Employer perspectives. *Transportation Journal*, 41(1), 16-26.

Knouse, S.B. & Fontenot, G. (2008). Benefits of the business college internship: A research review. *Journal of Employment Counseling*, 45, 61-66.

Knouse, S.B., Tanner, J.T., & Harris, E.W. (1999). The relation of college internships, college performance, and subsequent job opportunity. *Journal of Employment Counseling*, 36, 35-43.

Kolb, D.A. (1984). *Experiential learning*. Englewood Cliffs, NJ: Prentice Hall.

Kuh, G.D. (2008). High-impact educational practices: What they are, who has access to them, and why they matter. Washington, DC: Association of American Colleges and Universities. Retrieved from http://www.neasc. org/downloads/aacu_high_impact_2008_final.pdf

Lee, G., McGuiggan, R., & Holland, B. (2010). Balancing student learning and commercial outcomes in the workplace. *Higher Education Research & Development*, 29, 561-574.

Lipka, S. (2010, May 14). Would you like credit with that internship? *Chronicle of Higher Education*, pp. A1, A21.

Liu, Y., Xu, J., & Weitz, B.A. (2011). The role of emotional expression and mentoring in internship learning. *Academy of Management Learning & Education*, 10, 94-110.

Marshall, S. (2006, June 12). Internships drive students to NYC. *Crain's New York Business*, pp. 1-35.

Moghaddam, J.M. (2011). Perceived effectiveness of business internships: Student expectations, experiences, and personality traits. *International Journal of Management*, 28, 287-303.

Molseed, T.R., Alsup, J., & Voyles, J. (2003). The role of the employer in shaping students' work-related skills. *Journal of Employment Counseling*, 40, 161-171.

National Association of Colleges and Employers. (2011). A Position Statement on U.S. Internships. Retrieved from: http://www.naceweb.org/connections/advocacy/internship_position_paper/

Nair, S.K. & Ghosh, S. (2006). Factors affecting the placement prospects of MBA students: An exploratory study. *Vision*, 10(1), 41-49.

Nance-Nash, S. (2007, October). Internships and co-ops: No longer optional, they are absolutely essential. *Black Collegian*, pp. 63-66.

Narayanan, V.K., Olk, P.M., & Fukami, C.V. (2010). Determinants of internship effectiveness: An exploratory model. *Academy of Management Learning & Education*, 9, 61-80.

Neill, N. O. (2010). Internships as a high-impact practice: Some reflections on quality. *Peer Review*, 12(4), 4-8.

Perlin, R. (2011, April 29). Colleges shouldn't stick interns with the bill. *Chronicle of Higher Education*, pp. A23-A24.

Pierson, M., & Troppe, M. (2010). Curriculum to career. *Peer Review*, 12(4), 12-14.

Roever, C. (2000). Mead Corporation's creative approach to internships: Success in a unionized manufacturing plant. *Business Communication Quarterly*, 63, 90-100.

Rothman, M. (2007). Lessons learned: Advice to employers from interns. *Journal of Education for Business*, 82, 140-144.

Sapp, D.A. & Zhang, Q. (2009). Trends in industry supervisors' feedback on business communication internships. *Business Communication Quarterly*, 72, 274-288.

Smith, K., Clegg, S., Lawrence, E., & Todd, M.J. (2007). The challenges of reflection: Students learning from work placements. *Innovations in Education and Teaching International*, 44, 131-141.

Spooner, M., Flowers, C., Lambert, R., & Algozzine, B. (2008). Is more really better? Examining perceived benefits of an extended student teaching experience. *Clearing House*, 81, 263-269.

Steffes, J. S. (2004). Creating powerful learning environments beyond the classroom. *Change*, 36(3), 46.

Swail, W.S. & Kampits, E. (2004). *Work-based learning and higher education: A research perspective*. Washington, DC: Educational Policy Institute, Inc. Retrieved from http://www.eric.ed.gov/PDFS/ED499880.pdf

Taguchi, Sherrie Gong, "Summer Internship Programs: From Good to Great in Eight Essential Steps." *NACE Journal*, December 2006, 25 – 30.

Thiry, H., Laursen, S.L., & Hunter, A. (2011). What experiences help students become scientists? A comparative study of research and other sources of personal and professional gains for STEM undergraduates. *Journal of Higher Education*, 82, 357-388.

Timmers, S., Valcke, M., De Mil, K., & Baeyens, W.R.G. (2008). The impact of computer supported collaborative learning on internship outcomes of pharmacy students. *Interactive Learning Environments*, 16, 131-141.

Van Etten, S., Pressley, M., McInerney, D.M., & Liem, A.D. (2008). College seniors' theory of their academic motivation. *Journal of Educational Psychology*, 100, 812-828.

Vertreace, W.C. (2009, January). How to find your dream job in a nightmare economy. *Black Collegian*, pp. 36-39.

Warburton, E.C., Bugarin, R., & Nunez, A. (2001). Bridging the gap: Academic preparation and postsecondary success of first-generation students. (No. NCES 2001-153). U.S. Department of Education, National Center for Education Statistics. Washington D.C.: U.S. Government Printing Office.

Weible, R. (2010). Are universities reaping the available benefits internship programs offer? *Journal of Education for Business*, 85, 59-63.

Weible, R. & McClure, R. (2011). An exploration of the benefits of student internships to marketing departments. *Marketing Education Review*, 21(3), 229-240.

Wesley, S.C. & Bickle, M.C. (2005). Examination of a paradigm for preparing undergraduates for a career in the retailing industries: Mentors, curriculum, and an internship. *College Student Journal*, 39, 680-691.

Wilkinson, K. (2008). Using Breeze for communication and assessment of internships: An exploratory study. Journal of Educators Online, 5(2), 1-15.

Wilson, J.Q. (1989). Bureaucracy: what government agencies do and why they do it. New York, NY: Basic.

Wood, L. & Kaczynski, D. (2007). University students in USA and Australia: Anticipation and reflection on the transition to work. *International Journal of Employment Studies*, 15, 91-106.

Yagoda, B. (2008, March 21). Will work for academic credit. *Chronicle of Higher Education*, p. A36.

MY NOTES

MY NOTES

MY NOTES

**Our research and publications can only
be as good as your feedback.**

If you have any questions or comments,
please do not hesitate to contact us by emailing:
info@InternBridge.com.

We guarantee a personal response to each
and every email.

**Did you know that Intern Bridge provides consulting
services, expert speakers, and customized workshops?**

Contact us for more information:

www.internbridge.com
1.800.531.6091